The Godless Constitution
and the Providential Republic

EMORY UNIVERSITY STUDIES IN LAW AND RELIGION

John Witte Jr., General Editor

This series fosters exploration of the religious dimensions of law, the legal dimensions of religion, and the interaction of legal and religious ideas, institutions, and methods. Written by leading scholars of law, political science, and related fields, these volumes will help meet the growing demand for literature in the burgeoning interdisciplinary study of law and religion.

RECENTLY PUBLISHED

Liam de los Reyes, *The Earth Is the Lord's: A Natural Law Theory of Property*

Thomas C. Berg, *Religious Liberty in a Polarized Age*

Douglas Laycock, *Religious Liberty*, 5 vols.

For a complete list of published volumes in this series, see the back of the book.

The Godless Constitution and the Providential Republic

Steven D. Smith

William B. Eerdmans Publishing Company
Grand Rapids, Michigan

Wm. B. Eerdmans Publishing Co.
2006 44th Street SE, Grand Rapids, MI 49508
www.eerdmans.com

© 2025 Steven D. Smith
All rights reserved
Published 2025
Printed in the United States of America

31 30 29 28 27 26 25   1 2 3 4 5 6 7

ISBN 978-0-8028-8522-7

Library of Congress Cataloging-in-Publication Data

A catalog record for this book is available from the Library of Congress.

Contents

Prologue: Atheism and the Constitution — vii

PART 1: A GODLESS DOCUMENT? — 1

1. Atheist or Agnostic? — 9
2. The Establishment Clause in the Godless Constitution — 33

PART 2: THE PROVIDENTIAL REPUBLIC AND ITS (OFFICIAL) DEMISE — 51

3. Providentialism in America — 55
4. Civil Religion and Its Discontents — 89
5. Providence Banished — 112

PART 3: PROVIDENTIALISM AND THE TRAVAILS OF LIBERALISM — 141

6. Liberalism without Foundations — 151
7. Canceling the American Past? — 178

Epilogue: "Only a God Can Save Us" — 209
Acknowledgments — 215
Index — 217

PROLOGUE

Atheism and the Constitution

"Atheism is the public philosophy, established by law. The establishment was accomplished by the law of separation of church and state."

Who said this? Some ranting, right-wing religious extremist, maybe? The statement is reminiscent of a much-reported denunciation some years back by Florida official and Senate candidate Katherine Harris, who lambasted the "separation of church and state" as "a lie we have been told" that is contrary to both the Founders' intent and God's design.[1] Or perhaps the statement comes from the fulminations of the small band of neomedieval critics of the liberal order who pass under the label of "integralism" and who seemingly revel in being provocative and contrarian.[2]

But no. In fact, the claim that atheism has been established as the public philosophy by the law of separation of church and state issued from a more sober and surprising source. The contention was advanced during lectures

---

1. See Jim Stratton, "Rep. Harris Condemns Separation of Church, State," *Washington Post*, August 26, 2006, https://tinyurl.com/tfnrd5p9.

2. For a thorough description and sympathetic critique of this movement, see Kevin Vallier, *All the Kingdoms of the World: On Radical Religious Alternatives to Liberalism* (New York: Oxford University Press, 2023). For an analysis emphasizing perceived antiliberal and reactionary strands in the integralist position, see Richard Schragger and Micah Schwartzman, "Religious Antiliberalism and the First Amendment," *Minnesota Law Review* 104 (2020): 1375–81. For further discussion and criticism, see Steven D. Smith, "The Constitution, the Leviathan, and the Common Good," *Constitutional Commentary* 37 (2022): 459.

delivered at Yale University in 1962 by John Courtney Murray, SJ,[3] an eminent and erudite Jesuit theologian probably best known for his thoughtful defense of what he called "the American Proposition,"[4] including the Constitution and the First Amendment. Silenced by the church in the 1950s for his controversial advocacy of American-style religious freedom[5]—advocacy for which he was featured on the cover of *Time* magazine—Murray was seemingly vindicated in Vatican II as he was called upon to help draft *Dignitatis Humanae*, the Catholic Church's seminal endorsement of religious freedom.[6] More generally, Murray's efforts to reconcile the church with modern pluralism have sometimes led scholars to interpret him as a sort of Catholic forerunner of the hugely influential liberal philosopher John Rawls.[7]

So, then, why was Murray condemning the separation of church and state as the establishment of atheism?

American Exceptionalism?

Read in context, Murray's criticism seems directed primarily at particular instances of church-state separationism—those associated with the French Revolution, the Fascist regimes of the mid-twentieth century, and, above all, the Communist governments of Russia and Eastern Europe. By contrast, in his best-known book, *We Hold These Truths*, published two years earlier, Murray had defended the American constitutional design, including its provisions for disestablishment and free exercise of religion, as a proper allocation of the responsibilities of the independent spiritual and temporal authorities.[8]

---

3. John Courtney Murray, SJ, *The Problem of God: Yesterday and Today* (New Haven: Yale University Press), 99.

4. John Courtney Murray, SJ, *We Hold These Truths: Catholic Reflections on the American Proposition* (New York: Sheed & Ward, 1960).

5. See John T. McGreevy, *Catholicism and American Freedom: A History* (New York: Norton, 2003), 208.

6. McGreevy, *Catholicism and American Freedom*, 237.

7. See, e.g., Leslie Griffin, "Good Catholics Should Be Rawlsian Liberals," *Southern California Interdisciplinary Law Journal* 5 (1997): 297.

8. Murray, *We Hold These Truths*, 45–78, 197–217.

Atheism and the Constitution

In this respect, Murray was telling or tapping into a familiar story about the modern age. Modernity, the story goes, was born in and of "the Enlightenment," that intoxicating or, in any case, intoxicated[9] movement exuberantly dedicated to the pursuit of science and reason and to the elimination of superstition. A rejection of the authority and sometimes of the existence of God was a conspicuous feature of the Enlightenment, exemplified in different forms in defining figures like Denis Diderot and David Hume. And yet the Enlightenment was a complex phenomenon that could unfold in different ways. While Enlightened thinking sometimes moved in an atheistic direction, in the English-speaking world Enlightened thought generally embraced a providentialist view of the universe.[10]

Not surprisingly, therefore, the modernity that emerged from the Enlightenment could take different paths. The antireligious path was vividly apparent in the French Revolution, as well as in Communist nations. While these nations sometimes expressed a nominal commitment to religious freedom, in practice religion was persecuted; and the antireligious stance could sometimes appear explicitly in a constitution. For example, the Albanian Constitution of 1976 provided that "the state recognizes no religion whatever and supports atheist propaganda for the purpose of inculcating the scientific materialist outlook in people."[11]

In America, by contrast, the Declaration of Independence not only declined to reject God; it explicitly acknowledged and indeed depended on "Nature and Nature's God." The rights that "all men" enjoy on terms of equality, said the Declaration, are those with which they are "endowed by their Creator." In a similar spirit, Thomas Jefferson's seminal Virginia Statute

---

9. On the movement's intoxicated dimension, see James Q. Whitman, "Reason or Hermeticism?" *Southern California Interdisciplinary Law Journal* 5 (1997): 193.

10. A more recent interpretation by historian Jonathan Israel seems generally consistent with this account. Israel distinguishes between a "Radical Enlightenment" that was fundamentally atheistic and a "Moderate Enlightenment" that depended on the premise of a providential design. Jonathan Israel, *A Revolution of the Mind: Radical Enlightenment and the Intellectual Origins of Modern Democracy* (Princeton: Princeton University Press, 2010), 154–220. Israel argues that throughout the eighteenth and nineteenth centuries, mainstream thought in Britain, Ireland, and America rejected the radical, atheistic version of Enlightenment and embraced the moderate strand instead (235).

11. The Albanian Constitution of 1976, Article 37, https://tinyurl.com/bkedja6y.

for Religious Liberty began by declaring that "Almighty God hath made the mind free." Religious coercion was wrong, Jefferson contended, because it was "a departure from the plan of the Holy Author of our religion."[12]

By the mid-twentieth century, it had thus come to seem that modernity had moved in two different and indeed opposite directions. To the east, in Eastern Europe and Russia, modernity had taken an overtly antireligious turn. Conversely, to the west, at least and especially in America, modernity had adopted a more pious stance, in conscious contrast to the "godless Communism" of the East. The 1950s were the era of "piety on the Potomac": President Eisenhower conspicuously endorsed the importance of religion to American government, Congress added the words "under God" to the Pledge of Allegiance and adopted In God We Trust as the national motto, and the Supreme Court declared, "we are a religious people whose institutions presuppose a Supreme Being."[13]

In his Yale lectures, Murray appeared to be drawing on and reflecting this story about the directionally divided evolution of modernity. And yet, could he really let America off the hook so easily? If it is true that "the separation of church and state" amounts in its essence to the "establishment" of atheism as the public philosophy, how could America, reputed to be the pioneer and model of "separation of church and state," escape Murray's condemnation?

Murray was able to avoid an unhappy conclusion because he believed that in America, church-state separationism had taken a distinctive form. It had not been intended or understood to mean anything like public "secularism" in the modern sense of that term. On the contrary, he argued, church-state separationism "in the American sense" had permitted and indeed presupposed a nation constituted by an ongoing civil and public conversation grounded in truths—truths that were "self-evident," as the Declaration of Independence had asserted, or in any case knowable by reason, and that included the existence and authority of God and of a natural law understood to be a feature of God's providential order.[14] These truths

---

12. Virginia Act for Religious Freedom, reprinted in *Church and State in the Modern Age: A Documentary History*, ed. J. F. MacClear (New York: Oxford University Press, 1995), 63–64.
13. These developments are discussed in chapter 3.
14. Murray, *We Hold These Truths*, 8–15.

constituted, Murray wrote, "our essential patrimony, laboriously wrought out by centuries of thought, further refined and developed in our own land to fit the needs of the new American experiment in government."[15] And the sovereignty of God was preeminent among these truths: "The first truth to which the American Proposition makes appeal is stated in that landmark of Western political theory, the Declaration of Independence. It is a truth that lies beyond politics; it imparts to politics a fundamental human meaning. I mean the sovereignty of God over nations as well as over individual men. . . . The first article of the American political faith is that the political community, as a form of free and ordered human life, looks to the sovereignty of God as the first principle of its organization."[16]

Role Reversal: Godless West, Pious East?

We will look at the matter more closely, but suppose for a moment that Murray was right in his assessment of what the separation of church and state *had* meant in America. On that supposition Murray was also right, perhaps, in assuming that the American version of separationism did not imply any kind of public atheism. He was right for the time being, anyway.

But as an eminent minstrel put it the same year that Murray's Yale lectures were published, the times, they were a-changin'.

Even as Murray was defending "the American proposition" in this country and religious freedom in Catholic councils, the American Supreme Court and the legal profession were in the process of redefining the First Amendment and the separation of church and state. Wittingly or not, the Court and the profession were reconceiving the constitutional scheme in terms of the very political secularism that Murray perceived to be the establishment of atheism as "the public philosophy."

Conversely, in the East the denunciation of Stalinism by Premier Nikita Khrushchev foreshadowed developments that, three-plus decades later, would lead to the downfall of the Communist regimes of Russia and Eastern Europe. And the new post-Communist governments would in some

---

15. Murray, *We Hold These Truths*, 10.
16. Murray, *We Hold These Truths*, 28.

instances openly embrace the Christianity that the Marxist regimes had struggled vainly to expunge.

Taken together, these developments would signal the possibility of a dramatic reversal. Instead of a godless East set against a devout West, the opposite condition might come to prevail. If he had given his Yale lectures a half century later, therefore, Murray might well have directed his contention that "atheism is the public philosophy, established by law" not against the Eastern regimes but rather precisely against his own country—against the country that he had judiciously celebrated in *We Hold These Truths*.

Preview

In this book we will consider these developments and their far-reaching consequences. Part 1 ("A Godless Document?") will look closely at the American Constitution itself to assess the character of that document with respect to questions of religion and governance. Prominent scholars have contended that the Constitution was a "godless" document requiring a godless politics.[17] Is that description accurate?

We will see in part 1 that the answer to that question is . . . yes. And no. Sort of. We will see that the document adopted a simple stance with respect to God—deceptively simple, because the stance was also novel, and elusive, and easy to misunderstand. Before and since the framing of the American Constitution, national and state constitutions had and have often taken a position, for or against, with respect to God. Many have explicitly declared in *favor* of God. A few—in Communist countries mainly—have declared *against* God. More commonly, they have made no definite declaration either way—not in so many words, anyway—but have explicitly indicated that God has no place in the *public* domain. That government is to be secular. So God and religion are consigned (for their own good, perhaps?) to the private sphere. But the American Constitution did none of these things. It remained self-consciously, trenchantly silent on the subject. Agnostic.

This was a distinctive stance, deliberately adopted, with important implications that modern observers, including justices and lawyers and

---

17. Isaac Kramnick and R. Laurence Moore, *The Godless Constitution: A Moral Defense of the Secular State* (New York: Norton, 2005).

advocates of various kinds, have routinely failed to understand. The Constitution's agnostic stance meant that America would not endorse or support religion *as a constitutional matter* (as previous governments and constitutions in the West, including most state governments and constitutions, had nearly always done), but that governments had considerable freedom to endorse and support religion—or *not* to endorse and support religion—on a *nonconstitutional* level. The Constitution left both of those options open.

So then, which of the options did American governments choose? We will see in part 2 ("The Providential Republic and Its [Official] Demise") how for the first century and a half or so of the nation's existence, Americans often adopted a providentialist view of the world and the nation. They routinely did so in both their private and—this point is crucial—their public or official capacities and functions. Officials embraced and expressed a providentialist perspective in countless official actions and statements: prayers at official functions such as legislative sessions and presidential inaugurations were only the most conspicuous of these expressions. Governments and government officials adopted this providentialist stance, usually, without any sense that they were violating any constitutional prohibition, and indeed often with the understanding that they were carrying out a sacred duty.

Then, in the latter half of the twentieth century, the Supreme Court and the legal profession implemented a fundamental makeover of the Constitution, interpreting it to require government to be "neutral" toward religion and to confine itself to the domain of the secular. Under this new orthodoxy, providentialist actions and expressions that had characterized the republic for most of its history were now, in principle at least, constitutionally impermissible.

In effect, to borrow Murray's contention, the Court used the venerable idea of "separation of church and state" to establish *public* atheism as a component of the *public* philosophy. The word "public" needs to be underscored, because the Court never understood itself to be deprecating religion, as the Marxist regimes had done, or to be embracing atheism as a total or overall philosophy. On the contrary, the justices were self-consciously and from all appearances sincerely respectful and protective of religion *in the private sphere*. But (although implementation of this announced principle was always haphazard) invocations of deity were now deemed to be in principle impermissible *in the public or governmental sphere.*

The justices and their supporters declared, and may have actually believed, that in imposing public secularism on the nation they were acting on commitments made at the founding. By now it is close to axiomatic, among both political liberals and many political conservatives, that the Constitution was intended to establish "secular" and religiously "neutral" government. But however widely held, this particular axiom happens to be mistaken. Demonstrably mistaken. In fact, the Court's reconstruction of the Constitution was working a radical transformation, for better or for worse, not only in America's law but in its official self-conception. And this transformation has had momentous implications and consequences. Part 3 ("Providentialism and the Travails of Liberalism") will consider some of these consequences.

Part 1

A GODLESS DOCUMENT?

When the delegates to the Philadelphia convention finished their work and sent their newly devised constitution out to the states for ratification, their proposal immediately came in for heavy criticism. The Constitution, opponents complained, created an overly powerful central government, undermined the sovereignty of the states, failed to protect natural rights, and attempted to establish a republican form of government in a nation too large and diverse to sustain such a government.

These criticisms are familiar still, and resonate still. A different criticism hardly resonates at all and hence is largely forgotten. The Constitution, opponents charged, failed to pay its respects to God.

In this vein, a writer in a Boston newspaper predicted that because the Constitution refused to recognize God, God would decline to support the republic. The writer quoted the Old Testament prophet Samuel's warning to king Saul: "Because thou hast rejected the word of the Lord, he hath also rejected thee." A Pennsylvania pamphleteer going under the name of "Aristocrotis" objected that the "new Constitution, disdains . . . belief of a deity, the immortality of the soul, or the resurrection of the body, a day of judgement, or a future state of rewards and punishments." Other critics advanced similar objections.[1]

---

1. See Isaac Kramnick and R. Laurence Moore, *The Godless Constitution: A Moral Defense of the Secular State* (New York: Norton, 2005), 34–37. Compare David Sehat, *The Myth of American Religious Freedom* (New York: Oxford University Press, 2011), 42

PART 1

To the modern ear, these objections may sound like the epitome of artificial, contrived quibbling. True, the Constitution did not refer to God—with one small nonexception: the document recorded that it had been signed on "the Seventeenth Day of September in the *Year of our Lord* one thousand seven hundred and Eighty seven." But this was merely a conventional way of dating; the language was no more a serious religious invocation than are the letters BC or AD attached to a date.[2] So, yes, the Constitution omitted to acknowledge God. But then why on earth *should* it mention God? The Constitution was a legal document, after all, not a sermon or a summa; and legal documents—mortgages, insurance policies, merger agreements—typically do not say anything about God. Indeed, any such reference would seem weirdly out of place, maybe even sacrilegious, in a legal instrument designed to regulate this-worldly matters. So critics who objected to this omission were simply being churlish.

Or so it may seem to us. If we react to the criticism in this way, however, our reaction serves to demonstrate the cultural distance between us and the founding.

Imagine that you live in a world in which it is widely believed that an attentive, all-powerful deity is sovereign over and engaged in, well, everything. Not just church meetings and private devotions, not just the consciences of individual persons, but *everything*, including history and politics—and governance. In fact, as we will see, many in the founding generation, including not especially pious sorts such as George Washington and Thomas Jefferson, *did* believe something like this; or at least they said they did. On that assumption, in a landmark document meant to inaugurate and guide a new nation, it might seem entirely appropriate to acknowledge deity—and insolent and even dangerous to deliberately forgo any such acknowledgment. Nonrecognition might amount to a kind of snub. It would be as if the president or the chief justice or the queen—or the *generalissimo*—showed up at your city council meeting or school board

---

("To many religious leaders who lined up against the Constitution, the omission of God suggested a depraved sensibility that betokened the downfall of the Christian nation").

2. For analysis of the point, see Mark David Hall, *Did America Have a Christian Founding?* (Nashville: Nelson, 2019), 24–26.

session and you deliberately refused to introduce the person or acknowledge his or her presence.

And indeed, comparable documents at the time, and since, did and do acknowledge deity. The Declaration of Independence, arguably the nation's founding charter, invoked "Nature and Nature's God" and declared that the rights being asserted as a justification for the new nation were those with which people were "endowed by their Creator"; and the signatories to the revolutionary Declaration explicitly staked their lives, their fortunes, and their sacred honor based on "a firm reliance on the protection of divine Providence."

To be sure, the Declaration was more in the nature of a manifesto than of a practical legal instrument, as the Constitution was. But the Constitution's immediate and most equivalent predecessor, the Articles of Confederation, duly paid respect to "the Great Governor of the World."[3]

Every state constitution likewise offered (and still does offer) obeisance to "God," "Almighty God," "the Supreme Ruler of the Universe," or "the Sovereign Ruler of the Universe."[4] In the preamble to the Massachusetts Constitution of 1780, for example, the people "acknowledg[ed], with grateful hearts, the goodness of the Great Legislator of the Universe" and "devoutly implor[ed] His direction."[5] The Vermont Constitution, adopted in 1777, declared that the purpose of government is to enable citizens "to enjoy their natural rights, and the other blessings which the Author of existence has bestowed upon man."[6]

Nor is it only American constitutions, or eighteenth-century constitutions, that have acknowledged deity. The Canadian Constitution Act of 1982 declares that "Canada is founded upon principles that recognize the supremacy of God."[7] The preamble to the Irish Constitution of 1937 began

---

3. Articles of Confederation, Art. XIII.

4. For a compilation, see William J. Federer, *The Ten Commandments and Their Influence on American Law* (2003), 52–55.

5. *The Founders Constitution*, vol. 1, ed. Philip B. Kurland and Ralph Lerner (Chicago: University of Chicago Press, 1987), 11.

6. Constitution of Vermont, preamble, at https://tinyurl.com/bp7rcyz5.

7. Part 1 of the Constitution Act, 1982. For a discussion, see Jonathan W. Penney and Robert Jacob Danay, "The Embarrassing Preamble? Understanding the Supremacy of God and the Charter," *British Columbia Law Review* 39 (2006): 287.

by affirming: "In the Name of the Most Holy Trinity, from Whom is all authority and to Whom, as our final end, all actions both of men and States must be referred."[8] Eric Stein notes that in the European context, although the French and Italian constitutions are entirely secular, these are the exception; a "comparative survey of the constitutional systems of [European] Union members discloses that a majority embodies Christianity in one way or another (e.g., the German, Irish, Maltese, Greek, Danish and English)."[9] And the constitutions of Muslim nations declare a similar commitment—in Islamic vocabulary, of course. For example, the Enforced Constitution of Afghanistan began by proclaiming: "Praise be to Allah, the Cherisher and Sustainer of the Worlds," and the preamble proceeded to declare: "We the people of Afghanistan: Believing firmly in Almighty God, relying on His divine will and adhering to the Holy religion of Islam. . . ."[10]

So the critics were right in perceiving the omission of any acknowledgment of God as an audacious feature of the new American Constitution (as indeed the document's defenders unapologetically agreed).[11] Steven Waldman observes that "the US Constitution is stunningly secular. It doesn't mention Jesus, God, the Creator, or even Providence. In light of the unbroken record of invoking God's name in foundational documents throughout the world, throughout the colonies, and throughout history, the stubborn refusal of the US Constitution to invoke the Almighty is abnormal, historic, radical, and not accidental."[12]

All right. And yet . . . what exactly did the omission of any reference to God entail, or portend?

A couple of centuries later, in a much-discussed book, two scholars offered an answer to that question that many have found persuasive. In *The Godless Constitution*, Isaac Kramnick and R. Laurence Moore make essen-

---

8. Irish Constitution of 1937, https://tinyurl.com/7pa9rwyp.

9. Eric Stein, "The Church and the Constitution for Europe," *Columbia Journal of European Law* (2005): 451, 452.

10. Enforced Constitution of Afghanistan, https://tinyurl.com/2f9me34r.

11. See Kramnick and Moore, *The Godless Constitution*, 36–45. See also Steven K. Green, "The Legal Ramifications of Christian Nationalism," *Roger Williams University Law Review* 26 (2021): 430, 438–41.

12. Steven Waldman, *Founding Faith: How Our Founding Fathers Forged a Radical New Approach to Religious Freedom* (New York: Random House, 2008), 130–31.

tially two main claims. First, they say, the Constitution itself is a "godless" document; it is by deliberate design devoid of references to deity. Second, the godless quality of the Constitution entails or requires "godless" government and a "godless politics"[13]—that is, an exclusion or separation of God and religion from governance.

Although more nuance will in due course be called for, we might at the outset offer hasty reactions to these claims. Thus, we have already seen that the first of these claims is basically correct. (Someone might to be sure quarrel with the authors' provocative choice of the word "godless"; we will return to that question.) If the authors' first claim can be pronounced basically correct, however, the second claim seems on its face to be a brazen non sequitur.

From the fact that the Constitution itself lacks religious language, it does not logically follow that politics or governance generally was or is required to eschew religious language or beliefs. If the Constitution did not explicitly prescribe a religious orientation for government, neither did it disapprove or forbid such an orientation; nor did it prescribe any other worldview or normative system. The Constitution simply left all these possibilities open. It left the matter earnestly unresolved.

A comparison may be helpful. The Constitution did not and does not explicitly indicate any approval for utilitarianism, or the view that government along with other agents ought to act to promote the greatest good (defined, as utilitarian thinkers like John Stuart Mill have done, in terms of pleasure and the avoidance of pain) for the greatest number. But it hardly follows that governments cannot act on utilitarian considerations. The Constitution's silence on the subject means that American governments, national and state, may follow or not follow a utilitarian path, as they choose. The normatively noncommittal Constitution leaves that choice up to them. Same for religion.

Here is another way to look at the point. It is true that the Constitution could have acknowledged God (as other comparable documents did), and yet it declined to do so. Conversely, the Constitution could have explicitly required government to eschew religious considerations in governmental expressions and decisions—or, in other words, to be secular (as some other

---

13. Kramnick and Moore, *The Godless Constitution*, 151, 167–68.

nations' constitutions do).[14] But despite occasional modern representations to the contrary,[15] the Constitution did not do that either.

Some citizens in later generations agitated for both kinds of provisions; they advocated amendments to the Constitution that would have acknowledged God or Christianity or, conversely, that would have explicitly required that government in this country must be secular. Neither kind of proposal was ever adopted.[16] Indeed, organizations calling themselves the National Reform Association and the Liberal League held competing conventions in Philadelphia in 1876, timed to correlate with the Centennial Exposition, for the purpose of proposing amendments that would declare the republic to be, respectively, Christian or secular. The clashing conventions provoked considerable attention in the press, but neither group's agenda came close to being adopted.[17]

The upshot is that the framers enacted and later generations consciously retained a constitution that in its body and overall character—we will consider the First Amendment specifically in due course—was and is simply noncommittal with respect to God and to the role of religion in government.

To be sure, the original Constitution did prohibit the imposition of religious tests for holding federal office; so neither Congress nor a state could

---

14. For example, the preamble to the Indian Constitution declares: "We, the People of India, having solemnly resolved to constitute India into a sovereign socialist *secular* democratic Republic." Constitution of India (as of May 2022) (emphasis added), https://tinyurl.com/aehnk83k.

15. Professor Geoffrey Stone, for example, asserts that "the *stated purpose* of the Constitution was not to create a 'Government established according to God,' nor to establish a 'Christian nation,' but rather to create a secular state." Geoffrey R. Stone, "The World of the Framers: A Christian Nation?" *UCLA Law Review* 56 (2008): 5 (emphasis added). But Stone fails to quote any language from the Constitution that in fact states such a purpose or supports his description. For an exposition of the various ways in which Stone's presentation distorts the historical evidence, see Samuel W. Calhoun, "Getting the Framers Wrong: A Response to Professor Geoffrey Stone," *UCLA Law Review Discourse*, 2009, 1.

16. For discussion of these movements, see Philip Hamburger, *Separation of Church and State* (Cambridge, MA: Harvard University Press, 2002), 287–334.

17. For a detailed review of these movements, see Steven K. Green, *The Bible, the School, and the Constitution* (New York: Oxford University Press, 2012), 137–77.

limit eligibility for the presidency or the Senate or the House to, say, orthodox Christians (as states *could* do—and sometimes did—for state offices).[18] In addition, the later-adopted First Amendment, and more specifically that amendment's (non)establishment clause ("Congress shall make no law respecting an establishment of religion"), imposed an additional constitutional constraint of some kind. That amendment at least prohibited the establishment of any government-sponsored national church; whether it did more than that, and if so, how much more, will be taken up in chapter 2.

Beyond these specific provisions, though, the Constitution itself, although not a religious document, neither prescribed nor prohibited any particular governmental stance toward religion. It was like an agnostic parent who self-consciously leaves the children free to live a religious or a wholly secular life, as they may choose. So, yes, the Constitution left open the possibility of a "godless politics" and "godless" governance—evidently the course favored by Kramnick and Moore and many, many others, especially in recent decades. But the "godless" Constitution was also compatible with a more religion-infused governance and politics—which is in fact what ensued in the early republic and persisted for at least the next century and a half or so. (How to characterize the period since then presents a more complicated and debatable question, as we will see.)

Readers who are satisfied with this conclusion—that the Constitution itself with a couple of important but specific exceptions was mostly noncommittal on the role of religion in politics and governance—might accordingly skip over the next two chapters and go straight to parts 2 and 3, where the harmonies and tensions between the providential republic and the "godless" Constitution will be considered more directly. But in modern scholarship and jurisprudence, the conclusion just tentatively offered is in fact fiercely contested—or, more often, is simply rejected out of hand and scarcely even considered. Countless jurists, scholars, and citizens generally, both liberal and conservative, by now take it as virtually axiomatic

---

18. See Sehat, *The Myth of American Religious Freedom*, 29 ("Most [state] constitutions ratified before the 1787 U.S. Constitution . . . included limits on the kind of people who could be elected to office. Eleven of the fourteen constitutions prohibited Jews and agnostics from holding office. Seven of fourteen prohibited Catholic officeholders. Nine of the fourteen limited civil rights to Protestants (five), Christians (three), or theists (one)").

PART 1

that the Constitution mandated a "secular" and religiously "neutral" government. So a more sustained examination and defense seem called for. In addition, there are important qualifications, complications, and nuances that need to be noticed.

John Courtney Murray was correct in perceiving that the American Constitution, and the "separation of church and state" that it provided for, had a distinctive quality—a distinctive quality that has often been overlooked or misunderstood, including by the modern Supreme Court and leading constitutional scholars—and it will be helpful to consider that distinctive quality more closely. Which is the task of the following chapter.

CHAPTER 1

Atheist or Agnostic?

We sometimes describe a person as "religious," or perhaps "*deeply* religious." Or, conversely, as "not at all religious," or even "antireligious." We may offer similar descriptions for a book, a magazine, a piece of music, a university, or a cultural or political movement. So, can we use similar adjectives for a constitution? And if so, what sort of document is the American Constitution, religiously speaking? Is it a Christian or at least religious document, as some claim?[1] A "godless" document, as others assert?[2] Something in between? None of the above?

As we have seen already, in their book *The Godless Constitution*, Isaac Kramnick and R. Laurence Moore assert, first, that the Constitution is a "godless" document and, second, that the godless quality of the Constitution mandates a "godless politics" and governance. Other scholars and advocates make similar claims.[3] We have already said, in a hasty and conclusory preview, that the first of these claims is basically correct.

---

1. For a critical discussion of this claim and its various claimants, see John Fea, *Was America Founded as a Christian Nation? A Historical Introduction* (Louisville: Westminster John Knox, 2011), 57–75.

2. Isaac Kramnick and R. Laurence Moore, *The Godless Constitution: A Moral Defense of the Secular State* (New York: Norton, 2005).

3. See, e.g., Jared A. Goldstein, "How the Constitution Became Christian," *Hastings Law Journal* 68 (2017): 264 ("How did the godless Constitution condemned by nineteenth century Christian nationalists become the Constitution that more recent Christian nationalists laud as an expression of the nation's religious devotion?"); David Sehat, *The Myth of American Religious Freedom* (New York: Oxford University Press, 2011), 41; Steven K. Green, *The Second Disestablishment: Church and State in Nineteenth-Century*

PART 1: A GODLESS DOCUMENT?

But perhaps that observation was *too* hasty? The question will turn out to be key to understanding the distinctive but much-misapprehended character of the American Constitution, so it is worth taking a closer look.

A "GODLESS" CONSTITUTION?

It is true, as we have already seen, that the Constitution contained and (despite occasional efforts to correct the omission) still contains no meaningful acknowledgment of God. It is also true that this was a deliberate and in the historical context audacious omission. Does it follow that the Constitution is "godless" in character?

Maybe. But consider two possible objections.

First, the Constitution might have a religious quality—or, for that matter, an antireligious or atheistic quality—without explicitly declaring as much. We all know people who are deeply devout or, conversely, who disbelieve in God and religion but do not go around publicly proclaiming these views and commitments. Perhaps these people's convictions can be discerned in the way they live, or obliquely inferred from things they say; but we would not know of their faith or lack thereof just by listening to what they openly declare in public. Might not the same be true of the United States Constitution? Perhaps the Constitution rests on religious presuppositions—or atheistic presuppositions—that are unstated.[4]

America (New York: Oxford University Press, 2010), 55 (observing that "the Constitution was bereft of even a passing reference to a deity. No reference to a divine guiding hand or allusions to Providence appear in its provisions"); Susan Jacoby, *Freethinkers: A History of American Secularism* (New York: Metropolitan Books, 2004), 269, 358 (describing "the flourishing religious pluralism envisioned by the framers of the godless Constitution"); Daniel O. Conkle, "Religious Expression and Symbolism in the American Constitutional Tradition," *Indiana Journal of Global Legal Studies* 13 (2006): 417–18 ("We are committed to the idea of secular as opposed to religious government, and our national Constitution is itself a secular document"); Franklin Lambert, *The Founding Fathers and the Place of Religion in America* (Princeton: Princeton University Press, 2003), 246 ("The 'Godless' Constitution"); James E. Pfander, "So Help Me God: Religion and Presidential Oath-Taking," *Constitutional Commentary* 16 (1999): 551 (describing "the agnostic (if not downright atheistic) character of the Constitution").

4. Matthew Harris and Thomas Kidd assert that "although the Constitution said little about religion, religious beliefs still shadowed and shaped the Constitution." Mat-

Atheist or Agnostic?

How so? Well, here is one possibility. Each of the following propositions can claim considerable and distinguished support from the founding period.[5] First, the Constitution establishes a republican form of government for a free people. Second, this form of government necessarily depends on a virtuous citizenry. Third, as George Washington famously contended in his Farewell Address ("reason and experience both forbid us to expect that national morality can prevail in exclusion of religious principle"),[6] and as so many in the founding generation believed, a virtuous people necessarily depends on religion.[7] Suppose all of these contentions are correct; or rather, and less ambitiously, suppose that whether or not the contentions are correct, the framers and the founding generation *believed* them to be correct. The conclusion might be drawn that the Constitution was constructed on, or dependent on, religious assumptions or presuppositions. As John Adams put it, "our constitution was made only for a moral and religious people. It is wholly inadequate to the government of any other."[8]

Or someone might argue (as proponents sometimes did) that the influence of God was quietly at work in the proceedings that led to the drafting and enactment of the Constitution. Prominent federalists including Washington and Franklin pressed this point:[9] How else could anyone explain

---

thew L. Harris and Thomas S. Kidd, "Introduction: The Founding Fathers and Religion," in *The Founding Fathers and the Debate over Religion in Revolutionary America*, ed. Matthew L. Harris and Thomas S. Kidd (New York: Oxford University Press, 2012), 16. In this vein, Marci Hamilton argues that a significant number of the framers were Calvinists and that various features of the Constitution reflect Calvinist assumptions. See Marci Hamilton, "The Framers, Faith, and Tyranny," *Roger Williams University Law Review* 62 (2021): 495.

5. See Nathan S. Chapman and Michael W. McConnell, *Agreeing to Disagree: How the Establishment Clause Protects Religious Diversity and Freedom of Conscience* (New York: Oxford University Press, 2023), 32, 44.

6. "George Washington's Farewell Address," reprinted in *The Sacred Rights of Conscience*, ed. Daniel L. Dreisbach and Mark David Hall (Indianapolis: Liberty Fund, 2009), 468.

7. Ample support for each of these propositions with statements from founders is provided in Mark David Hall, *Did America Have a Christian Founding?* (Nashville: Nelson, 2019), 31–35. See also John A. Ragosta, "A Wall between a Secular Government and a Religious People," *Roger Williams University Law Review* 62 (2021): 545, 570–71.

8. Quoted in Hall, *Did America Have a Christian Founding?*, 32.

9. See Harris and Kidd, "Introduction," 16 ("Some of the framers, including Frank-

PART 1: A GODLESS DOCUMENT?

how the feisty, often fractious delegates to the Philadelphia convention had managed to converge on such a momentous and controversial proposal, and how ratification was ultimately achieved in all of the states even though it seems likely that most Americans didn't favor the new regime?[10] The very improbability of what happened might call for a providential explanation. Kramnick and Moore assert that the *Federalist Papers*, the classic essays written in support of ratification by James Madison, Alexander Hamilton, and John Jay, "fail to mention God anywhere."[11] But Kramnick and Moore are mistaken. Madison, in *Federalist* 37, after acknowledging the Constitution's imperfections, added, "The real wonder is that so many difficulties should have been surmounted, and surmounted with a unanimity almost as unprecedented as it must have been unexpected. It is impossible for any man of candor to reflect on this circumstance without partaking of the astonishment. It is impossible for the man of pious reflection not to perceive in it a finger of that Almighty hand which has been so frequently and signally extended to our relief in the critical stages of the revolution."[12]

---

lin, immediately began to suggest that the Constitution had somehow been blessed or given by God to America"). And in a letter to Jonathan Trumbull, Washington wrote that "we may, with a kind of pious and grateful exultation, trace the finger of Providence through those dark and mysterious events, which first induced the States to appoint a general convention, and then led them one after another, with such steps as were best calculated to effect the object, into an adoption of the system recommended by that general convention." Washington to Trumbull, reprinted in Harris and Kidd, *The Founding Fathers and the Debate over Religion in Revolutionary America*, 84.

10. Cf. Joseph J. Ellis, *The Quartet: Orchestrating the Second American Revolution, 1783–1789* (New York: Knopf, 2015), xiv: "The dominant historical forces in the 1780s were centrifugal rather than centripetal, meaning that the vast majority of citizens had no interest in American nationhood; indeed, they regarded the very idea of a national government as irrelevant to their local lives and ominously reminiscent of the British leviathan they had recently vanquished. There was no popular insurgency for a national government because such a thing was not popular."

11. Kramnick and Moore, *The Godless Constitution*, 31.

12. *Federalist* 37 (Madison), in *The Federalist Papers* (New York: Signet, 2003), 230–31. See also *Federalist* 2 (Jay), in *The Federalist Papers*, 38:

> Providence has in a particular manner blessed [the country] with a variety of soils and productions and watered it with innumerable streams for the delight and accommodation of its inhabitants. . . . Providence has been pleased to give this one connected country to one united people. . . . The

Atheist or Agnostic?

In sum, it might be that the Constitution is a religious document in some indirect or second-order sense not immediately evident on the face of the instrument.

Still, if we limit ourselves to examining the constitutional text, Kramnick and Moore seem to have a point. Whatever its presuppositions may have been, it might be argued, and whether or not a providential influence was silently at work in the process of its drafting and adoption, the Constitution just in itself was and is a godless document.

So consider a second objection. The term "godless" seems both gratuitously provocative and imprecise. Literally, the term simply means "without God"—a description that, as noted, arguably applies to the constitutional text. But the term also carries a tone of being opposed to God, as in the League of the Militant Godless that aggressively promoted atheism in the Soviet Union.[13] And there is not much semantic difference—is there?—between "godless" and "ungodly." Dictionaries list associated meanings such as "wicked" and "profane." These are common enough connotations, but they seem inapt for describing the Constitution; nor are they connotations that the proponents of secular government intend. The authors of *The Godless Constitution* are not condemning the document as wicked but rather celebrating and invoking it (as they understand it, anyway).

"Godless" can also seem almost synonymous with "atheistic." But if the Constitution does not mention God, neither does it say anything that denies or denigrates God.[14] It is simply silent on the subject of God.

So, although we can say loosely that the Constitution is "godless," a more

> country and this people seem to have been made for each other, and it appears as if it was the design of Providence that an inheritance so proper and convenient for a band of brethren, united to each other by the strongest ties, should never be split into a number of unsocial, jealous, and alien sovereignties.

13. See Daniel Peris, *Storming the Heavens: The Soviet League of the Militant Godless* (Ithaca, NY: Cornell University Press, 1998), 2 ("Created in 1925, the League of the Militant Godless was the nominally independent organization established by the Communist Party to promote atheism").

14. Compare Bruce Ledewitz, *American Religious Democracy: Coming to Terms with the End of Secular Politics* (Westport, CT: Praeger, 2007), 52 ("The Constitution is not an atheistic document, though it makes no reference to God"). See also Steven K. Green, "The Legal Ramifications of Christian Nationalism," *Roger Williams University*

eligible and precise term, it may seem, would be "agnostic." An agnostic, in popular parlance, is someone who takes no position on the existence of God—who refrains from either affirming or denying. Indeed, the term was invented, by Thomas Huxley, precisely to convey that "neither for nor against" position.[15] And this seems to be the stance taken by the Constitution.

So then, can we settle on the proposition that the Constitution is an "agnostic" document? Maybe, but before signing off on that description, let us again consider possible objections.

In the first place, not everything that omits to take a position on God is cogently described as agnostic. Most of the things we encounter in the world say nothing about God, and we do not typically describe all these things as "agnostic." So it would seem odd to talk about an agnostic automobile or an agnostic potato—or even (if we limit ourselves to linguistic expressions) an agnostic grocery list or meeting agenda. "Agnostic" is an apt description, it seems, for someone or something that might be expected to take a position about God, for or against, but deliberately abstains from doing so.

As we have seen, though, constitutions often did and do acknowledge deity; or, in Communist countries, they may declare their opposition to deity. Moreover, as we have also seen, citizens and organizations have campaigned to insert language into the Constitution that would acknowledge God or, conversely, explicitly declare the republic to be secular. But the Constitution

---

Law Review 26 (2021): 439 ("This does not mean that the drafters intended to create a 'Godless Constitution' in the sense of it being an antireligious or irreligious document").

15. Huxley explained how and why he came up with the term:

> When I reached intellectual maturity and began to ask myself whether I was an atheist, a theist, or a pantheist; a materialist or an idealist; a Christian or a freethinker; I found that the more I learned and reflected, the less ready was the answer.... The one thing in which most of these good people were agreed was the one thing in which I differed from them. They were quite sure they had successfully solved the problem of existence; while I was quite sure I had not, and had a pretty strong conviction that the problem was insoluble.

This stance proved embarrassing in the Metaphysical Society, however, where, said Huxley, "most of my colleagues [were] -ists of one sort or another." "So I took thought, and invented what I conceived to be the appropriate title of 'Agnostic.'" Thomas Henry Huxley, "Agnosticism" (1889), in *Agnosticism and Christianity and Other Essays* (Amherst, NY: Prometheus Books, 1992), 162–63.

Atheist or Agnostic?

studiously refrains from doing either of these things. In that sense, it seems fitting to describe the Constitution as agnostic. It *could* say something for or against God. Many people have *wanted* it to say something about God. Documents of its kind have often declared for or sometimes against God. But the American Constitution declines to do any of these things, instead maintaining a studied silence on the subject. It is . . . agnostic.

A different possible objection to this characterization is that "agnostic" is a misleading term, or a kind of cheat, because genuine agnosticism is an illusion.[16] In this vein, David Novak asserts that "despite the attempt to create a neutral position called 'agnosticism,' one can show that agnostics are really timid atheists."[17]

Novak's assertion will turn out to be at least partly mistaken, but it does prompt a closer look at agnosticism. It will become apparent that the agnostic position is more complicated than it may seem at first. Agnosticism does in one sense seem to be impossible, as Novak supposes; but in another sense it is not only possible but arguably even inevitable (at least for anyone who seriously engages with the question of God).

Impossible but also possible and maybe even inevitable? The description presents a paradox, and we will need to consider that paradox as well. In thinking through these complications, we will gain a clearer sense of how the Constitution is agnostic—and of the potential political implications of that agnosticism.

The Possibility—Inevitability?—of Agnosticism

On first inspection, it may seem obvious that agnosticism is at least a *possible* position. We know it is possible because, as in the joke about baptism by immersion, we've seen it done.[18] Indeed, many people may find that

---

16. Paul Horwitz considers this objection at length but ultimately finds it unconvincing. See Paul Horwitz, *The Agnostic Age: Law, Religion, and the Constitution* (New York: Oxford University Press, 2011), 98–104.

17. David Novak, "Law: Religious or Secular?" *Virginia Law Review* 86 (2000): 574. See also John Courtney Murray, SJ, *The Problem of God: Yesterday and Today* (New Haven: Yale University Press, 1964), 96 ("Agnosticism is atheism by default").

18. In one version of the joke, an old farmer is asked whether he believes in baptism by immersion. The farmer responds, "*Believe* in it? Hell, I've seen it done."

the term in its usual sense accurately describes their own way of thinking. They have reflected deeply, perhaps even prayerfully, without achieving any confidence about the answer.[19] They may have considered the standard arguments for and against the existence of God—the so-called ontological argument and the arguments from design and morality, on the one hand, and the argument from evil, on the other—and concluded that the arguments on each side of the question are less than compelling. And so they find that they are unable to decide one way or the other. Perhaps against their wishes and despite their best efforts, they are . . . agnostic. No other description seems to fit.

Indeed, it may even come to seem that agnosticism is not merely possible, but that it is the only position that a thoughtful person can honestly come to. If a mathematical demonstration is cogent, it will leave no intelligent dissenters. The conclusion will have been *proven*: no one who actually understands the proof will be able to resist the conclusion. Are there competent mathematicians who reject the demonstration of the Pythagorean theorem? Likewise, if the arguments either for or against God were compelling, they would have carried the day, it may seem; but in fact there are thoughtful, intelligent people who find all these arguments wanting. And given the lack of compelling arguments either way, agnosticism may seem the honorable default position. "In the absence of a convincing proof either of theism or of atheism," asks Anthony Kenny, "is not the rational position that of the agnostic, who refuses to place a bet either way?"[20]

True, there are people who claim to have certainty about God not so much from reasoning but rather from personal experience, or inspiration, or revelation. They prayed, perhaps, and felt within themselves a divine response.[21] But personal experience is subjective, and also in need of in-

---

19. Compare Hans Küng, *Does God Exist?*, trans. Edward Quinn (Eugene, OR: Wipf & Stock, 1978), 573 (observing that a person "can, perhaps utterly honestly and truthfully, declare his inability to know (agnosticism with a tendency to atheism)").

20. Anthony Kenny, *What I Believe* (London: Continuum, 2006), 46.

21. See, e.g., David Dollahite, "The Empirical Power of Spiritual Experience," *Public Square*, September 6, 2023, https://tinyurl.com/3tur2e2b. See also David Dollahite, "Sacred Encounters. Answered Prayers," *Public Square*, October 6, 2023, https://tnyurl.com/3p9a8azb. ("How does one determine the existence of God? Is it through philosophy, theology, science, logic, reason, experience, or any/all of these? I submit

terpretation; and the interpretations will always be contestable. What one person takes to be a personal encounter with God can always be given a more reductive psychological or neurological explanation: And can even the believer who is honest with herself be completely certain that the reductive explanation is not the correct one?

To be sure, some people on the basis of reasoning or personal experience will find the existence of God highly likely. Just as a subjective matter, perhaps, they feel no doubt at all; they would be lying if they pretended otherwise. They "know" (in a subjective sense) that God is real. Others will reach the opposite conclusion. There might conceivably be a God, they may admit—it is an abstract possibility—but considering all the horrors and undeserved suffering in the world that a God ought to prevent but manifestly doesn't.... And so forth. People who reach one of these conclusions will likely, and properly, describe themselves as theists, or as atheists.

And yet insofar as these descriptions are merely reporting estimates of likelihood, the believers or nonbelievers if they are honest must still acknowledge a lack of objective certainty, or of conclusive proof. Joseph Ratzinger explained the situation in this way: "Both the believer and the unbeliever share, each in his own way, doubt *and* belief, if they do not hide from themselves and from the truth of their being. Neither can quite escape either doubt or belief; for the one, faith is present *against* doubt; for the other, *through* doubt and in the *form* of doubt. It is the basic pattern of man's destiny only to be allowed to find the finality of his existence in this unceasing rivalry between doubt and belief, temptation and certainty."[22]

This mixture (in different proportions, to be sure) of faith and doubt—this lack of objective certainty—might be described as agnosticism. But

---

the most immediate and sure way is by having some kind of personal sacred encounter with God.")

22. Joseph Cardinal Ratzinger, *Introduction to Christianity*, trans. J. R. Foster (San Francisco: Ignatius, 1969), 46–47. Ratzinger added: "Perhaps in precisely this way doubt, which saves both sides from being shut up in their own worlds, could become the avenue of communication. It prevents both from enjoying complete self-satisfaction; it opens up the believer to the doubter and the doubter to the believer; for one, it is his share in the fate of the unbeliever; for the other, the form in which belief remains nevertheless a challenge for him."

among people who are thoughtful about the matter and honest with themselves, are there any who do not fit this description? And so it may seem that everyone who reflects on the matter and is brutally honest with himself or herself will be an agnostic. There will be theistically inclined agnostics and atheistically leaning agnostics. But everyone who is thoughtful and honest is an agnostic of one stripe or another.

Or perhaps this argument overreaches. Perhaps it construes the category of "agnosticism" too broadly. Someone might respond: "Look, there are many things which I believe without any doubt at all—which I *know*—and yet I might admit that, in the abstract, I *could* be mistaken. It's possible. I have not the slightest doubt that the sun is shining outside right now, that I have five toes on each of my feet, that I am at this moment eating a boiled egg. But of course I *could* be wrong. Like Descartes, 'in sleep I have often been deceived': this could all be an elaborate and extremely convincing dream. (Although I'm pretty sure it isn't.) Or I might just be a brain in a vat, and all of this stuff might be an illusion. So, if I admit this as an abstract possibility, does it follow that I am an agnostic about . . . everything? Isn't that stretching the term a little too far?"

Perhaps. If so, then the claim about agnosticism being inevitable would need to be retracted. Even so, it remains true that agnosticism is a possible position—and a position that many thoughtful people in fact occupy, and sincerely claim.

The Impossibility of Agnosticism

And yet from a different perspective, even that more modest proposition may seem mistaken. Agnosticism may seem not to be possible at all. To see how, consider a well-known essay by the psychologist and philosopher William James called "The Will to Believe,"[23] which was itself written in response to a vigorous plea for agnosticism by the British mathematician William Clifford.[24]

---

23. William James, "The Will to Believe," in *The Will to Believe and Other Essays in Popular Philosophy and Human Immortality* (New York: Dover, 1956), 1.

24. William Clifford, "The Ethics of Belief," reprinted in *Philosophy of Religion: Selected Readings*, ed. Michael Peterson et al. (New York: Oxford University Press, 2001), 80.

Atheist or Agnostic?

The central premise of Clifford's essay, entitled "The Ethics of Belief," was that "it is wrong to believe anything upon insufficient evidence." Actually, that description is too tame. In fact, Clifford vehemently contended, to believe without sufficient evidence is not only unwarranted; it is "wrong, always, everywhere, and for anyone." Believing without sufficient proof is "sinful," "dishonest," "wicked," and "a great wrong towards Man." "The credulous man is father to the liar and the cheat."

Clifford understood that given the limitations of human life, people would often be unable to do the full investigation necessary to decide conclusively whether a particular proposition is true or false. In that case, they should simply forgo believing. If someone does not have time fully to investigate a question, "then he should have no time to believe."[25]

The truculent certainty in Clifford's denunciation of unwarranted certainty may seem ironic, and James wryly noted that there was "somewhat too much of robustious pathos in the voice."[26] More substantively, James argued that Clifford's "agnostic rules for truth-seeking"[27] were fundamentally unsound. Although James presented an array of objections, for our purposes his most pertinent objection asserted that in life we are sometimes confronted with "forced options"—with propositions that demand a "yes or no," "for or against" response. Such propositions leave us no practical option of simply suspending judgment, or remaining neutral, because anything other than a yes answer will for all practical purposes be equivalent to a no answer.[28]

To be sure, many questions that confront us—most of them, probably—do not have this forced character. Did William Shakespeare actually write all the plays attributed to him? Did Lee Harvey Oswald act alone in shooting John Kennedy, or did he have accomplices or sponsors? Are Bigfoot and the Loch Ness monster real? With respect to all of these and countless other questions, nothing seems to prevent someone from saying,

---

25. Clifford, "The Ethics of Belief," 84–85.
26. James, "The Will to Believe," 8.
27. James, "The Will to Believe," 28.
28. See James, "The Will to Believe," 3: "But if I say, 'Either accept this truth or go without it,' I put on you a forced option, for there is no standing place outside of the alternative. Every dilemma based on a complete logical disjunction, with possibility of not choosing, is an option of this forced kind."

PART 1: A GODLESS DOCUMENT?

"I don't know. Maybe, maybe not." Often, as James acknowledged and indeed insisted, that is the sensible position to take.[29]

But many other questions—including some of the most important or existentially pressing ones—do seem to have the "forced" quality described by James. James gave an imaginative example in which you are invited to accompany an expedition to the North Pole.[30] A commitment is required, so if you say you can't decide, that will amount to saying no: you won't be going on the expedition.[31] A similar logic would apply to a variety of more mundane practical propositions—to the propositions contained in a job offer, for example, or a marriage proposal, an investment opportunity, or a house that you might purchase. *Not* to decide is to decide—to decide *against*. Dithering endlessly over whether the proposer of marriage is worthy of your commitment is equivalent for practical purposes to concluding that he or she is *not* worthy—even if you never consciously draw that conclusion.

Religious questions will sometimes be of this character.[32] Not always: undoubtedly there are numerous abstruse theological disputes about which most of us can say, "I don't know, and I don't need to know: it makes no difference to me." But if a preacher tells me, "Accept and follow Jesus and you will be saved; if you don't accept Jesus you will be damned,"[33] I am faced with a forced choice. Because simply to say "I can't decide" is the same as a refusal to accept. If the preacher happens to be correct, the honest, humble agnostic will be in the same unhappy position as the militant atheist.

Or we might put it this way: Relative to the preacher's proposition, as a practical matter, the option of simply suspending judgment seemingly

---

29. See James, "The Will to Believe," 20.

30. James, "The Will to Believe," 4.

31. "He who refuses a unique opportunity loses the prize as surely as if he tried and failed." James, "The Will to Believe," 4.

32. James, "The Will to Believe," 26 ("We cannot escape the issue by remaining sceptical and waiting for more light, because, although we do avoid error in that way if religion be untrue, we lose the good, if it be true, just as certainly as if we positively chose to disbelieve").

33. Compare Mark 16:16 ("He that believeth and is baptized shall be saved; but he that believeth not shall be damned," KJV).

becomes unavailable. "He that is not with me is against me," Jesus said,[34] leaving no neutral middle ground for the undecided. With respect to this kind of proposition, it seems that agnosticism is not an option.

Layered Believing

And yet we can imagine the sincere agnostic complaining: "How can you say that agnosticism is impossible, even in these existentially pressing cases, when I'm telling you that this is in fact what I think: I honestly don't know, and I can see no way of determining whether the preacher's proposition is true or not. Agnosticism *must be* possible because, once again, we've seen it done. Behold . . . me!—exhibit A. Nor is it accurate to say that agnosticism is equivalent to atheism. My atheist friend confidently asserts that there is no God, and hence that the man called Jesus could not have been divine. I don't assert any such thing; I'm genuinely unsure. So the atheist and I are very different in what we believe."

The objection points to a paradox in which the previous discussion seems to land us. We have seen that agnosticism seems to be at least possible, and perhaps even unavoidable (at least for some sincere and thoughtful people). And yet agnosticism also seems to be impossible, and what we might call agnosticism turns out to be equivalent to atheism.

We can dissolve this paradox, though, by acknowledging what any introspective person surely knows from personal experience—namely, that believing is a complex, textured, multilevel phenomenon. So it is possible to believe something in one sense or on one level while disbelieving (or at least suspending judgment) in a different sense or on a different level. Alec Ryrie makes the point with admirably convoluted clarity: with respect to some difficult and disputed religious questions, he says, "the only conclusion must be that a great many people do not truly believe what they believe they believe. It could even be hard to believe that you yourself believe what you believe you believe."[35] The French poet Charles Peguy

---

34. Matt. 12:30. Unless otherwise indicated, Bible references in this book come from the King James Version.

35. Alec Ryrie, *Unbelievers: An Emotional History of Doubt* (Cambridge, MA: Belknap Press of Harvard University Press, 2019), 78–79.

contended that many Christians are actually in this position: the modern Christian, Peguy said, does not believe what he believes.[36]

More specifically, we might distinguish between what we could call "abstract" or perhaps "detached" beliefs and "operative" beliefs. (In reality, beliefs do not sort themselves into two clean categories, but the distinction is serviceable for our purposes.) Abstract or detached beliefs are those that a person would affirm if she is acting simply as a detached thinker—or, as William James put it, a "purely judging mind," or as if "we are passive portions of the universe."[37] Operative beliefs, by contrast, crop up to inform and guide our practical decisions and actions. We implicitly invoke this distinction when we say, for example, that something is a "working assumption." At an abstract level, you may be unsure whether proposition X is ultimately true, but you adopt X anyway—you treat it *as* true—for certain practical or operational purposes.[38]

Any given person will likely hold both kinds of beliefs—detached and operative beliefs (and, again, in reality beliefs exist in various forms and on a multitude of levels)—and the interaction between these beliefs can be complex. Some detached beliefs simply do not make contact with a person's operative beliefs. You probably believe a whole host of things—that the universe began billions of years ago with a big bang, that the square root of 10,000 is 100, that Julius Caesar was murdered by a cabal led by Brutus and Cassius—that simply have no bearing on any life choices you have to make. (Unless you happen to be a contestant on *Jeopardy!*) You could change your mind about any of these things, and the change would make no difference to the way you live.[39]

---

36. Quoted in Michael Hanby, "The Crisis of Catholic Atheism," *Lamp*, no. 17 (2023): 32.

37. James, "The Will to Believe," 21, 28.

38. A familiar instance would be what is sometimes called "methodological naturalism." Whether or not a naturalistic view of the world as fully reducible to forces and particles in motion is ultimately true, a scientist might say, it is a picture that has much to recommend it and that works well for purposes of science. And so in doing science the scientist will treat that view *as* true, while perhaps suspending judgment about whether ultimately or for all purposes the naturalistic view is true or not.

39. Compare James, "The Will to Believe," 20: "What difference, indeed, does it make to most of us whether we have or have not a theory of the Rongten rays, whether

Atheist or Agnostic?

But other detached beliefs *do* make contact with—or even collide with—operative beliefs. They concern matters that affect life decisions, and about which you also have operative beliefs. And these detached beliefs may reinforce or be consistent with your operative beliefs—that is the desirable or least dissonant situation, probably—or they may stand in tension with or even in contradiction to your operative beliefs.

Suppose you have taken on the job of campaign manager for Adam Adams, who is running for the Senate. It will be very helpful if you believe, at least as a working assumption or operative belief, that Adams has a chance to win the election. That is because as campaign manager you will be required to do and say a lot of things—inspire the volunteers to work long hours for Adams, ask people to contribute large sums of money to Adams's campaign, and many other things—that make sense on the assumption that Adams can win, and that make less or no sense if Adams has no chance of winning. And so as a working assumption or operative belief, you will act on the assumption that Adams has a chance to win. (And the "has a chance" is important because if Adams is *certain* to win, then again there might be little reason for anyone to work hard or to sacrifice financially to secure an outcome that is predetermined anyway.)

Adams has a chance to win: this is your operative belief, or practical assumption. But is it also your detached belief? Maybe, maybe not. Maybe you try to avoid the question, much in the way a defense attorney avoids asking her client whether he is really guilty. Still, the question may arise: Does Adams actually have a chance? In the best case or least conflicted scenario, you can sincerely say that the polls or other evidence shows that Adams does indeed have an excellent or at least realistic chance of winning. Or maybe on the detached level you are uncertain: you don't trust the polls, maybe, and so although you work to secure Adams's election, you really have no idea whether he has a chance or not. The situation of greatest dissonance is one in which the evidence makes it very clear to you that Adams has no chance. You need the job of campaign manager, maybe, or you like and respect Adams and want to support him, and so you talk

---

we believe or not in mind-stuff, or have a conviction about the causality of conscious states? It makes no difference. Such opinions are not forced on us."

and act as if you believe he can win. But "off the record," you would say, "Of course he can't actually win. Not a prayer."

Similar possibilities apply in many life situations. A coach or player on a football team, a teacher trying to teach calculus to students, a lawyer litigating a tough case, a person who has agreed to marry a particular suitor: in these and countless other situations, people may have comparatively detached beliefs that support, or that remain uncertain about, or that contradict and undermine their operative beliefs.

With respect to the question of God, likewise, all of these possibilities are present. A person may live in ways that reflect an operative belief in God—she goes to church, perhaps, or fasts, or tithes—and this same person might in a candid "off the record" moment (or speaking under the influence of a truth serum) confess that she does indeed fervently believe in God, or that she is uncertain, or that she doubts very much whether God exists. (In the last scenario, she goes to church from habit, maybe, or to accommodate a spouse or parent, or for some other reason.) Conversely, someone (Fyodor Karamazov, perhaps) might live as if there is no God—he lives a purely selfish and hedonistic life, maybe, cheating and exploiting others for personal gain—and yet in an honest moment admit that he is unsure, or even that he believes there is a God, alas, who will ultimately hold him warmly accountable for his ungodly behavior.

Agnostic Atheists, Agnostic Theists

As our discussion has suggested, it is possible for a person to be agnostic at one level and yet atheistic—or, conversely, theistic—at another level. In common usage, the former possibility is widely appreciated. Agnosticism is commonly thought to be closely associated with atheism (as David Novak's comment suggested): an agnostic is pretty much a timid atheist—one who hedges his bets, or his atheistic opinions. Probably there is good reason for this familiar association. Someone who *calls himself* an agnostic is likely to lean toward atheism. Or put it this way: a person who says she is an agnostic is likely to be someone who lives *as if* there is no God. She probably does not go to church, or tithe, or pray.

And yet she *might*. The philosopher Anthony Kenny, who self-identifies as an agnostic, argues that an agnostic can consistently and in good conscience pray to God. For an agnostic to pray is no more illogical, Kenny argues, than for a person in distress to call out for help even though she does not know whether anyone is around to respond.[40]

Recognizing these levels of belief and the resulting possibilities suggests a redrawing of the common one-level picture in which, relative to the question of God, people fall onto a continuum ranging from hardened atheists at one end to indecisive agnostics in the middle to dogmatic religious believers at the other end. Now these terms become potentially usable at both levels—at the detached level and at the operative level. So we could have atheist/atheists (i.e., people who are atheists at both the detached and operative levels), theist/theists, atheist/theists, and so forth.

The categories could be multiplied beyond easy comprehension, and some of the possible categories would be quite perplexing in themselves. (Which is not to deny that there may be people who fit into these categories: theist/atheist, for example—a paradoxical category that arguably applies to countless religious believers who declare, sincerely, as they suppose, that they believe in God but who for all practical purposes live *and think* as if God does not exist or does not matter.) For our purposes, though (because once again, we are exploring this matter for use in understanding our agnostic *Constitution*), we need not attempt to survey all the possibilities. The important thing is to recognize the possibility of two hybrid agnostic categories—the categories of agnostic/atheists and agnostic/theists. Of people who are ultimately unsure about God, and hence take no position on the question, but who also for practical purposes think, or suspect, or at least live on the working assumption that God *does not* exist (the agnostic/atheists)—or that he *does* (the agnostic/theists).

Nor are these merely empty or abstract categories. Surely there are people—millions of them, probably—who fall into these categories. People who are ultimately unsure but who live on the working assumption that there is no God. And people who are unsure but who live (perhaps on the logic of Pascal's famous wager)[41] on the assumption that God is real.

---

40. Kenny, *What I Believe*, 64.
41. For description and discussion, see James A. Connor, *Pascal's Wager: The Man Who Played Dice with God* (San Francisco: HarperCollins, 2006).

PART 1: A GODLESS DOCUMENT?

The Impossibility of Operative Agnosticism

Before applying these distinctions to the Constitution, we need to emphasize one further point. Earlier we considered the objection that agnosticism is impossible, and we saw how at least with respect to some religious questions, William James's analysis of "forced options" would support that objection. Once again, if the evangelist says, "Accept Jesus with all of your heart and you will be saved; if you do not accept Jesus, you will be lost," then *relative to that proposition*, operative agnosticism is seemingly unavailable—because not to decide amounts to not accepting Jesus. So if the evangelist is right, then the indecisive waffler will be lost along with the belligerent skeptic. We then revived the possibility of agnosticism by distinguishing between detached and operative beliefs. It is possible to be agnostic at the detached level, we said, even if at the practical or operative level one faces a "forced option" and thus must either believe or disbelieve.

At *that* level, however—at the operative level—it seems that James's point still holds. You may be unsure in a detached sense whether the evangelist is correct, but you will still, of necessity, proceed to live *as if* he is correct or as if he is incorrect. So at that level, it seems that David Novak is basically right, after all: there is no neutral or agnostic option left to you. You will have to accept the proposition or not; to remain undecided is the same as not accepting it.

So we said earlier that it is possible to be an agnostic and yet be an atheist, or a theist. Now we can add that agnostics not only *can* be one of these things; it seems they *cannot escape* being one of these things. They can of course vacillate, as many of us do; they can switch from one side of the divide to the other. But on the operative level, they cannot escape the "forced option" of theism or atheism.[42]

---

42. Compare Christine L. Niles, "Epistemological Nonsense? The Secular/Religious Distinction," *Notre Dame Journal of Law, Ethics and Public Policy* 17 (2003): 574 ("The man who says 'I do not know' with his mouth declares with his life the opposite. Thus, the agnostic is not neutral, as he proclaims to be").

Atheist or Agnostic?

The Constitution as Agnostic

In the *Republic*, Plato tried to discern what justice means for individual persons by reflecting on what justice means in the polis. Here we have been following the opposite course, from personal to political: we have been reflecting on what agnosticism means for individuals as a way of discerning what it might mean in a constitution. We have seen that believing and disbelieving have a layered quality for human beings. And similar possibilities can be projected onto the "godless" or agnostic Constitution—or at least onto the legal and political system governed by that Constitution. Just as believing as it occurs in human beings has a layered quality, so the Constitution is part of a multitiered or layered legal system in which a proposition can be accepted or asserted on one level but not on other levels.

Adjustments are required, to be sure. It may seem inapt to treat the Constitution as a set of "detached" propositions, in contrast to "operative" propositions of statutory law and case law or executive policy, because the document is not just a set of abstract propositions; it is a binding legal instrument. Such is the celebrated teaching of *Marbury v. Madison*. Even so, the Constitution is law at the highest level, and it leaves a great deal to be decided by legislatures and other government officials, at a variety of lower levels—national, state, and local. With respect to decisions made at these levels, the Constitution sets outer limits while leaving most matters to be decided as people and officials at those levels see fit. The Constitution might be described as "detached"—or as "agnostic"—relative to the multitude of questions that arise within the outer limits that it sets and for which it neither prescribes nor prohibits anything one way or the other.

So the Constitution itself might be "godless"—and indeed it is, as we have seen—but it is godless in a specific sense. The Constitution is not godless in the sense of being affirmatively atheistic. With respect to the matter of God, it is demurely agnostic. The Constitution itself does not take a position for or against God, and it thus leaves undecided what the posture toward God will be not only for individuals but for other political contexts and at other levels of government. For individual persons, as we have seen, it is possible to be an agnostic/atheist (i.e., agnostic at the detached level but atheist at the operative level) or an agnostic/theist. The multitiered constitutional system creates similar possibilities for the republic itself.

PART 1: A GODLESS DOCUMENT?

A "Godless" Politics?

This discussion allows us to appreciate the essential error in Kramnick and Moore's second basic claim—that because the Constitution is godless, politics and governance in America must be godless as well. As we saw earlier, just on its face, this claim seems a blatant non sequitur. From the fact that the Constitution itself lacks religious language, it simply does not follow that politics or governance generally was or is required to eschew religious language or beliefs.

Kramnick and Moore's error might be attributable to the provocative imprecision of their term "godless." If the Constitution were godless in the sense of being atheistic, or of affirmatively embracing atheism, the inference that the document sponsors a godless politics would be more plausible. But the Constitution itself is not atheistic; it in no way declares against God. And if we understand the term more precisely to mean "agnostic," then it seems that governments under an agnostic Constitution have the same options open to individuals who are agnostic at a detached level. As we have seen, an individual may find that in a detached reflection she cannot confidently either affirm or deny the existence of God; but in practice she still has the choice—indeed, she can hardly avoid the choice—of believing or living on the working assumption that there is a God or that there is not. Similarly, agnosticism at a constitutional level is compatible with governance at other levels that either does or does not make reliance on God an operative reality.

And in fact, this distinctively layered and tolerantly agnostic quality is the reason why John Courtney Murray could exempt the American constitutional system from his charge that the separation of church and state amounts to the "establishment" of atheism as a "public philosophy." The agnostic American Constitution *permits* governments and public discourse to embrace atheism as a public philosophy, just as it permits individuals to adopt atheism as a personal philosophy. But it does not require any such policy, and it accordingly does not *establish* any public or political philosophy of atheism.

Or at least it *did not* establish atheism. We will see in a later chapter how the modern Supreme Court transformed the Constitution in this respect.

Atheist or Agnostic?

The Virtues of Constitutional Agnosticism

Before moving on, however, we should pause to appreciate the virtues of an agnostic Constitution that leaves open various possibilities at different levels of government.[43] The fact is that in many matters, and *a fortiori* in matters of religion, the American republic has been pluralistic from the beginning; and this pluralism has if anything intensified with the passing of the decades. How to maintain the allegiance of such a diverse citizenry has been a central challenge of our constitutional tradition. And the multilevel structure of governance has been a key component in meeting that challenge.

With respect to matters on which citizens disagree, this structure allows, within limits, for one answer to prevail in one context and for a different answer to be adopted in a different context. And even for a single jurisdiction, the tiered structure presided over by an agnostic Constitution has allowed for multiple answers. More specifically, with particular respect to religion, this multilevel constitutional structure has allowed government to be openly supportive of religion (typically in a "nonsectarian" sense)[44] in situations where that stance is called for by and is likely to elicit the allegiance of citizens, while softening the effect of this support for differently minded citizens by assuring them that on a more fundamental level the nation itself is *not* formally committed to or constituted by any particular religion, or by religion at all.

So suppose you are a citizen who believes that a sovereign God rules over everything—the natural creation, human beings, churches, nations. You believe that, as President George Washington asserted in an early proclamation, "it is the duty of all Nations"—not merely of individuals, notice, but of *Nations*—"to acknowledge the providence of Almighty God, to obey his will, to be grateful for his benefits, and humbly to implore his protection and favor."[45] So it would be difficult for you to give your

---

43. For elaboration, see Steven D. Smith, "Our Agnostic Constitution," *New York University Law Review* (2008): 120.

44. See Steven D. Smith, "Nonestablishment 'under God'? The Nonsectarian Principle," *Villanova Law Review* 50 (2005): 1.

45. "Thanksgiving Proclamation," George Washington, October 3, 1789, reprinted in Dreisbach and Hall, *The Sacred Rights of Conscience*, 453 (emphasis added). Wash-

allegiance to a government that shirked this essential duty by refusing to acknowledge God's sovereignty. But although the Constitution itself does not make any such acknowledgment (as other constitutions have done, and as you might believe the Constitution itself ideally should do), you can nonetheless take comfort in the fact that God is officially recognized in other ways and places—in the national motto (In God We Trust), perhaps, or in the Pledge of Allegiance ("one nation, under God"), or perhaps in your state constitution. These acknowledgments may be sufficient to make a claim upon your loyalty.

Or suppose to the contrary that you are an aggressive, Christopher Hitchens–type atheist who thinks that "religion poisons everything."[46] Governmental declarations of support for religion may leave you feeling angry, excluded, and alienated.[47] So you will no doubt deplore the religious expressions noted above. Even so, you can take comfort in the fact that presiding over the whole structure is a Constitution that studiously eschews any mention of God. To be sure, you may still resent the religious expressions in the national motto and the Pledge of Allegiance and such—and who among us does not find many official acts and expressions irksome?—but the agnostic Constitution provides assurance that at the most fundamental level the republic is not officially *constituted* on the basis of religion.

It is a subtle and complicated strategy for addressing the challenge of pluralism—one that many, including the modern Supreme Court and the

---

ington's successor, John Adams, issued a similar proclamation declaring that "the safety and prosperity of nations ultimately and essentially depend on the protection and the blessing of Almighty God, and the national acknowledgment of this truth is . . . an indispensable duty which the people owe to Him." Reprinted in John T. Noonan Jr. and Edward McGlynn Gaffney Jr., *Religious Freedom: History, Cases, and Other Materials on the Interaction of Law and Religion* (New York: Foundation, 2001), 202–3.

46. Christopher Hitchens, *God Is Not Great: How Religion Poisons Everything* (New York: Twelve, 2007).

47. Stephen Gey notes that "the government has gone so far as to insert the words 'under God' in the official Pledge of Allegiance and place 'in God we trust' on its currency," and he infers that "in these respects, atheists are effectively precluded from participating fully in the public life of their country." Stephen G. Gey, "Atheism and the Freedom of Religion," in *The Cambridge Companion to Atheism*, ed. Michael Martin (New York: Cambridge University Press, 2007), 264.

proponents of the Kramnick-Moore thesis, have often failed to comprehend. Nor is there any guarantee that it will succeed in securing the allegiance of the citizenry. More zealously devout citizens might find the incidental religious expressions insufficient: only explicit acknowledgment of God *in the Constitution itself*, they might think, will work to discharge the national duty and hence to merit *their* allegiance. Conversely, citizens who are sufficiently offended by expressions like the national motto or the Pledge of Allegiance might say that their resentment is not assuaged by the fact of an agnostic Constitution. A government must forgo these religious expressions altogether, they might insist, or forfeit their support.

Citizens who take these more hard-line positions are seemingly atypical, however. If they were more numerous, the Constitution presumably *would* acknowledge God; or, conversely, the national motto and the pledge would be modified to delete the offensive religious language. As we have seen, though, when such proposals have been offered, they have been rejected by the electorate. And so through much of our history, the multilevel strategy in which God could be publicly acknowledged on some levels or in some ways or contexts but not in others has arguably worked tolerably well to secure the support of the citizenry.

Until recently, at least.

What about the First Amendment?

Our discussion in this chapter, prompted by the claim of Kramnick and Moore and others that America is governed by a "godless" Constitution that mandates a "godless politics," has led us to the conclusion that at least in its text the Constitution is indeed godless in a literal sense. But the Constitution is not atheistic; rather, it is simply agnostic with respect to God. The Constitution's agnosticism leaves open the possibility that governments will embrace a "godless" politics. But it also leaves open the possibility of a more religiously infused politics.

And yet this discussion may seem to have mostly ignored, with only an occasional sideways glance, the elephant in the room. Namely, the First Amendment, with its establishment clause ("Congress shall make no law respecting an establishment of religion . . ."). Most often when modern justices and advocates say that government is constitutionally required to

PART 1: A GODLESS DOCUMENT?

maintain secular governance or politics, they have drawn that conclusion not so much from the "godless" quality of the Constitution itself (as Kramnick and Moore do), or at least not *only* from the "godless" Constitution, but rather from the more specific prohibition of the First Amendment. Before proceeding to consider how American governments have claimed and used the options allowed them by the agnostic Constitution, therefore, we should take a more direct look at the establishment clause.

CHAPTER 2

The Establishment Clause in the Godless Constitution

In the previous chapter, we considered the claim that the Constitution itself, in its original form, was a "godless" document that thereby mandated a "godless politics" or governance. Examining this claim, we saw that although the original Constitution was indeed "godless" in a strictly literal sense—it did not meaningfully invoke or acknowledge God—the document was agnostic rather than atheistic in character; and this agnosticism was compatible either with a "godless" politics—a purely secular politics, that is—or with a more religion-infused governance. The Constitution was like an agnostic parent who permits the children to follow a religious or a nonreligious path, as they choose.

But even if this conclusion holds for the original Constitution, it might be that later additions—and specifically the establishment clause of the First Amendment ("Congress shall make no law respecting an establishment of religion . . .")—implemented a fundamental change in this respect. And in fact, countless modern justices, scholars, and advocates have claimed as much. Government must remain removed from religion, they have argued, because the establishment clause so mandates.

So, did the establishment clause alter the basic character of the Constitution, such that one of the options permitted under the original, agnostic Constitution—the option of a religion-infused politics and governance— was taken off the table?

The question may seem a daunting one, because it implicates what are by now virtual libraries of scholarly, judicial, and lawyerly work specifically devoted to arguing about what the establishment clause meant or did or

PART 1: A GODLESS DOCUMENT?

prohibited.[1] Moreover, the question also implicates an even larger body of work and commentary that argues about the proper mode of interpreting the Constitution generally. But it would be futile and even foolhardy—wouldn't it?—to attempt to take on those massive literatures in one relatively short chapter of a modestly sized book.

In this situation, one might wish for some way of addressing the basic question—and even of arriving at a modest answer sufficient for present purposes—while bypassing the morass of scholarly commentary and advocacy. But is there any way of doing that?

How about this? We know that the First Amendment *can* be interpreted to require religion-free governance (or "godless politics," as Kramnick and Moore put it);[2] and, alternatively, we know that it *can* be interpreted to allow a greater role for religion in governance. We know that each of these possibilities exists because, once again, we've seen them done (as chapters 3 and 4 will elaborate). Could we simply say this much and then proceed, in part 2, to consider what *has* been done?

But this observation about what *can* be done is too modest, even for our purposes. Because although history may indeed establish that each of these interpretations is a real possibility that has in fact been adopted at different times, it might be that one interpretation is demonstrably correct and the other is demonstrably wrong. If someone says that "we know 2 and 2 *can* be added together to make 5 because some people—first-graders—have sometimes actually done that," this observation will seem merely obtuse. True, some first-graders might say that "2 plus 2 equals 5"—but they would be wrong! Similarly, when courts and other Americans have interpreted the Constitution to require or not to require a religion-free politics, maybe they were simply mistaken.

So then, is there any other way to address the question—the question of what the establishment clause did to the Constitution—while avoiding

---

1. I have contributed more than my fair allotment of pages to this debate. See, e.g., Steven D. Smith, *The Rise and Decline of American Religious Freedom* (Cambridge, MA: Harvard University Press, 2014), chapter 2; Steven D. Smith, "The Jurisdictional Establishment Clause: A Reappraisal," *Notre Dame Law Review* 81 (2006): 1843; Steven D. Smith, *Foreordained Failure: The Quest for a Constitutional Principle of Religious Freedom* (New York: Oxford University Press, 1995).

2. Isaac Kramnick and R. Laurence Moore, *The Godless Constitution: A Moral Defense of the Secular State* (New York: Norton, 2005), 151, 167–68.

The Establishment Clause in the Godless Constitution

the unmanageable task of directly engaging with and assessing the vast literatures on the establishment clause specifically and constitutional interpretation more generally?

Maybe there is.

Let us start with an observation: *If* the First Amendment somehow required a "godless politics," or, in other words, if the amendment contained some general prohibition or principle precluding the government from drawing on, promoting, expressing, or endorsing religion, then it seems apparent that the people who were on the scene—the people who wrote and enacted that amendment or who were immediately subject to it—were either unaware of this prohibition or else pretended to be unaware of it. We will consider the voluminous evidence for this proposition more fully in chapter 3. For now, it should be enough to notice what is pretty much undisputed and indisputable—namely, that early national officials both executive and legislative almost immediately and repeatedly and unapologetically brought religion into governance in a variety of ways. So did their successors. Almost simultaneously with approving the First Amendment, for example, both houses of Congress appointed chaplains to begin sessions with prayer. The same Congress requested the president to declare a national day of thanksgiving and prayer,[3] and President Washington unhesitatingly complied with this request (asserting in his Declaration that "it is the duty of all *Nations* to acknowledge the providence of Almighty God, to obey his will, to be grateful for his benefits, and humbly to implore his protection and favor").[4] Every president beginning with Washington and including supposed separationists like Jefferson (author of the famous "wall of separation" letter) and Madison included prayer and overt religious language and ritual in their inauguration ceremonies.[5]

Such instances of the mixture of religion and governance could be multiplied almost indefinitely. Moreover, this mixing continued throughout the nineteenth and into the twentieth century, and beyond. And although decades after the fact and in a private memorandum that was not made

---

3. These events are discussed in chapter 3.
4. George Washington, "Thanksgiving Proclamation," October 3, 1789, reprinted in *The Sacred Rights of Conscience*, ed. Daniel L. Dreisbach and Mark David Hall (Indianapolis: Liberty Fund, 2009), 453 (emphasis added).
5. For a more detailed discussion, see chapter 3.

PART 1: A GODLESS DOCUMENT?

public until many years later, James Madison might express doubts about some of these measures—legislative chaplains in particular—congressmen at the time the chaplains were instituted seemed to suppose that no constitutional prohibition was implicated. Madison himself was on the House committee that proposed appointment of a chaplain, and he seems to have raised no objection.[6]

These facts are well known: advocates of more religion-friendly constitutional interpretations (like Justices William Rehnquist and Antonin Scalia) have tended to invoke such facts while more secularly inclined interpreters (such as Justices William Brennan and David Souter) have attempted to explain them away. A more theory-innocent and commonsensical observer, though, might ask: How can the First Amendment as enacted have contained a prohibition on the involvement of religion in governance if the people who were there at the time, and who wrote and debated and voted for the amendment, did not understand it to contain such a prohibition? How could the provision have meant something that no one at the time understood it to mean?

It is a challenging question; a commonsense observer might even think it is a decisive one. Maybe it should be. But our discussion cannot end here, because modern advocates have developed a variety of responses to that challenge. Setting aside the response of outright misrepresentation,[7] we might classify the leading responses under three (partially overlapping) headings, which we could call the "hypocrisy" story, the "undetected meaning" explanation, and the "evolution" story. Let us consider each of these responses in turn.

The Hypocrisy Story

One response has it that although the First Amendment *did* actually prohibit the use or involvement of religion in governance, and although the enactors and others in the founding generation and afterward in some sense understood or should have understood that the amendment contained this prohibition, early officials were unhappy with the restriction

---

6. See Mark David Hall, *Did America Have a Christian Founding?* (Nashville: Nelson, 2019), 82.

7. See "Postscript: The Orwellian Rewriting of History," pp. 204–8.

and thus proceeded to ignore and violate it. And they thereby set a disturbing precedent for later generations.

In this vein, Douglas Laycock, a leading religion clause scholar, has suggested that when early governments and officials supported or endorsed or drew on religion, they were acting not on the basis of their constitutional understanding but rather from "unreflective bigotry."[8] Other scholars offer similar characterizations.[9] Indeed, it is a sometimes unspoken implication of much modern establishment clause scholarship and jurisprudence that American governments for decades were regularly and rampantly engaged in violating the establishment clause's ostensible prohibition on government involvement with religion.

But if we try to step back and consider it from a detached perspective, this story—the story of how Americans deliberately adopted a constitutional provision mandating religion-free governance and then almost immediately and flagrantly proceeded to violate that provision, over and over again, for decade after decade—seems, as John Marshall might have put it, "too extravagant to be maintained."[10] Why would Americans—why would anyone—do such a thing? The usual suggestion is that Americans failed to honor the constitutional prohibition because governmental religious actions and utterances were such a familiar part of their political inheritance that these practices seemed to them natural and proper.[11] But that

---

8. Douglas Laycock, "'Nonpreferential' Aid to Religion: A False Claim about Original Intent," *William and Mary Law Review* 27 (1986): 919.

9. See, e.g., Howard Gillman and Erwin Chemerinsky, *The Religion Clauses: The Case for Separating Church and State* (New York: Oxford University Press, 2020), 41–42 ("Just as our credo that 'all men are created equal' was corrupted, assaulted, and tormented by a history that assumed America was a country for the white race, so too was our secular republic corrupted, assaulted, and tormented by illegitimate assumptions that (nevertheless) America was a Christian nation"); David Sehat, *The Myth of American Religious Freedom* (New York: Oxford University Press, 2011), 159 (criticizing "the hypocrisy of the moral establishment, which maintained an establishment of religion but denied it"). Compare Martha C. Nussbaum, *Liberty of Conscience: In Defense of America's Tradition of Religious Equality* (New York: Basic Books, 2008), 113 (asserting that "the early history [of government interactions with religion] shows us something we already knew about people: that they often act unreflectively").

10. Marbury v. Madison, 5 U.S. 137, 179 (1803).

11. See, e.g., Thomas J. Curry, *The First Freedoms: Church and State in America to the Passage of the First Amendment* (New York: Oxford University Press, 1986), 218.

PART 1: A GODLESS DOCUMENT?

explanation seems suspect on its face. If we suppose that most Americans including governmental officials regarded such religious practices as natural and proper, then why on earth would they have knowingly prohibited such practices—and then have immediately proceeded to ignore the prohibition that they themselves had adopted? The story simply doesn't make sense.

The charge of hypocrisy may seem to gain credibility from a comparison to the issues of equality and race, where an often-told and superficially analogous story seems more credible. Thus, it is commonly and plausibly believed that the Constitution (or if not the Constitution itself, then the Declaration of Independence) expressed commitments to equality, including by logical implication racial equality, but that American governments especially in the southern states routinely violated these commitments by maintaining systems of slavery and then, even after the Thirteenth and Fourteenth Amendments, of legally imposed racial segregation. It was only in the mid-twentieth century—*Brown v. Board of Education* was a monumental turning point—that the nation began to attempt to take the originary commitment to equality seriously. Perhaps the same trajectory holds with respect to religion?[12]

But this comparison seems flawed; if anything, it serves to undermine the hypocrisy story in the area of religion. Thus, the glaring conflict between the basic American commitment to equality and official racial discrimination in the form of slavery and, later, state-imposed segregation was obvious from the outset, and was vehemently and indignantly condemned by numerous critics, including by slaveholders such as Thomas Jefferson,[13] and including in the Constitutional Convention itself. In the convention, Gouverneur Morris denounced slavery as "a nefarious institution" that would bring down "the curse of heaven on the states where it prevailed." Constitutional accommodations for slavery amounted to "a sacrifice of every principle of right, of every impulse of humanity."[14] Luther Martin pro-

---

12. For instances of this argument, see Steven K. Green, *The Second Disestablishment: Church and State in Nineteenth-Century America* (New York: Oxford University Press, 2010), 72; Gillman and Chemerinsky, *The Religion Clauses*, 41–42.

13. See Thomas Jefferson, *Notes on the State of Virginia*, ed. Frank C. Shuffleton (New York: Penguin Books, 1999; original 1785), 169 (declaring, with reference to slavery, "I tremble for my country when I reflect that God is just: that his justice cannot sleep forever").

14. Edward J. Larson and Michael P. Winship, *The Constitutional Convention: A Narrative History from the Notes of James Madison* (New York: Modern Library, 2005), 112–13.

tested that constitutional provisions protecting slavery were "inconsistent with the principles of the revolution and dishonorable to the American character."[15] George Mason (himself a slaveholder) declaimed at length on the moral, cultural, economic, and political evils of slavery and declared that the institution would "bring[ ] the judgment of heaven on a country." His ominous prediction turned out to be prophetic: "By an inevitable chain of causes and effects, providence punishes national sins by national calamities."[16] In the area of religion, by contrast, when both houses of Congress appointed chaplains or when presidents proclaimed days of thanksgiving, there was little if any publicly expressed sense of any tension between these actions and the requirements of the Constitution.

We might put the point this way: although American governments for many decades violated the founding commitment to equality, this deviation was recognized from the start and was frequently denounced as a shameful betrayal of basic principle. The hypocrisy was manifest. By contrast, with possible minor exceptions,[17] American officials and legislators who drew upon or endorsed religion in their official functions—Americans like Washington, Adams, Lincoln, even (as we will see) Jefferson—were not being hypocrites. They did not consider themselves to be departing from any constitutional principle; on the contrary, as we will see in chapter 3, they regarded themselves as discharging a sacred duty.

The "Undetected Meaning" Explanation

So then, perhaps the founding-era officials who mixed religion with politics and governance were not hypocrites, exactly; but might they nonetheless have been violating a constitutional prohibition of which they were

---

15. Larson and Winship, *The Constitutional Convention*, 128.

16. Larson and Winship, *The Constitutional Convention*, 130.

17. James Madison as president proclaimed national days of fasting and prayer, but years later he privately reasoned that such proclamations were contrary to the First Amendment. See James Madison, "Detached Memoranda," reprinted in *The Founders Constitution*, ed. Philip B. Kurland and Ralph Lerner, vol. 5 (Chicago: University of Chicago Press, 1987), document 64. Perhaps Madison's thinking on the subject had evolved; conversely, it is at least possible that Madison as president may have been acting against his principles in response to cultural or political pressure, and that his proclamations could thus be deemed hypocritical.

PART 1: A GODLESS DOCUMENT?

innocently unaware? Perhaps the First Amendment in reality contained a prohibition of religion in governance, but this prohibition somehow escaped the attention or the consciousness of early officials—Congress, presidents, and others.

From one perspective, this suggestion also might be peremptorily dismissed as nonsensical on its face. Language is not some Platonic emanation in which words have some ideal and true meaning independent of what the humans who use the words understand them to mean. On the contrary, language is a conventional construction used by human beings to communicate with each other; and words accordingly have those meanings and only those meanings that humans ascribe to them. To be sure, some theorists associate linguistic meanings with what *speakers* intend, while others emphasize the meanings that *hearers*—or "the public," or the competent user of the language—would understand the words to carry.[18] Either way, if the people who wrote and voted for the First Amendment and the people who were subject to it did not understand the provision to contain any general prohibition on religion in governance, it would be merely nonsensical to suppose that, unbeknownst to the people who were actually using the language, the amendment did somehow contain such a prohibition.

Once again, perhaps this objection should be decisive. And yet there are formalist (or "objectivist," or "object-ist")[19] theories of language that say or imply that combinations of words—sentences and such—can have meanings that are neither intended by the speakers nor perceived by the hearers. Even, or especially, in the realm of law.

A vivid if deservedly controversial example is the Supreme Court's relatively recent decision in a case called *Bostock v. Clayton County*.[20] The

---

18. These different perspectives are manifest in debates over constitutional interpretation: the speakers' meaning view is manifest in what is often called "intentionalist" theories of interpretation, while the hearers' or readers' perspective is manifest in what is often called textualism or "original public meaning" positions. For explanation and discussion, see Steven D. Smith, *Fictions, Lies, and the Authority of Law* (Notre Dame: University of Notre Dame Press, 2021), 55–60.

19. See Perry Dane, "The Nagging in Our Ears and Original Public Meaning," *Marquette Law Review* 106 (2023): 767.

20. 590 U.S. 644 (2020).

question was whether language in the 1964 Civil Rights Act prohibiting employers from discriminating on the basis of "sex" also forbade discrimination on the basis of sexual orientation. It was generally conceded that the members of Congress who enacted the law did not intend or understand it to have any such meaning. Nor had other officials, or courts, or the public generally perceived any such meaning; indeed, Congress had repeatedly considered proposals to amend the law by extending its prohibition to cover sexual orientation discrimination—and had consistently rejected those proposals. Nonetheless, the *Bostock* Court ruled that the words of the statute, taken literally, applied to sexual orientation discrimination, and indeed had all along applied to sexual orientation discrimination— even if no one involved had intended or perceived this application. If you just look carefully at the words of the law and think hard about them—in particular the words "sex" and "discrimination"—you will see that sexual orientation discrimination is prohibited, even if the legislators and pretty much everybody else somehow failed to notice that prohibition. So wrote Justice Neil Gorsuch for the *Bostock* majority.

This is a contestable approach to interpretation, to say the least;[21] but once again, we've seen it done. So perhaps a similar argument could be made about the establishment clause. Perhaps the language of the clause prohibits government from drawing on or endorsing or promoting religion even if no one at the time wanted or intended or perceived such a prohibition.

The problem is that the language does *not* support any such interpretation. It would have been possible to draft such language. "Congress shall make no law endorsing or promoting religion," maybe. But in fact, the clause did not and does not contain such language.

Actually, at one point in its deliberations on what became the First Amendment,[22] the House of Representatives considered a proposal that might more plausibly have been construed to require religion-free gov-

---

21. I have elsewhere criticized the decision. See Steven D. Smith, "The Mindlessness of *Bostock*," *Law and Liberty*, July 9, 2020, https://tinyurl.com/4kwyye8a.

22. For a detailed discussion of the proceedings, see Vincent Phillip Munoz, *Religious Liberty and the American Founding: Natural Rights and the Original Meanings of the Religion Clauses* (Chicago: University of Chicago Press, 2022), 125–82.

ernment. Samuel Livermore of New Hampshire offered the following wording: "Congress shall make no law *touching religion*, or infringing the rights of conscience."[23] Probably the congressmen did not understand Livermore's proposal to ban every sort of governmental involvement with religion—such a prohibition would have seemed radical, and no one in the House made any such objection—but if the proposal had been adopted, a later court might have more plausibly said, *Bostock*-fashion, "This may not be what the legislators intended, but it is what their language means." It is an academic question, however, because Livermore's proposal was briefly adopted but then almost immediately rejected.

Instead, Congress ultimately settled on the narrower wording contained in the Constitution today: "Congress shall make no law respecting an establishment of religion . . ." Donald Drakeman cogently explains what these words meant to people at the time.

> It is important to appreciate that [the First Amendment establishment clause] was not the statement of a principle of secularism, separation, disestablishment, or anything else. It was the answer to a very specific question: Would the new national government countenance a move by the larger Protestant denominations to join together and form a national church? The answer was no. . . .
>
> At the time it was adopted, the establishment clause addressed one simple noncontroversial issue, and the list of those who supported it demonstrates that it cannot reasonably be seen as encompassing a philosophy about church and state.[24]

Attempting to use the text to support a broader meaning, proponents of more modern and expansive interpretations sometimes put great weight on the word "respecting"; they suggest the clause means that Congress cannot

23. For discussion, see Munoz, *Religious Liberty*, 155–57.
24. Donald L. Drakeman, *Church, State, and Original Intent* (New York: Cambridge University Press, 2010), 330. Drakeman updates his analysis and defends his interpretation against competitors in Donald Drakeman, "Which Original Meaning of the Establishment Clause Is the Right One?" in *The Cambridge Companion to the First Amendment and Religious Liberty*, ed. Michael D. Breidenbach and Owen Anderson (Cambridge: Cambridge University Press, 2020), 365.

set up a national church or do anything *tending toward* or approximating such an establishment.[25] Even today this interpretation is hardly a plausible interpretation of "respecting." If the framers had intended such a meaning, they might easily and much more clearly have used words like "tending toward"; or, more straightforwardly, they might have simply adopted something like the wording offered by Livermore. In fact, in the historical context, the term "respecting" had a different and readily understandable function; it served economically to convey that Congress was forbidden *either* to set up a national church *or* to interfere in the religious establishments that some states continued to maintain.[26] Either kind of law would have been a law "*respecting* an establishment of religion," and hence was forbidden.

Even on a formalist or *Bostock*-style understanding of how language works, in short, the argument that the First Amendment prohibited any governmental involvement with religion even though people at the time did not intend or perceive such a prohibition fails for a simple reason: the words of the provision simply do not cooperate in supporting such an interpretation.

THE MINIMALIST ESTABLISHMENT CLAUSE

The discussion thus far has suggested that in its original historical context, the First Amendment's establishment clause imposed an important but relatively narrow prohibition: it meant that the national government was forbidden to set up any sort of official church, as England and several of the states had done, and was also precluded from interfering in religious establishments at the state level.[27] This would also mean that if the provi-

---

25. See Nussbaum, *Liberty of Conscience*, 101; see also Everson v. Board of Education, 330 U.S. 1, 31 (1947) (Rutledge, J., dissenting) ("Not simply an established church, but any law respecting an establishment of religion, is forbidden").

26. Compare Nathan S. Chapman and Michael W. McConnell, *Agreeing to Disagree: How the Establishment Clause Protects Religious Diversity and Freedom of Conscience* (New York: Oxford University Press, 2023), 76 ("That is why the language was revised to forbid Congress from making any law 'respecting' an establishment of religion. . . . This prohibited two things: (1) any establishment of religion at the national level and (2) any federal interference with state establishments").

27. I have elsewhere argued for a slightly broader variation on this interpretation: the clause meant that Congress had *no jurisdiction* over establishments of religion. See Smith,

PART 1: A GODLESS DOCUMENT?

sion was later extended to the states, as eventually happened, state governments would likewise be forbidden to set up any sort of official church, or to interfere in the administration of churches. That was pretty much it.

And so Americans seem to have understood the measure, for decades. Indeed, for over a century and a half. And since Americans of the period were already moving away from government-established churches even without judicial prodding, Supreme Court cases from this period addressing establishment clause challenges are accordingly scarce, and scarcely memorable. In *Bradfield v. Roberts*,[28] the Court tersely and unanimously dismissed an establishment clause challenge to congressional appropriations for support of a Catholic hospital in the District of Columbia. We are talking about a hospital, the Court said, not a church. In *Reuben Quick Bear v. Leupp*,[29] the Supreme Court rejected without dissent a challenge to the expenditure of public money in support of the St. Francis Mission Boarding School on an Indian reservation in South Dakota. The plaintiffs' unsuccessful legal challenge was based not on the First Amendment but rather on statutory restrictions in a series of Indian Appropriation Acts. The possibility of any constitutional restriction was deemed too insubstantial to require analysis: citing *Bradfield*, the Court observed dismissively that "it is not contended that [the expenditure] is unconstitutional, nor could it be."[30]

That is pretty much all there is from this period (which even now spans well over half of the republic's existence). And there is nary a hint that the numerous and sundry prayers or religious expressions from the president or Congress or other officials might be constitutionally problematic; indeed, it was the Court itself that declared that "this is a Christian nation"[31] and, later, more ecumenically, that "we are a religious people whose institutions presuppose a Supreme Being."[32]

Rise and Decline, 48–66; Smith, *Foreordained Failure*, 17–34. On this interpretation, Congress would be unable to set up a national church but Congress would also be forbidden to interfere in the affairs of churches. This jurisdictional interpretation would have important implications in some contexts, see, e.g., Hosanna-Tabor Evangelical Lutheran Church v. EEOC, 565 U.S. 171 (2012), but it is not of great importance to the themes of this book.

28. 175 U.S. 291 (1899).
29. 210 U.S. 50 (1908).
30. 210 U.S. at 81.
31. Holy Trinity Church v. United States, 143 U.S. 457, 471 (1892).
32. Zorach v. Clauson, 343 U.S. 306, 312 (1952).

The Establishment Clause in the Godless Constitution

If we want to endow the establishment clause with a different and broader meaning, therefore (and nearly everyone, especially including the justices of the Supreme Court, *has* wanted to do this for the last half century or so), we will need to find a different approach to constitutional interpretation. And as it turns out, there is a candidate for that role that has seemed to many to be perfect for the purpose.

THE EVOLUTIONARY EXPLANATION

The "hypocrisy" and "undetected meaning" accounts of how the First Amendment transformed the Constitution seem demonstrably implausible, and so it is not surprising that proponents of more expansionary and secularizing interpretations have more often relied on a different sort of account: they have contended that even if the establishment clause's prohibition was initially limited to something like the creation of a national church, the meaning of the clause evolved and expanded as the nation itself grew.[33] As Martha Nussbaum asserts, "our understanding of constitutional meaning evolves with new historical experiences."[34]

This sort of approach is associated with the notion, or slogan, of a "living Constitution." So labeled, the approach is controversial; it implicates well-known debates between constitutional "originalists" such as Justice Antonin Scalia and devotees of a "living Constitution" such as Justice William Brennan. Within the legal academy, those debates have become sufficiently refined and scholastic that it is difficult to enter into them without having a PhD in philosophy or linguistics.[35] And yet there may be less disagreement than meets the eye.

That is because both originalists and "nonoriginalists" or "living constitutionalists" tend to agree that at least some constitutional provisions should be understood as expressions of "principles"—principles like equal-

---

33. Compare Green, *The Second Disestablishment*, 8 ("To the founders, the separation of church and state was an unfolding idea, not an accomplished reality").

34. Nussbaum, *Liberty of Conscience*, 100.

35. For discussion of the growing complexities, see Steven D. Smith, "That Old-Time Originalism," in *The Challenge of Originalism: Essays in Constitutional Theory*, ed. Grant Huscroft and Bradley W. Miller (New York: Cambridge University Press, 2012). Not surprisingly, the sophistication of the debate has advanced measurably since this essay was written.

ity or "human dignity" (as Justice Brennan liked to say)[36]—and that their interpretation involves not just a reading of the literal words but an attempt to understand and apply the principles contained in the provisions. This "principles" approach to constitutional interpretation allows later readers or courts to expand the meaning of a provision beyond what people at the time of enactment intended or understood while continuing to claim continuity with the text or original understanding.[37] Such expansions may be justified in either of two ways.

First, it may be argued that as time has passed, later generations have come to understand the basic principle more fully than did the enactors who originally approved the principle and put it into the Constitution. For example, it might be that the Eighth Amendment's prohibition of "cruel and unusual punishments" expresses a principle of humane punishment, or something of that sort; and it might also be that this principle is violated by capital punishment even though the amendment's enactors, living in a more violent and vengeful time (when, for example, executions could be a macabre but popular form of public entertainment),[38] had not yet grasped this implication. To take another example, it might be that the people who enacted the Fourteenth Amendment's equal protection clause, while adopting a constitutional commitment to equality, were thinking of racial equality but did not yet understand that discrimination based on sex or sexual orientation also violated that constitutional principle. It took the passage and experience of decades, perhaps, before this implication of the principle came to be understood. Such arguments are by now standard fare in constitutional discussions.

Second, it might be that facts and conditions in the world have changed in a way that requires applications of a principle that were not contemplated or called for at earlier periods. Again, the equal protection clause

---

36. See Seth Stern and Stephen Wermeil, *Justice Brennan: Liberal Champion* (Lawrence: University Press of Kansas, 2010), 418.

37. For a critical discussion of some of the leading proponents of interpreting the Constitution as a repository of principles, see Steven D. Smith, "The Not-Your-Ancestors' Principle-Plush Constitution," in Steven D. Smith et al., *A Constitution of Principles? Four Skeptical Views* (Lanham, MD: Lexington Books, 2022), 39.

38. See, e.g., "Connecticut Draws the Curtain on Public Executions," Connecticut History.org, August 15, 2021, https://tinyurl.com/yc5ypxf4.

provides a possible example. At a time when education did not have the central role in society that it later came to have, the framers of that clause might plausibly have supposed that racially segregated schools were not implicated by the measure; but as public education became a more integral and essential part of life and society, the principle came to entail the unconstitutionality of such programs.

For better or worse, such arguments from and about "principle" are by now the daily bread and butter of constitutional scholars and lawyers. And the principles approach to constitutional interpretation provides ample resources for arguments about an expansionary establishment clause.

The first step is to say or assume that however narrow its immediate and understood purpose and application may have been, the establishment clause embodied or reflected a broader principle—or perhaps more than one principle.[39] And what was that principle, exactly, or what were those principles? The contemporary advocate has an abundance of options from which to choose. Maybe it was a principle of "nondivisiveness": the goal was to prevent religion from being a divisive force in American society, as it had been in Europe over the previous centuries. (Justice Stephen Breyer advocated such a reading.)[40] Or maybe it was a principle of "inclusiveness": the goal was to prevent anyone from feeling like an "outsider" because of her religion. (This was a favorite theme of Justice Sandra Day O'Connor.)[41] The principle might have been one of, say, "equal respect." (This is a preferred position for many modern scholars.)[42] And there are other possibilities.[43]

---

39. See Mitchell N. Berman, "Religious Liberty and the Constitution: Of Rules and Principles, Fixity and Change," *University of Pennsylvania Journal of Constitutional Law* 26 (2024): 4; John Witte Jr., *Religion and the American Constitutional Experiment* (New York: Oxford, 2000).

40. For a critical discussion of this rationale and of Justice Breyer's use of it, see Richard W. Garnett, "Religion, Division, and the First Amendment," *Georgetown Law Journal* 94 (2005–2006): 1667.

41. See, e.g., Lynch v. Donnelly, 465 U.S. 668, 688 (1984) (O'Connor, J., concurring).

42. See, e.g., Nussbaum, *Liberty of Conscience*; Christopher L. Eisgruber and Lawrence G. Sager, *Religious Freedom and the Constitution* (Cambridge, MA: Harvard University Press, 2010).

43. For example, Ira Lupu and Robert Tuttle, two prominent First Amendment scholars, contend that the purpose of the establishment clause was to "place[] ulti-

PART 1: A GODLESS DOCUMENT?

By any of these readings, it can be argued that although the establishment clause may not originally have worked to keep government separated from religion, even so, as the nation became more religiously diverse, its underlying principle or principles came to dictate some such prohibition. When everyone—or nearly everyone, or nearly everyone who was deemed to matter—was some version of Protestant, the "nondivisiveness" or "inclusiveness" or "equal respect" principles seemed consistent, maybe, with generically Protestant actions and utterances by government. But in a world composed of Protestants and Catholics and Jews and Muslims, and also agnostics and atheists and "nones" and "spiritual but not religious" folks, those same principles entail that government must stay out of religion altogether.

These sorts of arguments are familiar enough. Of course, every one of these interpretations might also be—and indeed has been—the subject of criticism. Lively debates thus swirl around all of these interpretations. More generally, the overall approach to constitutional interpretation that emphasizes "principles" over text or original understanding more narrowly conceived is itself eminently contestable[44] (although, as noted, self-identifying originalists are hardly averse to using the "principles" approach where this seems to them sensible).

These debates are all serious and important. But for our purposes, fortunately, we need not enter into or take sides in these intricate debates.

Why not? Well, think of it this way: let us grant for purposes of argument that the common contemporary practice of interpreting the Constitution as an expression of broad principles is to be accepted. In that case, as Ronald Dworkin (perhaps the leading theorist of the principled approach) explained, while trying to maintain some connection to (or, as Dworkin put it, "fit" with) the constitutional text, we will also try to interpret the Constitution to be "the best it can be." We will try to interpret the Constitution to make it square with what seems to us the best political-moral philosophy,[45] or the demands of modern society. With respect to

---

mate transcendent concerns beyond the reach of government." Ira C. Lupu and Robert W. Tuttle, "The Remains of the Establishment Clause," *Hastings Law Journal* 74 (2023): 1765.

44. See, e.g., the various criticisms in Smith, *A Constitution of Principles?*
45. See generally Ronald Dworkin, *Freedom's Law: The Moral Reading of the Con-*

The Establishment Clause in the Godless Constitution

the establishment clause specifically, therefore, if we believe that religion-free governance is most consistent with justice and sound policy, either in general or under contemporary circumstances, then we will interpret the Constitution to entail that conclusion. And the constitutional text is probably malleable enough, just barely, to support such a reading, so long as we are willing to read it loosely. Here, for example, we might treat the amendment's language about *"respecting* an establishment" to mean "tending toward," even if that is not what the enactors meant by the word.

Conversely, if some involvement of religion in politics and governance seems consistent with principle and policy, then we can easily conclude that the First Amendment allows for such involvement. All that is needed is to adhere to something like the original understanding of the provision as something like a narrow prohibition of an established national church.

BACK TO THE AGNOSTIC CONSTITUTION

But this conclusion brings us full circle, back to the position we started from. We saw in the previous chapter that the original "godless" or agnostic Constitution allowed for different governmental stances toward religion. It allowed for religion-free governance and politics; conversely, subject to some specific exceptions (in particular the prohibition on "religious tests" for officeholding), it was also permissive of and consistent with a more religion-infused governance and politics. And it turns out that the addition of the First Amendment did not fundamentally alter the Constitution's position in this respect. Initially and then for a century and a half, the amendment was *not* understood to require "godless politics and governance," and it need not be so understood today if that conclusion would be unwelcome or unattractive or unjust. Indeed, it takes considerable intellectual or rhetorical work even to impose such a construction on an unsupportive text and history. Still, there are people—many of them, in fact, capable and highly placed—who are eager to do exactly that work, and who in fact have been doing that work since the mid-twentieth century or before. And at least under a loose "principles" approach, the text

---

stitution (Cambridge, MA: Harvard University Press, 1997); Ronald Dworkin, *Law's Empire* (Cambridge, MA: Belknap Press of Harvard University Press, 1986).

arguably provides enough material to support such a construction *if* that construction seems more consistent with justice and good policy. We've seen it done. (And we *will* see it done, in chapter 4.)

So we might put the point this way: under a "principles" approach to constitutional interpretation, the First Amendment or the Constitution as a whole can be interpreted to require godless or secular governance *if* this interpretation would serve to make the instrument "the best it can be." Conversely, the First Amendment need not and should not be interpreted to require godless or secular governance if this interpretation would *not* make the instrument "the best it can be." But whether a secularizing interpretation would make the Constitution the best it can be is not a question that we can answer just by looking at the text itself, or even just by looking at the text in its founding-era historical context. We would need instead to see what has happened in the nation since that time, and what the national situation is today; and then we would need to ask whether purely secular governance would be the most attractive or prudent or fair. And so, that is a task that we will defer until later chapters.

For now, what we can say is that, a modern consensus to the contrary notwithstanding, the Constitution itself—the original text—did *not* in itself require secular governance. It was an agnostic document, not an atheistic one. And the addition of the First Amendment did not change anything in this respect. Whether a more secularizing interpretation is warranted *today* is a question that will need to be answered based on later developments—on developments that we will consider in upcoming chapters.

Part 2

THE PROVIDENTIAL REPUBLIC AND ITS (OFFICIAL) DEMISE

The chapters in this part recount how the America republic officially *was*, and then officially was *not*, "providentialist" in character. That terse preview, however, may stir up associations with a number of familiar, sometimes frustrating, often seemingly futile debates on which, fortunately, we need not attempt to take sides.

For clarity's sake, and to avoid being led down paths that we do not need to take, let us notice some of these at-times impassioned debates about which we can remain blissfully noncommittal. Were the Founding Fathers, as we often call them, Christians?[1] Was the American republic founded as a "Christian nation" (as the Supreme Court once declared it to be)?[2] Was the founding generation "religious" in the sense of being a pious and churchgoing people,[3] or were founding-era Americans rather

---

1. Compare, e.g., Isaac Kramnick and R. Laurence Moore, *The Godless Constitution: A Moral Defense of the Secular State* (New York: Norton, 2005), with Mark David Hall, *Did America Have a Christian Founding?* (Nashville: Nelson, 2019).

2. Holy Trinity Church v. United States, 143 U.S. 457, 471 (1892). For discussion of various aspects of the question, see John Fea, *Was America Founded as a Christian Nation? A Historical Introduction* (Louisville: Westminster John Knox, 2011).

3. Estimates by respectable historians of the percentage of Americans in the founding generation who belonged to and attended churches range from 15 to 20 percent to upward of 60 percent. See Roger Finke and Rodney Stark, *The Churching of America, 1776–2005* (New Brunswick, NJ: Rutgers University Press, 2005), 27–35. For an examination of some of the methodological assumptions (and a criticism of the lower

"secular" in their orientation? Was the Supreme Court correct, and if so in what sense, when it declared in 1952, "we are a religious people whose institutions presuppose a Supreme Being"?[4]

As noted, we will not in this section be weighing in on these debates. It is not that the discussions surrounding these questions are irrelevant to our subject here: they *are* relevant, and we will freely draw upon such discussions where appropriate. And yet these debates are not our question or theme, and they might even distract us from that theme.

How so? These familiar debates in various ways address the connection between America and *Christianity*, or between America and *religion*. And the proposition that America has been a "religious" nation is in fact one about which historians have written prolifically, and that is almost surely true in some complicated but meaningful sense. This feature was one that struck astute foreign visitors like Hector St. John de Crevecoeur, Alexis de Tocqueville, and Frances Trollope as conspicuous and remarkable.[5] The

---

estimates), see Mark David Hall, "Was the Founding Generation 'Churched'?" *Law and Liberty*, October 16, 2024, https://tinyurl.com/3kanha8r.

4. Zorach v. Clauson, 343 U.S. 306, 312 (1952).

5. See Patricia Bonomi, *Under the Cope of Heaven: Religion, Society, and Politics in Colonial America* (New York: Oxford University Press, 1986), 218–19. Tocqueville's remarkable report on Sabbath observance based on his visit in the 1830s—though surely idealized?—is memorable:

> In the United States, when the seventh day comes, trade and industry seem suspended throughout the nation. All noise stops. A deep repose, or rather solemn contemplation, takes its place. At last the soul comes into its own and meditates upon itself.
>
> On this day places of business are deserted; every citizen, accompanied by his children, goes to a church; there he listens to strange language apparently hardly suited to his ear. He is told of the countless evils brought on by pride and covetousness. He is reminded of the need to check his desires and told of the finer delights which go with virtue alone, and the true happiness they bring.
>
> When he gets home he does not hurry to his business ledgers. He opens the book of Holy Scripture and there finds sublime and touching accounts of the greatness and goodness of the Creator, of the infinite magnificence of the works of God, of the high destiny reserved for men, of their duties and their claims to immortality.
>
> Thus it is that the American in some degree from time to time escapes

The Providential Republic and Its (Official) Demise

country's complex but discernible religious character, historically at least, is relevant to our concern in part 2. And yet it may also distract us from that concern. That is because the central thesis here is not that America in its early decades or thereafter was a *religious* nation. The proposition, rather, which is both narrower and broader, is that America was a nation grounded in a *providentialist* perspective, in a sense that we will explain more carefully in chapter 3.

Providentialism and religion tend to go together, to be sure, and Christianity often has provided the form and content of American providentialist thought. And yet providentialism is not the same thing as Christianity, and it is not even the same thing as religion. In a book called *Providence Lost*, philosopher Genevieve Lloyd discusses the Western providentialist tradition as developed and expounded by a series of philosophers from Plato to Marcus Aurelius to Descartes and Spinoza.[6] Most of these providentialist thinkers were not Christian and may not have been "religious" at all in any conventional sense. In a similar vein, Arthur Lovejoy's classic *The Great Chain of Being*[7] amounts to an exploration of how a particular kind of essentially providentialist perspective decisively shaped Western thinking from antiquity until relatively modern times. Lovejoy traced this way of thinking back not to the Bible but rather to Plato's *Timaeus*. Such studies show that religion and providentialism are not identical.

Current usage and observation support the same conclusion. People whom you or I know might be religious in the sense that they believe in God, say prayers at meals or before going to bed, attend religious services on Sundays (or Saturdays, or Fridays), even pay tithes or donations to a religious institution or congregation; and yet they might not live with a "providentialist" orientation. This description very likely fits many church-

---

from himself, and for a moment free from the petty passions that trouble his life and the passing interests that fill it, he suddenly breaks into an ideal world where all is great, pure, and eternal.

Alexis de Tocqueville, *Democracy in America*, trans. George Lawrence (New York: Harper & Row, 1988), 542.

6. Genevieve Lloyd, *Providence Lost* (Cambridge, MA: Harvard University Press, 2008), 11.

7. Arthur O. Lovejoy, *The Great Chain of Being* (Cambridge, MA: Harvard University Press, 1936).

goers today if, as Genevieve Lloyd contends, "we have largely lost the frame of providence."[8]

Conversely, people might live under an apprehension of providence even if they do not say or do or even believe conventionally religious things. Think, for example, of common everyday invocations of "karma." Something bad happens to someone, and she or maybe someone else attributes the misfortune to "bad karma." Such references have a vaguely providentialist tone or tinge, in the sense in which Lloyd defines providentialism in terms of a sense of "cosmic justice" based on the premise of "a moral order implicit in the world itself."[9] But are they really "religious"? Or think of phrases like "It wasn't meant to be"—wasn't meant *how*, or by *whom*?—or "It's destiny." ("Luke, ... *Lu-u-uke*, it is your destiny.") Such expressions are evidence of, or at least holdovers from, a providentialist perspective.[10] But do they necessarily convey any sense of "religion"?

So religion will be relevant to our discussion here. And yet our deeper concern will be not with religion per se (whatever that turbulent term may mean), but rather and more specifically with providentialism. We will be considering how providentialism—sometimes in a Christian form, sometimes not—was crucial to America's constitution, self-understanding, and development.

Up until the time when ... it wasn't?

8. Lloyd, *Providence Lost*, 11.
9. Lloyd, *Providence Lost*, 15–16.
10. Compare Lloyd, *Providence Lost*, 1 ("Providence may now be largely 'lost' from our secular consciousness; but it continues to exert an influence on our thought and on our lives").

CHAPTER 3

Providentialism in America

It may be useful to start by reiterating what the thesis of this chapter is *not*. At its founding and for at least many decades thereafter, America was a "religious" nation: that proposition in some sense may be true enough, but it is not the proposition that this chapter seeks to explain and defend. Not exactly. The thesis of this chapter, rather, is that America was founded and for decades maintained on *providentialist* premises and with a providentialist self-conception.

Meaning . . . what?

In his acclaimed history of the American Revolution, Robert Middlekauf explains:

> Almost all Americans—from the Calvinists in New England searching Scripture for the will of God to the rationalists in Virginia studying the divine mechanics in nature—agreed that all things fell within the providential design. Providence ordered the greatest and smallest events of men's lives; Providence controlled the workings of the universe from the turning of the planets to the flight of a bird. Men might disagree about the meaning of the occurrences of their lives, some of which seemed surprising, even inexplicable—early deaths, epidemics, droughts, plagues, wars, evil as well as good. Such things men might wonder at and even describe as judgments, or afflictions, or marvels, or mysteries. Yet they did not doubt that these things had meaning.[1]

---

1. Robert Middlekauf, *The Glorious Cause: The American Revolution, 1763–1789* (New York: Oxford University Press, 2005), 4.

PART 2: THE PROVIDENTIAL REPUBLIC AND ITS (OFFICIAL) DEMISE

It is not that all Americans were pious in a churchy sense. Some were; some weren't. "Perhaps few sustained great religious passion for long," Middlekauf observes, "but they did retain faith in providential order." Moreover, "the order that began with the divine and expressed itself in the lives of a people *embraced their government*."[2]

In a study entitled *Providence and the Invention of the United States*, historian Nicholas Guyatt offers some helpful refinements and distinctions. Defining providentialism as "the belief that God controls everything that happens on earth," Guyatt distinguishes between "personal providentialism," or the belief that God guides the lives of *individuals*, and "national providentialism," which holds that God governs the destinies of *nations*. In the colonial and founding periods, Guyatt observes, "many Britons and Americans came to regard personal providentialism as superstitious and backward even as they continued to believe that God directed the fates of nations."[3]

Guyatt further distinguishes between two strands of national providentialism that have been powerfully influential in American history.[4] What he calls "historical providentialism" might be thought of as a sort of "special mission" conception: the central idea is that "God imagined a special role for certain nations in improving the world and tailored their history to prepare them for the achievement of this mission." America, in this view, is one such nation with a "special role": exactly what that role or mission is has been a subject of divergent interpretations.[5] (Of sometimes murderously divergent interpretations—as in the Civil War.) The other strand, which Guyatt calls "judicial providentialism," and which is more uniformly applicable across nations and societies, holds that God rewards and punishes nations based on "the virtues of their people and leaders."[6]

---

2. Middlekauf, *The Glorious Cause*, 4, 5 (emphasis added).

3. Nicholas Guyatt, *Providence and the Invention of the United States, 1607–1876* (New York: Cambridge University Press, 2007), 5.

4. Actually, Guyatt distinguishes among three versions, but the third—what he calls "apocalyptic providentialism"—appears to be a variation of "historical providentialism" informed by a focus on the biblical book of Revelation. Guyatt, *Providence and the Invention*, 6.

5. Compare Conrad Cherry, introduction to *God's New Israel: Religious Interpretations of American Destiny*, ed. Conrad Cherry (Chapel Hill: University of North Carolina Press, 1998), 19 ("Americans have been deeply divided over the meaning of the national mission").

6. Guyatt, *Providence and the Invention*, 6.

These two strands—the historical and the judicial—are often interwoven. Together they have constituted an understanding that through much of the nation's history was not merely an incidental or contingent feature of American society. On the contrary, providentialism was central to "the Invention of the United States," as Guyatt puts it—and to its ongoing self-conception.[7] Providentialist premises shaped public discourse, inspired hope and resolve in difficult or desperate times, and conferred on Americans a sense that their nation was not merely an association formed for mutual self-interest but rather a divinely ordained entity with a providential role in the history of the world.[8]

THE PRACTICE OF PROVIDENTIALISM

Both the historical and judicial strains of national providentialism were conspicuously on display in what might be viewed as the country's first official act. In the inaugural presidential address,[9] the man unanimously chosen to lead the new nation began by confessing his inadequacy to the great task. How could any mere mortal have the wisdom and strength requisite for such a daunting challenge? President George Washington then simultaneously answered his own question and discharged an obligation: he declared, "It would be peculiarly improper to omit in this first official Act"—note that he was speaking officially, not (as later dismissive interpreters sometimes suggest) in some sort of private-citizen aside[10]—"my

---

7. See also Kody W. Cooper and Justin Buckley Dyer, *The Classical and Christian Origins of American Politics: Political Theology, Natural Law, and the American Founding* (Cambridge: Cambridge University Press, 2022), 212: "Nearly all of the founders affirmed a Creator God who was above and beyond nature, particularly providential in the governance of human affairs, legislator of the natural moral law and its derivative natural rights, just judge [of] nations and persons, and benevolent enforcer of the moral order. Such a public theology was part of America's providential constitution."

8. Compare Stephen H. Webb, *American Providence: A Nation with a Mission* (New York: Continuum, 2004), 29 (asserting that "an orthodox theology of providence lies at or near the heart of much American history.... Providence defines America as a nation").

9. George Washington, "The First Inaugural Address" (1789), reprinted in *The Sacred Rights of Conscience*, ed. Daniel L. Dreisbach and Mark David Hall (Indianapolis: Liberty Fund, 2009), 446–47.

10. This and other similar instances and statements thus do not support John Ragosta's claim that early officials were acting on the premise that "an official can pray,

fervent supplications to that Almighty Being who rules over the Universe, who presides in the Councils of Nations, and whose providential aids can supply every human defect, that his benediction may consecrate to the liberties and happiness of the People of the United States, a Government instituted by themselves for these essential purposes.... In tendering this homage to the Great Author of every public and private good, I assure myself that it expresses your sentiments not less than my own."

Washington went on to elaborate briefly on the nation's dependence on and duty of gratitude to the "Almighty Being." Speaking as the man who had held together the hungry, tattered troops at Valley Forge and thereafter,[11] and who had later presided over a contentious constitutional convention that had more than once seemed on the brink of disintegration,[12] he was convinced that "no People can be bound to acknowledge and adore the invisible hand, which conducts the affairs of men more than the People of the United States." By any merely human calculation, after all, a happy outcome could hardly have been predicted in the war against Britain, or in the constitutional convention. And yet these developments had been blessed by a "providential agency" that beyond human reckoning had secured their success. Washington concluded this reverent meditation by emphasizing that his words were not merely pious stuffing. "These reflections, arising out of the present crisis, have forced themselves too strongly on my mind to be suppressed."

Washington's providentialist perspective was expressed through a prayer or, as he put it, a "homage" and "supplication"; and that form of expression was apt for the purpose. Prayer is perhaps the quintessential

---

even publicly, but he or she cannot pray officially." John A. Ragosta, "A Wall between a Secular Government and a Religious People," *Roger Williams University Law Review* 62 (2021): 545, 597–99.

11. Compare Middlekauf, *The Glorious Cause*, 302: "And now in 1775 ... [Washington] was called upon to lead forces of doubtful quality, supported by colonies of still unknown resolve, against the greatest power in Europe. Those strong inner resources of mind and character which had developed so slowly in Washington sustained him in the eight years of war that followed. So also did at least two profound convictions. The first was that he was an instrument of Providence in the struggle."

12. See Steven D. Smith, "Unpretentious Beginnings: The Merely Legal Constitution," in Steven D. Smith et al., *A Constitution of Principles? Four Skeptical Views* (Lanham, MD: Lexington Books, 2022), 5, 16, 22–25.

manifestation of a providentialist orientation, because it is in prayer that a person or a community acknowledges the authority of deity and requests divine guidance or assistance. This same orientation was likewise expressed in the first Congress, which as one of its first matters of business appointed chaplains in both branches to begin sessions with prayer.[13]

In engaging in public prayer, and in their providentialism generally, founding-era Americans were continuing a tradition that had been manifest in America from colonial times (although of course colonial providentialism was not projected onto an *America* that did not yet exist as a nation). John Winthrop's well-known "City on a Hill" address was a classic instance.[14] But a providentialist perspective had been virtually ubiquitous in the Puritan period.[15] The perspective radiated in the very first lines of Cotton Mather's history of New England, entitled *Magnalia Christi Americana*:

> It hath been deservedly esteemed, one of the great and wonderful Works of God in this Last Age, that the Lord stirred up the Spirits of so many Thousands of his Servants, to leave the Pleasant Land of England, . . . and to transport themselves, and Families, over the Ocean Sea, into a Desert Land, in America, . . . trusting in God for That, in the way of seeking first the Kingdom of God, . . . and that the Lord has added so many of the Blessings of Heaven and Earth for the comfortable subsistence of his People in these Ends of the Earth. Surely of this Work, and of this Time, it shall be said What hath God Wrought? And, This is the Lord's doings, it is marvelous in our Eyes![16]

---

13. Thomas J. Curry, *The First Freedoms: Church and State in America to the Passage of the First Amendment* (New York: Oxford University Press, 1986), 216–18.

14. Winthrop's providentialist aspirations for his colony led him to expel troublesome dissenters—like Roger Williams, who departed to found a city named . . . Providence. My thanks to Don Drakeman for pointing out this irony to me.

15. See Philip Gorski, *American Covenant: A History of Civil Religion from the Puritans to the Present* (Princeton: Princeton University Press, 2017), 37–59. See also Conrad Cherry, "The Colonial Errand into the Wilderness," in Cherry, *God's New Israel*: "The most self-conscious pursuit of destiny under God in the New World was enacted by the Puritans of Massachusetts Bay. . . . They envisioned their journey to these shores less as an escape from religious persecution than as a positive mission for the construction of a model Christian society."

16. Cotton Mather, *Magnalia Christi Americana, or The Ecclesiastical History of New-*

PART 2: THE PROVIDENTIAL REPUBLIC AND ITS (OFFICIAL) DEMISE

Later, a similar, albeit less sectarian, orientation had been pervasively manifest in the revolutionary struggle.[17] The Continental Congress had officially declared that "God Almighty . . . superintends and governs men and their actions," and that "our dependence was not upon man; it was upon Him who hath commanded us to love our enemies, and to render good for evil."[18] In declaring their independence from England, as Guyatt explains, patriots had acted on the reassuring conviction that "the very recent turn toward American independence had been in God's plans all along."[19]

As Abraham Keteltas, a New York politician and minister, put it: "I think we have reason to conclude, that the cause of this American continent, against the measures of a cruel, bloody, and vindictive ministry, is the cause of God. We are contending for the rights of mankind, for the welfare of millions now living, and for the happiness of millions yet unborn. . . . The war carried on against us, is unjust and unwarrantable, and our cause is not only righteous, but most important: It is God's own cause; it is the grand cause of the whole human race."[20]

For their part, Americans loyal to Britain attempted to articulate an alternative interpretation of the providential design more favorable to the Mother Country—but with less success.[21] The prevailing American view was colorfully expressed in a popular hymn known as "Chester":

England, from Its First Planting in the Year 1620 unto the Year of our Lord 1698 (1702), https://tinyurl.com/yc6ktjz4.

17. See Middlekauf, *The Glorious Cause*, 52: "The generation that made the Revolution were the children of the twice-born, the heirs of this seventeenth-century religious tradition. George Washington, Thomas Jefferson, John Adams, Benjamin Franklin, and many who followed them into revolution may not have been men moved by religious passions. But all had been marked by the moral dispositions of a passionate Protestantism. They could not escape this culture; nor did they try. . . . Their responses [to the political crisis]—the actions of men who felt that Providence had set them apart for great purposes—gave the revolution much of its intensity and much of its idealism."

18. Quoted in John Fea, *Was America Founded as a Christian Nation? A Historical Introduction* (Louisville: Westminster John Knox, 2011), 123–24.

19. Guyatt, *Providence and the Invention*, 95.

20. Abraham Keteltas, "God Arising and Pleading His People's Cause" (1777), in *Political Sermons of the Founding Era, 1730–1805*, ed. Ellis Sandoz, vol. 1 (Indianapolis: Liberty Fund, 1998), 595.

21. Guyatt, *Providence and the Invention*, 108–14.

> Let tyrants shake their iron rod
> And slav'ry Clank her galling Chains
> We fear them not we trust in god
> New englands god for ever reigns.[22]

Still, Americans could not simply count on their special role in God's plan to secure divine support; they needed to live so as to be worthy of such support. In an expression of providentialism's "judicial" strain, Henry Cumings, a prominent Massachusetts minister, observed, "[Although] from the good things which God has done for us, we are encouraged to hope," nonetheless "[a] good cause often suffers, and is sometimes lost, by means of the sin and folly of those who are engaged in it." "Nothing darkens our prospects more," Cumings pleaded, "or gives us more reason to be fearful, as to the event of the present contest, than the great and general prevalence of unrighteousness among us."[23]

In this spirit, John Adams believed that the Americans' only chance of victory against England would be if they "fear God and repent [their] sins."[24] In the same vein, General Washington declared, "We can have but little hopes of the blessing of heaven on our Arms, if we insult it by our impiety and folly"; and so he implored his troops "to endeavor to live and act as becomes a Christian soldier" and to avoid "the foolish and wicked practice of profane cursing and swearing."[25]

On the same premise, Washington urged his men to embrace special days of fasting, which would "incline the Lord, and Giver of Victory, to prosper [their] arms."[26] And both Congress and the states sponsored numerous such days of national fasting and prayer.[27] As the resolution of the Continental

---

22. Quoted in Mark A. Noll, *America's God: From Jonathan Edwards to Abraham Lincoln* (New York: Oxford University Press, 2005), 16.

23. Henry Cumings, "A Sermon Preached at Lexington on the 19th of April" (1781), in Sandoz, *Political Sermons of the Founding Era, 1730–1805*, 677.

24. Steven Waldman, *Founding Faith: How Our Founding Fathers Forged a Radical New Approach to Religious Freedom* (New York: Random House, 2008), 70.

25. Waldman, *Founding Faith*, 69.

26. Waldman, *Founding Faith*, 69.

27. Guyatt, *Providence and the Invention*, 104. See also Fea, *Was America Founded?*, 125: "Throughout the war, Congress appointed committees to write resolutions for days

PART 2: THE PROVIDENTIAL REPUBLIC AND ITS (OFFICIAL) DEMISE

Congress in 1776 put it: in times of peril "it is the indispensable duty of these hitherto free and happy colonies, with true penitence of heart, and the most reverent devotion, publickly to acknowledge the over ruling providence of God; to confess and deplore [their] offences against him; and to supplicate his interposition for averting the threatened danger, and prospering [their] strenuous efforts in the cause of freedom, virtue, and posterity."[28]

Summarizing the situation, Guyatt observes that "the sheer profusion of providential language in early America demonstrates a broad public audience for these ideas." He goes on, "In many cases, we can be confident that a particular person who used providential ideas was a committed believer in God's control over history. Even those whose public piety diverged from their private convictions—like Thomas Paine—adopted providential language precisely because they realized that many Americans accepted its premises."[29]

And these themes would continue into the new republic. In a sermon preached before the governor and General Assembly of Connecticut and entitled "The United States Elevated to Glory and Honour," minister and Yale president Ezra Stiles offered a detailed and thoroughly providentialist interpretation of the revolutionary struggle, and he added, "we have reason to hope, and I believe to expect, that God has still greater blessings in store for this vine which his hand hath planted."[30]

Expressions of providentialism from this period, often not specifically Christian, are so numerous that it would be pointless to try to recite them.[31] But as one illustrative instance, consider Thomas Jefferson—a sig-

---

of 'fasting and humiliation' in which Americans were urged to cease their labor, go to church, and pray for the nation."

28. "Religion and the Continental Congress," in *The Founding Fathers and the Debate over Religion in Revolutionary America*, ed. Matthew L. Harris and Thomas S. Kidd (New York: Oxford University Press, 2012), 24–25.

29. Guyatt, *Providence and the Invention*, 8. Steven Green, while arguing strenuously that the founders and the Constitution established a secular republic, acknowledges that "without question, a dynamic religious environment informed republican ideology by providing the Revolution with a greater, transhistorical meaning, one that explained events as part of a continuum reaching back to biblical times." Steven K. Green, *The Second Disestablishment: Church and State in Nineteenth-Century America* (New York: Oxford University Press, 2010), 21.

30. Ezra Stiles, "The United States Elevated to Glory and Honour," reprinted in Cherry, *God's New Israel*, 83.

31. Laura Underkuffler-Freund explains that at the time of the founding

nificant instance because he was philosophically and religiously quite different from Washington and, *a fortiori*, from more pious or evangelical Christians like Cumings or Stiles, and indeed he was viewed by his political opponents as an infidel.[32] Jefferson is typically invoked in modern thinking and jurisprudence as a proponent of separationism and secular government.[33] Nonetheless, in his first presidential inaugural address Jefferson acknowledged "an overruling Providence, which by all its dispensations proves that it delights in the happiness of man here and his greater happiness hereafter."[34] In his second inaugural address, Jefferson returned to the theme. "I shall need," he told the citizenry, "the favor of that Being in whose hands we are, who led our fathers, as Israel of old, from their native land and planted them in a country flowing with all the necessaries and comforts of life, who has covered our infancy with His providence and our riper years with His wisdom and power, and to whose goodness I ask you to join in supplications with me."[35]

Another manifestation of the providentialist perspective was the frequent days of national fasting, prayer, and thanksgiving that, as noted, began in prerepublic America and continued with some regularity thereafter.

---

governmental papers were replete with mention of "God," "Nature's God," "Providence," and other religious references. Religious references on the Great Seal of the United States were apparently deemed desirable by conservatives and reformers alike. When proposed designs were solicited, Franklin suggested an image of Moses lifting up his wand and dividing the Red Sea, with the motto "Rebellion to tyrants is obedience to God," and Jefferson proposed the children of Israel in the wilderness "led by cloud by day and a pillar of fire by night." Reformers tolerated such references, apparently, because they were not believed to implicate core concerns.
Laura Underkuffler-Freund, "The Separation of the Religious and the Secular," *William & Mary Law Review* 36 (1995): 954–55 (footnotes omitted).

32. Isaac Kramnick and R. Laurence Moore, *The Godless Constitution: A Moral Defense of the Secular State* (New York: Norton, 2005), 88–109.

33. See, e.g., Kramnick and Moore, *The Godless Constitution*; Jack N. Rakove, *Beyond Belief, beyond Conscience: The Radical Significance of the Free Exercise of Religion* (New York: Oxford University Press, 2020), 99.

34. Reprinted in John T. Noonan Jr. and Edward McGlynn Gaffney Jr., *Religious Freedom: History, Cases, and Other Materials on the Interaction of Law and Religion* (New York: Foundation, 2001), 205.

35. Noonan and Gaffney, *Religious Freedom*, 206.

James Madison, for example, another of the founders who is often enlisted in modern jurisprudence on the side of church-state separationism, prescribed a number of such observances during his presidency[36] (although in a private memorandum written some years later he questioned the propriety of such prescriptions).[37]

Whether the leaders who made such statements and sponsored such practices were themselves wholly earnest in their reverent declamations is of course difficult to know, in some cases anyway. Although (as we will see) Jefferson embraced a providentialist perspective in understanding everything from natural science to government and rights, he privately described one official fast in terms that carry a tone of cynicism.[38]

Expressions mainly calculated to please the public are no doubt common enough with politicians; but if a particular politician's expression is more calculated than sincere, the expression nonetheless (or perhaps *a fortiori*) serves as evidence of the beliefs of the constituency to which the politician caters. Steven Green argues strenuously in favor of a secular Constitution and a secular founding, but his attempt to explain away the pervasive evidence to the contrary is distinctly odd. "Undue significance can be imputed to the founders' use of religious language and their willingness to speak in providential terms," Green contends. "In light of the extraordinary times and the prevalence of religious discourse it would have been remarkable if the founders had *not* employed biblical terminology in their public statements."[39] Precisely.

The Protean Character of American Providentialism

As noted above, providentialism is not necessarily tied to Christianity, or to any particular scripture or religion. In the early American republic, to be sure, providentialism was powerfully shaped by Christianity, and by

---

36. Noonan and Gaffney, *Religious Freedom*, 207; Mark A. Noll, *America's Book: The Rise and Decline of a Bible Civilization, 1789–1911* (New York: Oxford University Press, 2022), 111.

37. James Madison, "Detached Memoranda," reprinted in *The Founders' Constitution*, ed. Philip B. Kurland and Ralph Lerner, vol. 5 (Chicago: University of Chicago Press, 1987), document 64.

38. See Ragosta, "A Wall," 593–94.

39. Green, *The Second Disestablishment*, 23.

the Bible. And yet the most high-profile and insistent exponents of the providentialist perspective—Thomas Jefferson and, later, Abraham Lincoln—were not Christians, at least in any orthodox sense. Considering these different versions of providentialism helps to illuminate the protean and inclusive character of the providentialist perspective in America.

Providentialism and the Bible

In a recent massive study, Mark Noll shows how Americans set out to create a "Bible civilization."[40] The Bible was overwhelmingly the most published, purchased, read, and cited book in the early republic,[41] and biblical thought and language saturated American discourse, both public and private: "It is difficult to overestimate the casual regularity with which antebellum Americans salted their day-to-day communications with the Bible. As it was for the founding generation of Washington, Franklin, Adams, Jefferson, Jay, Dickinson, and Witherspoon, so it continued. To speak in public was, time after time, to exploit biblical paraphrases, allusions, cadences, or quotations. To write for private or public purposes was to draw from the same source."[42] And "implicit in these widely deployed biblical tropes was the assumption that God took special care of the American nation."[43]

Following earlier historians like Perry Miller, Noll observes that in the early republic, Americans drew more heavily for public purposes on the Hebrew scripture that Christians call the Old Testament than on the more Christian New Testament.[44] And the Old Testament is chock-full of teach-

---

40. Noll, *America's Book*.
41. Noll, *America's Book*, 130, 133.
42. Noll, *America's Book*, 122.
43. Noll, *America's Book*, 127.
44. Noll, *America's Book*, 19, 119. In this respect, Americans were continuing in a movement that had begun in the late sixteenth and seventeenth centuries. Eric Nelson has shown how Protestants in particular began in this period to turn to the Old Testament for political guidance. "In the wake of the Reformation," Nelson explains, "readers began to see in the five books of Moses not just political wisdom, but a political constitution. No longer regarding the Hebrew Bible as the Old Law... they increasingly came to see it as a set of political laws that God himself had given to the Israelites as their civil

ings and stories that emphatically communicate a message of national historical providentialism. "Blessed is the nation whose God is the Lord."[45]

Thus, the Pentateuch builds up to a Deuteronomic conclusion comprised of alternately hopeful and frightful verses[46] in which God, speaking through Moses, explains at length and in vivid, indelible detail that if Israel—Israel as a people or nation—worships God and complies with his law, the nation will prosper and will be protected against its enemies. "Blessed shalt thou be in the city, and blessed shalt thou be in the field. . . . Blessed shalt thou be when thou comest in, and blessed shalt thou be when thou goest out. The Lord shall cause thine enemies that rise up against thee to be smitten before thy face; they shall come out against thee one way, and flee before thee seven ways."[47] Conversely, if the nation turns from God to pursue other deities and other pleasures, all of these blessings will be inverted—turned into curses. "And it shall come to pass, that as the Lord rejoiced over you to do you good, and to multiply you; so the Lord will rejoice over you to destroy you, and to bring you to nought; and ye shall be plucked from off the land."[48]

Later books in the Bible not only reaffirm this message of blessing and cursing; they purport to corroborate it, over and over again, with historical experience. When Israel honors God, it prospers and prevails over its foes; when it neglects or deviates from the divine mandates, the nation falls under the oppressive governance of outside enemies—the Philistines, the Assyrians, the Babylonians.

Americans routinely compared their own fledgling nation to a new Israel,[49] and they assumed that the same promises and curses applied equally to them.

Actually, however, the Bible's providentialism is not parochial; its Deu-

---

sovereign." Eric Nelson, *The Hebrew Republic: Jewish Sources and the Transformation of European Political Thought* (Cambridge, MA: Harvard University Press, 2010), 16.

45. Ps. 33:12.
46. Deut. 28.
47. Deut. 28:3–7.
48. Deut. 28:63.
49. See the array of readings collected in Cherry, *God's New Israel*. See also Joshua Zeitz, *Lincoln's God: How Faith Transformed a President and a Nation* (New York: Viking, 2023), 74.

teronomic blessings and cursings are not limited to Israel. The prophet Isaiah extends the blessings and especially the cursings to neighboring nations.[50] And the book of Daniel recounts how the Babylonian king Nebuchadnezzar is deprived of his throne—and of his reason—for arrogantly failing to acknowledge that "the most High ruleth in the kingdom of men, and giveth it to whomsoever he will."[51] After being humbled for a period and then acknowledging the sovereignty of providence, Nebuchadnezzar is restored to his sanity and his kingship: "And at the end of the days I Nebuchadnezzar lifted up mine eyes unto heaven, and mine understanding returned unto me, and I blessed the most High, and I praised and honoured him that liveth for ever, whose dominion is an everlasting dominion, and his kingdom is from generation to generation: And all the inhabitants of the earth are reputed as nothing: and he doeth according to his will."[52]

Nor was it only Americans of European descent for whom the Bible provided the basic template for life. On the contrary, Noll points out that for African peoples brought to this country as slaves and for their children, the Bible became if anything an even more constant and authoritative guide to understanding life in the new land in which they involuntarily found themselves.[53] Among Black Americans, "the scriptural presence stretched from the intellectual elite to those without formal learning."[54]

Unsurprisingly, enslaved peoples often took different lessons from the Scripture than did their overlords. "The Bible [became] a unique source of light for a population groping in the darkness of race prejudice and enslavement. No other source of hope, inspiration, psychological support, and guide for action came even close."[55] Joshua Zeitz reports that "for Black evangelicals, the message of Christian perfectionism carried less resonance than Old Testament stories of God's retributive justice against the wicked— both wicked individuals and wicked nations." In this vein, Frederick Douglass "was a devout churchgoer who wove biblical themes and imagery into

---

50. See, e.g., Isa. 7:18–25 (Assyria); 13:1–14:27 (Babylon); 14:28–32 (the Philistines); 15:1–16:13 (Moab); 17:1–14 (Damascus); 18:1–7 (Cush); 19:11–25 (Egypt).
51. Dan. 4:25.
52. Dan. 4:34–35.
53. Noll, *America's Book*, 177–84.
54. Noll, *America's Book*, 178.
55. Noll, *America's Book*, 184.

his writings. Like other Black evangelicals, he frequently invoked the prophetic tradition of the Old Testament and patterned his lectures after Puritan jeremiads, with their warnings of societal decline in the face of iniquity."[56]

To be sure, the biblically based vision could turn violent, the most dramatic instance being Nat Turner's uprising. Turner, a slave who preached, prophesied, and baptized, derived from his close study of the Bible an apocalyptic vision of an impending judgment day in which divine retribution would be imposed for the evils of slavery. After preparing himself through fasting and prayer, he led a group of slaves in a revolt seeking to capture the nearby county seat (portentously named Jerusalem). Scores of men, women, and children died in the revolt and its suppression, and atrocities were committed by both the rebels and their suppressors. Captured and awaiting trial, Turner was asked whether he now admitted his mistake. His response was succinct: "Was not Christ crucified?"[57]

Optimistic Heterodox Providentialism—Jefferson

Despite the pervasiveness of the biblical orientation in the early republic, however, it would be a mistake simply to identify or equate American providentialism with the Bible, or with Christianity. Indeed, perhaps the nation's two preeminent providentialist thinkers—Thomas Jefferson and Abraham Lincoln—were flagrant exceptions to the orthodox Protestantism of their time. Both men studied the Bible intensely, and quoted it. And both reasoned and spoke from within a thoroughly providentialist framework of assumptions. But neither was an orthodox Christian, and each adopted heterodox (albeit dramatically different) approaches to understanding and applying the ways of providence. Noticing these variations can help to provide a more full and nuanced picture of the encompassing character of American providentialism.

Modern secularists often adopt Thomas Jefferson as a sort of representative of a secular outlook, and with some warrant: he was an enthusi-

---

56. Zeitz, *Lincoln's God*, 95.
57. Daniel Walker Howe, *What Hath God Wrought? The Transformation of America, 1815–1848* (New York: Oxford University Press, 2007), 323–27.

astic proponent of "reason" over authority, Scripture, or tradition.[58] And yet historian Daniel Boorstin explains that "Jefferson on more than one occasion declared 'the eternal pre-existence of God, and his creation of the world' to be the foundation of his philosophy."[59] Jefferson contended that even without any appeal to revelation, the rational human mind in contemplating the universe could not fail to perceive "an ultimate cause, a fabricator of all things, . . . an intelligent and powerful Agent," who superintends all that transpires in the cosmos.[60]

Nor was this a merely abstract commitment: the providentialist framework shaped Jefferson's concrete conclusions on matters ranging from natural science to politics and governance. Two characteristic if curious examples from the field of natural science can serve to illustrate Jefferson's providentialist mind-set.

Take first a specialized and somewhat exotic question: Do mammoths still exist? Yes, they do, Jefferson confidently declared.[61] But how could he be so sure? Well, we know that mammoths existed at one time, because we have discovered their fossils. And if mammoths existed once, then they must exist still (probably somewhere in the continent's as yet unexplored northern or western regions);[62] that is because nature conceived of in

---

58. Compare Noble E. Cunningham Jr., *In Pursuit of Reason: The Life of Thomas Jefferson* (New York: Random House, 1987), xiii ("As a man of the Enlightenment who believed in the application of reason to society as well as to nature, Jefferson throughout his life pursued the use of reason as the means by which mankind could obtain a more perfect society").

59. Daniel J. Boorstin, *The Lost World of Thomas Jefferson* (Chicago: University of Chicago Press, 1993), 30. See also Cooper and Dyer, *Classical and Christian Origins*, 76 (arguing that "Jefferson—admittedly among the most religiously skeptical of the founders— . . . understood Nature's God to be a creating, particularly providential, and moralistic being whose existence and causal relation to the world was essential to the foundations of natural rights republicanism").

60. Quoted in Waldman, *Founding Faith*, 83–84.

61. Thomas Jefferson, *Notes on the State of Virginia*, ed. Frank C. Shuffleton (New York: Penguin Books, 1999; original 1785), 55–57.

62. Jefferson offered a possible explanation for the species' migration away from the more densely inhabited eastern sections. Mammoths might be carnivorous, he hypothesized, and since the Indians tend to overhunt and thus deplete the stock of wildlife in regions where animal skins can be exchanged with white men for hatchets

providentialist and personalist—and feminine—terms simply would not allow any of her creations to perish. "Such is the oeconomy of nature," he explained, "that no instance can be produced of her having permitted any one race of her animals to become extinct, of her having formed any link in her great work so weak as to be broken."[63]

Take another question that was debated then and is debated now, by scientists and others: How old is the earth? Not very old, Jefferson at one point asserted. The earth with its plants and animals had been created all at once; it had not evolved in stages over long stretches of time, as some theorists mistakenly claimed. No biblical literalist, Jefferson did not base this conclusion on Scripture. Instead he reasoned again from the nature of a now masculine providence (and on a sort of Occam's razor premise):

> I give one answer to all these theorists. . . . They all suppose the earth a created existence. They must suppose a creator then; and that he possessed power and wisdom to a great degree. As he intended the earth for the habitation of animals and vegetables, is it reasonable to suppose, he made two jobs of his creation, that he first made a chaotic lump and set it into rotary motion, and then waited the millions of ages necessary for it to form itself? That when it had done this, he stepped in a second time, to create the animals and plants which were to inhabit it? As the hand of a creator is to be called in, it may as well be called in at one stage of the process as another. We may as well suppose he created the earth at once, nearly in the state in which we see it, fit for the preservation of the beings he placed on it.[64]

Although Jefferson was highly regarded in his day as an amateur scientist,[65] today of course, it is not for his scientific opinions but rather for his political pronouncements and achievements that he is taken seriously. But Jefferson's political views were equally beholden to his providential-

---

and guns and such, this depletion would naturally tend to drive the colossi away from the colonized areas. Jefferson, *Notes on the State of Virginia*, 56.

63. Jefferson, *Notes on the State of Virginia*, 55.
64. Quoted in Boorstin, *The Lost World*, 31.
65. Compare Boorstin, *The Lost World*, 25 (noting that "among his contemporaries who were competent to judge, Jefferson had a considerable reputation as a naturalist").

ist assumptions. As Boorstin shows with abundant evidence, Jefferson's thinking on governance and equality and human rights and American destiny was every bit as dependent on deducing conclusions from a posited providential design as was his thinking about mammoths and the age of the earth. Even more so, in fact. Boorstin observes that for Jefferson, "political theory" was "a way of discovering the plan implicit in nature."[66] In a similar vein, Henry May explains that "[a] benign God, a purposeful universe, and a universal moral sense are necessary at all points to Jefferson's political system."[67]

Take two of the most essential and celebrated themes in Jefferson's political thought: equality and rights. The claim that human beings are equal would seem, just on the face of things, and not to put too fine a point on it . . . preposterous. It seems undeniable, rather, that humans differ drastically from each other in every dimension—physical, intellectual, artistic, moral. And yet they are equal, said Jefferson in drafting the Declaration of Independence, because they are "created equal." "Behind those created equal," George Fletcher explains, "stands a Creator—the source as well of our basic human rights."[68]

But in what sense or respect are human beings equal? The Declaration goes on to explain: despite their manifest differences, humans are equal in the sense that, as noted, they are "endowed by their creator with certain unalienable rights." Rich or poor, strong or weak, clever or inept, we all have the same rights; in that sense we are equal. And notice the ground or source of those rights: they come from the "creator." "The word 'right' was always a signpost pointing back to the divine plan of the Creation," Boorstin explains, and "no claims [of right] could be validated except by the Creator's plan."[69]

---

66. Boorstin, *The Lost World*, 171–72.

67. Henry F. May, *The Enlightenment in America* (New York: Oxford University Press, 1976), 302.

68. George Fletcher, *Our Secret Constitution: How Lincoln Redefined American Democracy* (New York: Oxford University Press, 2001), 102.

69. Boorstin, *The Lost World*, 194–95. Given this understanding of rights, Jefferson was untroubled by the concern of some contemporary legal scholars that rights will come into conflict, and hence will produce social dissension and even breakdown. See, e.g., Jamal Greene, *How Rights Went Wrong: Why Our Obsession with Rights Is Tearing*

PART 2: THE PROVIDENTIAL REPUBLIC AND ITS (OFFICIAL) DEMISE

But it was not only human equality and not just a fixed set of universal and equally shared human rights that Jefferson derived from the divine design. In the vast expanse and natural wealth of the American continent he perceived a developing providential destiny for his own country—a destiny that would benefit not only Americans but the entire world by manifesting the possibility of republican government and natural rights.[70] Similarly, in the prosperity of American enterprises Jefferson perceived "the Creator's approval of the American experiment."[71]

For the most part, Jefferson's providential vision seems to have been markedly optimistic. Even, one might say, childlike. The providential design was a wholly beneficent one: there is "an overruling Providence, which by all its dispensations proves that it delights in the happiness of man here and his greater happiness hereafter."[72] No agonized struggle with the "problem of evil" here! Moreover, providence and its designs are readily knowable to and by anyone—the plowman as well as the professor.[73] That is because providence had needed to—and therefore did—endow all humans with a moral sense or faculty for discerning moral truths; were it otherwise, Jefferson said, "He who made us would have been a pitiful bungler."[74] Daniel Boorstin explains how Jefferson and his intellectual circle, rejecting dark Calvinistic notions of an inscrutable divine Sovereign, held that "God could be neither unpredictable nor malevolent," but must instead be "benign and intelligible."[75]

In this respect, the providentialism of Jefferson's most distinguished presidential successor was utterly different.

America Apart (Boston: Houghton Mifflin Harcourt, 2021). The Sage's "belief in rights was . . . supported by faith in a benevolent God whose design had made the claims of individual men harmonious." Boorstin, *The Lost World*, 245.

70. Boorstin, *The Lost World*, 226–29.

71. Boorstin, *The Lost World*, 229.

72. Reprinted in Noonan and Gaffney, *Religious Freedom*, 205.

73. See "Letter to Peter Carr," August 10, 1787, reprinted in *The Portable Thomas Jefferson*, ed. Merrill D. Peterson (New York: Penguin Classics, 1977) 423, 425 ("State a moral case to a ploughman and a professor. The former will decide it as well, and often better than the latter, because he has not been led astray by artificial rules").

74. Quoted in Richard K. Matthews, *The Radical Politics of Thomas Jefferson: A Revisionist View* (Lawrence: University Press of Kansas, 1984), 58.

75. Boorstin, *The Lost World*, 152. See also 239 ("The God invoked by the Jeffersonian was necessarily an intelligible being").

The Anguished Providentialism of Abraham Lincoln

In marked contrast to Jefferson's, Lincoln's vision was much more troubled and even tortured in quality. Although he repudiated his Calvinist upbringing, refrained from joining any church,[76] and rejected central Christian doctrines such as the divinity of Christ,[77] his mature outlook was profoundly providentialist in character.[78] His law partner William Herndon reported that Lincoln had "no faith in the Christian sense of that term"; even so, "no man had a stronger or firmer faith in Providence" than Lincoln.[79] Another associate reported that Lincoln "fully believed in a Superintending & overruling Providence, that guides & controls the operations of the world."[80]

As president, Lincoln aspired to be, as he said, "an humble instrument in the hands of the Almighty,"[81] and he became convinced that "nothing in [his] power whatever would . . . succeed without the direct assistance of the

---

76. See Allen C. Guelzo, *Abraham Lincoln: Redeemer President* (Grand Rapids: Eerdmans, 1999), 19: "Intellectually, [Lincoln] was stamped from his earliest days by the Calvinism of his parents. But he rebelled vigorously against that influence in adolescence, declined to join his parents' church, and turned instead toward the Enlightenment as his intellectual guide, toward 'infidelity,' 'atheism,' and Tom Paine in religion, to Benthamite utilitarianism in legal philosophy, and to 'Reason, all-conquering Reason' in everything else."

77. John Stuart, Lincoln's law partner, recalled that "Lincoln always denied that Jesus was the Christ of God. . . . [He] denied that Jesus was the son of God as understood and maintained by the Christian world." Zeitz, *Lincoln's God*, 121. A friend recalled that Lincoln denied "the innate depravity of Man, the character & office of the great head of the Church, the atonement, the infallibility of the written revelation, the performance of myricles, the nature & design of present and future rewards & punishments . . . and many other subjects." Zeitz, 66.

78. See generally Elton Trueblood, *Abraham Lincoln: Theologian of American Anguish* (New York: HarperCollins, 1973). Compare Cooper and Dyer, *Classical and Christian Origins*, 211 ("A search of Lincoln's collected works . . . uncovers over 300 invocations of God (and hundreds more if we include terms like 'Almighty' or 'Creator'), but few even indirect references to Jesus").

79. See Guelzo, *Abraham Lincoln*, 152.

80. Zeitz, *Lincoln's God*, 68.

81. "Address to the New Jersey State Senate," February 21, 1861, reprinted at https://tinyurl.com/7mfxbxvf.

PART 2: THE PROVIDENTIAL REPUBLIC AND ITS (OFFICIAL) DEMISE

Almighty."[82] When constituents urged him to emancipate the slaves, he explained: "it is my earnest desire to know the will of Providence in this matter. And if I can learn what it is I will do it!"[83] When his wife, Mary, questioned him critically about the Emancipation Proclamation, the president simply looked heavenward and declared, "I am under orders, I cannot do otherwise."[84]

Nor was this merely a private commitment for himself as an individual. Much like Washington and Adams and other predecessors, Lincoln asserted in an official presidential proclamation that "it is the *duty of nations as well as of men* to own dependence upon the overruling power of God, to confess their sins and transgressions, in humble sorrow, yet with assured hope that genuine repentance will lead to mercy and pardon."[85]

So the nation and its president should follow the divine will. But what was that will, exactly? And had the nation perhaps forfeited its providential calling through its injustices and iniquities, especially including slavery?[86]

Maybe it had. Lincoln wasn't sure. As the staggering losses of the Civil War converged with personal family tragedy, Lincoln did not lose his belief in a divine design—on the contrary—but he became less and less sure that this design was neatly benign or discernible by mere mortals like himself. And he was accordingly more critical of people who confidently claimed to know the divine will.[87] The death of his son Willie from typhoid fever led to

---

82. Quoted in Jon Meacham, *And There Was Light: Abraham Lincoln and the American Struggle* (New York: Random House, 2022), 15.

83. Zeitz, *Lincoln's God*, 164. See also Meacham, *And There Was Light*, 15 (observing that Lincoln "moved toward emancipation amid a deepening sense that his duty lay in attempting to discern and to apply the will of the divine to human affairs").

84. Guelzo, *Abraham Lincoln*, 345.

85. Quoted in Mark A. Noll, *One Nation under God? Christian Faith and Political Action in America* (New York: HarperCollins, 1988), 98 (emphasis added).

86. Compare Zeitz, *Lincoln's God*, 167: "Lincoln, for his part, never shared in this certainty that the Union's cause was God's cause. Speaking the familiar language of the Puritan jeremiad, he deemed the conflict a 'terrible visitation' from God and bade Americans to reflect 'in sorrowful remembrance of our own faults and crimes as a nation and as individuals, to humble ourselves before Him, and to pray for His mercy—to pray that we may be spared further punishment, though most justly deserved.'"

87. Compare Trueblood, *Abraham Lincoln*, 6 (explaining that Lincoln was "deeply convinced of the reality of the divine will" but "had no patience at all with any who were sure they knew the details of the divine will").

agonized reflections:[88] Lincoln locked himself in his departed son's bedroom every Thursday and sometimes visited his grave alone, while Mary began holding séances in the White House (at least one of which Lincoln attended) in an attempt to contact her son.[89] And the Union army's defeat at Fredericksburg, only the latest in a series of crushing disappointments, prompted Lincoln to confess: "We are now on the brink of destruction. It appears to me the Almighty is against us, and I can hardly see a ray of hope."[90]

In 1862, in a private memorandum, Lincoln reflected:

> The will of God prevails. In great contests each party claims to act in accordance with the will of God. Both *may* be, and one *must* be wrong. God can not be *for*, and *against* the same thing at the same time. In the present civil war it is quite possible that God's purpose is something different from the purpose of either party—and yet the human instrumentalities, working just as they do, are of the best adaptation to effect His purpose. I am almost ready to say that this is probably true—that God wills this contest, and wills that it shall not end yet. By his merely quiet power, on the minds of the now contestants, He could have either *saved* or *destroyed* the Union without a human contest. Yet the contest began. And having begun He could give the final victory to either side any day. Yet the contest proceeds.[91]

This understanding—or this confession of uncertainty—achieved its public expression in Lincoln's magisterial Second Inaugural Address. Lincoln acknowledged a commonality in the contestants: both the North and the South had "read the same Bible and prayed to the same God." While conveying his own conviction of the injustice of slavery, Lincoln humbly declined to condemn those who had defended the institution ("It may seem strange that any men should dare to ask a just God's assistance in wringing their bread from the sweat of other men's faces, but let us judge

---

88. See David Herbert Donald, *Lincoln* (New York: Simon & Schuster, 1995), 336–38.
89. Zeitz, *Lincoln's God*, 144–45.
90. Quoted in Meacham, *And There Was Light*, 13.
91. Noll, *America's God*, 431.

not, that we be not judged"). And unlike nearly everyone else at the time, in both the North and the South, Lincoln did not purport to comprehend God's design, or to claim God's unqualified support for his own side. "The Almighty has his own purposes."

It was possible that the war was a divine punishment for the sin of slavery, and that with emancipation that punishment might come to an end. Possible—but not certain: "Fondly do we hope, fervently do we pray, that this mighty scourge of war may speedily pass away. Yet, if God wills that it continue until all the wealth piled by the bondsman's two hundred and fifty years of unrequited toil shall be sunk, and until every drop of blood drawn with the lash shall be paid by another drawn with the sword, as was said three thousand years ago, so still it must be said 'the judgments of the Lord are true and righteous altogether.'"

And rather than taking vengeance on the sinful oppressors, the nation must try to follow a more magnanimous course: "With malice toward none, with charity for all, with firmness in the right as God gives us to see the right, let us strive on to finish the work we are in, to bind up the nation's wounds, to care for him who shall have borne the battle and for his widow and his orphan, to do all which may achieve and cherish a just and lasting peace among ourselves and with all nations." Frederick Douglass said of Lincoln's address: "These solemn words . . . struck me at the time, and have seemed to me ever since to contain more vital substance than I have ever seen compressed in a space so narrow."[92]

The Essential Functions of Providence

Thus far we have noticed the pervasiveness of providentialism, in Christian but also more heterodox forms, in early American history. But was providentialism actually essential to the American project and tradition? After all, a quality or feature can be pervasive and yet not truly essential, or constitutive.

Consider a couple of comparisons. Throughout the country's history, it seems safe to say, most Americans have eaten meat; and they have also spoken English (in one or another dialect). These practices are a conspicu-

---

92. Quoted in Meacham, *And There Was Light*, 24.

ous and pervasive part of American culture, but are they truly *constitutive*? Suppose that some sort of moral awakening or scientific finding were to convince most citizens to become vegetarians. Would this development reflect any fundamental change in the meaning of America? Or imagine, somewhat improbably, that Americans generally decided that it would be better to speak Spanish instead of English—perhaps on the assumption that Spanish spelling and grammar are more regular, making Spanish easier for children and others to learn. So instead of "home," Americans begin to say "casa"—instead of "mother," "madre." Would anything truly essential to the country have been lost?

As a contrast: If the country somehow chose to abandon elections and representative government in favor of entrusting all power to a (hopefully) benevolent despot, we could plausibly say that America itself is no longer what it once was. Its constitutive essence of being "of the people, by the people, for the people" would have been forfeited. But if Americans chose to stop eating meat, or to communicate in a different language, nothing really essential would have changed. Or so one might plausibly think.

Perhaps the providentialist dimension of American history is another such pervasive but inessential feature? True, presidents and politicians, and citizens generally, have often used religious language or made pious references to some supposed providential design. But if the nation's self-understanding and discourse were to shift so that appeals to providence dropped out, it would still be the same people and the same country. Wouldn't it?

Well . . . maybe not. To address the question, though, we need to go beyond noticing that providentialist thinking has been pervasive in American history and ask what functions such thinking has served. So then, what were the uses of providentialist rhetoric and reasoning in the American tradition? There is no need to attempt any exhaustive list here; it will be sufficient to notice several of the principal (albeit overlapping) functions that providentialism has performed.

National Purpose

Understood from a providentialist perspective, the American republic is not something that simply evolved through the random unfolding of history. Neither is it merely a political association formed by men and

PART 2: THE PROVIDENTIAL REPUBLIC AND ITS (OFFICIAL) DEMISE

women, perhaps in some sort of "social contract," to promote the interests of the contracting parties. On the contrary, the republic was in a sense foreordained for a higher or transcendent purpose or mission. It is part of a divine plan.

To be sure, Americans might not agree on exactly what this purpose was, or is. Some Americans—the New England Puritans, for example—have conceived of it in specifically Christian terms; others have understood the purpose in more ecumenical and secular terms as the maintenance of freedom and republican government, or enlightenment.[93] "I always consider the settlement of America as the opening of a grand scheme and design in Providence," said John Adams, "for the illumination of the ignorant and the emancipation of the slavish part of mankind all over the earth."[94] That conception may be condescending, but it is not parochial or sectarian.

Still others—perhaps Lincoln in his last years, as we have seen—have believed in a providential purpose while confessing their incomprehension of exactly what that purpose might be. One can have a sense or even a conviction of purpose without having any clear conception of precisely what that purpose is.

Even without any precise formulation, however, a sense of purpose can be an existentially crucial fact, for an individual or for a nation.[95] A person with a conviction of purpose will not just wake up and ask, "What do I feel like doing today?" Instead she will try to discern what her purpose is and how she can carry it out. She is like an actor in a play who cannot just do

---

93. See Conrad Cherry, "Revolution, Constitution, and a New Nation's Destiny," in Cherry, *God's New Israel*, 61 ("Victory [in the Revolutionary War] was interpreted as . . . a proof of God's blessing on American tasks. The achievement of constitutional government was seen as the first step to a bold experiment that would assure basic human freedoms"). See also Lyman Beecher, "A Plea for the West," in Cherry, *God's New Israel*, 123 (suggesting that "this nation is, in the providence of God, destined to lead the way in the moral and political emancipation of the world").

94. Quoted in Robert N. Bellah, *The Broken Covenant: American Civil Religion in Time of Trial*, 2nd ed. (Chicago: University of Chicago Press, 1992), 33.

95. Genevieve Lloyd observes, "ideas of providence have strong emotional and imaginative force—whether in their evocation of a loving God or through the wonder elicited by ancient visions of a cosmos structured in accordance with necessary order." Genevieve Lloyd, *Providence Lost* (Cambridge, MA: Harvard University Press, 2008), 3.

and say whatever she pleases: she must perform the assigned part, follow the script. Same for a nation.

Thus, a sense of purpose will naturally provide guidance or at least orientation when difficult decisions are to be made. A person or a nation with a purpose will make choices so as to further that purpose.

Moreover, a sense of purpose will provide motivation to persist when difficulties or disagreements arise, as well as hope that such difficulties or disagreements can be overcome.[96] As John Witherspoon, president of Princeton and a delegate to the Continental Congress, put it in a sermon preached on the eve of what might have seemed a reckless revolution: "if to the justice of your cause, and the purity of your principles, you add prudence in your conduct, there will be the greatest reason to hope, by the blessing of God, for prosperity and success."[97]

This motivating function has been starkly evident at times when the nation faced serious possibilities of defeat or disintegration. We have noted how a sense of providential purpose and support helped sustain Washington and his troops—and Americans generally—through the adversities of the Revolution. Providentialism again featured strongly in the War of 1812. Mark Noll observes that "political-religious controversy during the War of 1812 illustrated both the widespread belief in God's special attention to the nation as well as confidence in the human ability to discern the hand of God in history." On this providentialist premise (and possibly despite private misgivings), President James Madison declared three days of national fasting with the purpose of securing divine favor for the nation and its cause.[98]

Similarly, when upon Lincoln's election the Southern states seceded, the new president might have acquiesced in this severance and concentrated on promoting the prosperity of the Northern, nonslavery states. There were those in the North (especially among the abolitionists) who

---

96. Compare George M. Frederickson, *The Inner Civil War: Northern Intellectuals and the Crisis of the Union* (New York: Harper & Row, 1968), 7 (observing that the "pervasive millennialism which looked hopefully on the American future as the fulfillment of divine promise" endowed Americans with a sense of "cosmic optimism").

97. John Witherspoon, "The Dominion of Providence over the Passions of Men," in Sandoz, *Political Sermons of the Founding Era, 1730–1805*, 552.

98. Noll, *America's Book*, 111.

urged him to do just that;[99] and considering the horrific violence and exorbitant cost of the Civil War in blood and resources, one might wonder whether, all things considered, this might have been the more prudent course. But Lincoln's determination to preserve the union, whatever the cost, was based on his conviction that America had a providential mission to fulfill—a mission that would be defeated or compromised if the union were permitted to disintegrate. This conception was manifest in perhaps his most celebrated speech—the Gettysburg Address. The war was being fought, and the "honored dead" had paid their "last full measure of devotion," in behalf of a nation "under God"—a nation with an "unfinished work" and with a "great task remaining before [it]." Namely (as he supposed at that point), the task of ensuring that "government of the people, by the people, for the people, shall not perish from the earth."[100]

Discourse

As we have already seen, the providential perspective informed (though it surely did not exhaust) discourse in America—political discourse in particular. To be sure, Americans argued about elections and political decisions and policies in pragmatic and consequentialist terms then just as they do today. Would a particular policy—a proposed tariff, or a subsidy for "internal improvements" such as roads or canals—promote peace and prosperity? Would it cost more than it was worth? These kinds of utilitarian considerations are perfectly familiar now and were common enough in past generations as well. But especially in the most crucial matters—whether to incur the deadly risks of declaring independence from England, whether to maintain or curtail the institution of slavery, whether to fight a horrendously bloody war to preserve the union—Americans pervasively argued about which course would be in accordance with the design of providence. The more pragmatic arguments operated within the encompassing framework of that assumed design.

Indeed, we already saw this tendency in founding-era Americans who, in denouncing the institution of slavery, did not merely declare the institution to be unjust or inhumane. Often, rather, they phrased their opposition

99. Frederickson, *The Inner Civil War*, 58.
100. "The Gettysburg Address," Abraham Lincoln online, November 19, 1863, https://tinyurl.com/57srrkpz.

Providentialism in America

by invoking the providential design. With reference to slavery, Thomas Jefferson said, "I tremble for my country when I reflect that God is just: that his justice cannot sleep forever."[101] In the Philadelphia convention, Gouverneur Morris denounced slavery as "a nefarious institution" that would bring down "the curse of heaven on the states where it prevailed."[102] And George Mason predicted that slavery would "bring[] the judgment of heaven on a country. . . . By an inevitable chain of causes and effects, providence punishes national sins by national calamities."[103]

Many debates, then as now, were of course conducted in the vocabulary of "rights." But at least to Americans like Jefferson, this vocabulary itself presupposed a providential design in which such rights were grounded.[104] So stated the nation's original founding document—the Declaration of Independence: the people's rights were those by which they were "endowed by the Creator." Arguments over rights were thus a kind of providentialism at one short remove.

Both epic national debates[105] and mundane court cases[106] also frequently deployed the vocabulary of "natural law," which again was understood to be grounded in the providential design. Legal historian Stuart Banner has shown that a common assumption of eighteenth- and nineteenth-century lawyers and judges (though here Jefferson was an outlier) was that Chris-

---

101. Jefferson, *Notes on the State of Virginia*, 169.

102. Edward J. Larson and Michael P. Winship, *The Constitutional Convention: A Narrative History from the Notes of James Madison* (New York: Modern Library, 2005), 112–13.

103. Larson and Winship, *The Constitutional Convention*, 130.

104. Compare Cooper and Dyer, *Classical and Christian Origins*, 76 (arguing that "Jefferson understood Nature's God to be a creating, particularly providential, and moralistic being whose existence and causal relation to the world was essential to the foundations of natural-rights republicanism").

105. See Cooper and Dyer, *Classical and Christian Origins*, 21: "The idiom of natural law and natural rights deployed by the Americans in the Imperial Crisis of the 1760s and the 1770s is only fully intelligible within the colonists' shared theological framework, reflected in the moral philosophy curriculum of the colonial colleges, that emphasized God's ongoing providential role in ruling creation according to the pattern of his own goodness, a rule that human beings could participate in through the exercise of their God-given faculty of reason."

106. See R. M. Helmholz, *Natural Law in Court: A History of Legal Theory in Practice* (Cambridge, MA: Harvard University Press, 2015), 142–72.

PART 2: THE PROVIDENTIAL REPUBLIC AND ITS (OFFICIAL) DEMISE

tianity is built into the common law.[107] This widely held belief, Banner explains, was not so much a particular legal doctrine as a metadoctrine; it served to support a "nonpositivist" view of the common law "as having an existence independent of the statements of judges,"[108] and hence as something that was there to be "discovered,"[109] not made.

Public discourse grounded in providentialist premises was wide-ranging and, sometimes, profound. John Coleman observes that "the strongest American voices for a compassionate just community always appealed in public to religious imagery and sentiments, from Winthrop and Sam Adams, Melville and Lincoln of the second inaugural address, to Walter Rauschenbusch and Reinhold Niebuhr and Frederick Douglass and Martin Luther King.... The American religious ethic and rhetoric contain rich, polyvalent symbolic power to command commitments of emotional depth, when compared to 'secular' language."[110]

Constituting Community

And yet providentialism performed an even more fundamental role in the republic: it not only served to guide national debate and decisions, but it was essential in leading Americans to regard themselves as a nation at all.

An influential scholarly study explains that political communities are "imagined."[111] They exist not as physical facts—a community is not just a collection of *Homo sapiens* living in physical proximity to each other—but as constructs in the minds of their citizens. A community is a community because people think of it as one, or *imagine it* as one. So then, what is it—or what *was* it—that led Americans to think of themselves as a community?

107. Stuart Banner, *The Decline of Natural Law: How American Lawyers Once Used Natural Law and Why They Stopped* (New York: Oxford University Press, 2021), 96–110.
108. Stuart Banner, "When Christianity Was Part of the Common Law," *Law & History Review* 16 (1998): 27, 61, 50.
109. Banner, "When Christianity Was Part," 60.
110. John Coleman, *An American Strategic Theology* (Eugene, OR: Wipf & Stock, 2005), 193–94.
111. Benedict Anderson, *Imagined Communities: Reflections on the Origin and Spread of Nationalism* (London: Verso, 2006).

Many things, no doubt: but belief in the nation as having a providentially ordained role was a significant factor in supporting such a conception. Thus, although highly critical of contemporary invocations and uses of the "Christian nation" concept, historian John Fea reports that "the idea that the United States was a 'Christian nation' was central to American identity in the years between the Revolution and the Civil War."[112] This notion "was freighted with the idea that the United States had a special role to play in the plan of God. . . . Moreover, when nineteenth-century Americans talked about living in a 'Christian nation' they rarely used the term in a polemical way. In other words, they were not trying to defend the label against those who did not believe the United States was a Christian nation. Instead, they used the phrase as if it were a well-known, generally accepted fact."[113]

Thus, in the revolutionary and founding periods, as documented above, the idea that America was part of a providential plan with a divinely ordained destiny was a significant factor in holding the people of the various states together through the war, and then in consolidating the victory by binding themselves together under the Constitution. Even so, nationhood was hardly a secure achievement. "United States" at that time was still a plural term,[114] and many citizens surely identified primarily with their states—they thought of themselves as Virginians or Pennsylvanians or Georgians—and only secondarily and precariously with the nation. Not even after the federalists by persuasion and by hook and by crook secured adoption of the Constitution was unified nationhood secure.[115]

In the founding period, the largely common English heritage and the common experience of the Revolution worked to forge a sense of commonality, but there were also important cultural and commercial differences—and of course, the huge dividing factor of slavery. In later times, and with increasing immigration from various lands, the English heritage

112. Fea, *Was America Founded?*, 4.
113. Fea, *Was America Founded?*, 5.
114. See Harry S. Stout, *Upon the Altar of the Nation: A Moral History of the Civil War* (New York: Viking Penguin, 2006), xxi ("Before the Civil War, Americans would routinely say 'the United States are a republic.' After the war they would instinctively come to say 'the United States is a republic'").
115. Noll, *America's Book*, 31, 100–103.

receded as a salient source of unity, but a partly shared history and tradition helped to bring the disparate peoples into communion. At the same time, regional cultural and economic differences—again emphatically including slavery—pushed the states apart. Traveling through the country in the 1830s, the French visitor Alexis de Tocqueville observed that the centrifugal forces were stronger than the centripetal forces: the federal government "is tending to get daily weaker" while "the feeling of independence [is] becoming more and more lively in the states." Tocqueville could see "nothing to stop this general tendency"—unless it should be a "profound aberration in [the country's] basic structure, a change of opinion, an *internal crisis*, or a *war*."[116]

And in this, as in so much else, Tocqueville proved to be prescient. "In 1860 no coherent nation commanded the sacred allegiance of all Americans over and against their states and regions," historian Harry Stout observes. "Apart from federal election days and trips to the post office, most antebellum Americans had no real sense of belonging to a vast nation-state whose central government acted directly on its citizens. Their imagined community could not easily stretch beyond their local boundaries."[117] Stout discerns in the horrific slaughter of the Civil War the effective source of a religious understanding that transformed the disparate populations into a national community. "Only as casualties rose to unimaginable levels did it dawn on some people that something mystically religious was taking place, a sort of massive sacrifice on the national altar. The Civil War taught Americans that they really were a Union, and it absolutely required a baptism of blood to unveil transcendent dimensions of that union."[118]

Beyond the Civil War

Stout's volume deals with the Civil War; Guyatt's study of American providentialism likewise extends from the colonial period through the

---

116. Alexis de Tocqueville, *Democracy in America*, trans. George Lawrence (New York: Harper & Row, 1988), 394 (emphasis added).
117. Stout, *Upon the Altar*, xxi.
118. Stout, *Upon the Altar*, xxi. Compare Zeitz, *Lincoln's God*, 140 ("The Bible—particularly the Old Testament—increasingly offered a lens through which ordinary Americans in the North (as well as the South) observed and assessed the unimaginable drama in which each citizen now played a part").

founding and antebellum periods. But did a providentialist perspective persist beyond the Civil War period—into the Gilded Age and the twentieth century?

Mark Noll argues that the specific form of providentialism aiming at what he calls a "Bible civilization" did *not* survive the war. Differences of biblical interpretation—and in particular, vehement disagreements about what the Bible taught with regard to slavery—sharply divided Americans and fragmented church denominations; and these disagreements meant that the Bible could no longer serve as the common authoritative source or guide that it had been in the republic's early decades.[119] Noll observes that America remained in many respects a "Bible nation," even if it was no longer aspirationally a "Bible civilization."[120] Bibles in large quantities continued to be published, purchased, read, quoted, and revered. But the Bible was no longer serving the central civic function that it once had done.

And yet, even if the specifically biblical vision that had once prevailed now receded, a more ecumenical providentialism remained very much alive. To be sure, as immigration brought more and more Catholics and also Jews to the country, the Protestant quasi monopoly was broken. But growing pluralism served to reveal the adaptable and protean character of American providentialism. American culture evolved in the twentieth century into what one scholar has called "Tri-Faith America."[121] But the religious and indeed providentialist orientation continued.

Indeed, it might be argued that providentialism reached its high point in the 1950s—the era of a "piety on the Potomac" that was joined in by all branches of government.[122] President Dwight D. Eisenhower repeatedly endorsed the importance of religion to the American way of life. "Without God," the president asserted, "there could be no American form of govern-

---

119. Noll, *America's Book*, 473–74.

120. Noll, *America's Book*, 585.

121. Kevin M. Schultz, *Tri-Faith America: How Catholics and Jews Held Postwar America to Its Protestant Promise* (New York: Oxford University Press, 2011). See also Andrew Koppelman, *Defending American Religious Neutrality* (Cambridge, MA: Harvard University Press, 2013), 28–42.

122. For a somewhat disdainful contemporary account, see William Lee Miller, *Piety along the Potomac: Notes on Politics and Morals in the '50s* (New York: Houghton Mifflin, 1964).

ment, nor an American way of life."[123] Congress added the words "under God" to the Pledge of Allegiance (echoing the "this nation, under God" of Lincoln's Gettysburg Address) and ratified the national motto (already announced as such many decades earlier in Francis Scott Key's national anthem): In God We Trust.[124] And the Supreme Court declared, not that we are a "Christian nation," as the Court had said in 1892,[125] but rather and more ecumenically that "we are a religious people whose institutions presuppose a Supreme Being."[126]

This new situation was astutely captured in Will Herberg's *Protestant-Catholic-Jew*. Herberg eloquently described an America constituted by a "conception of the three 'communions'—Protestantism, Catholicism, Judaism—as three diverse, but equally legitimate, equally American, expressions of an over-all American religion."[127] Although even this "three communion" conception would become cramped as the proliferation of homegrown American religions such as Mormonism and Adventism and the growing presence of other world religions such as Islam continued to expand the country's religious diversity.

To be sure, the conspicuous and even ostentatious public expressions of providentialism of the 1950s may cover over a more ambiguous underlying reality. Although Americans, including American leaders, might continue to acknowledge God and supplicate God's help for the nation, it also seems possible and even likely that many Americans did not habitually view the world through the same pervasively providentialist lens that (as noted at the beginning of this chapter) Professor Middlekauf described with respect

---

123. Quoted in Fea, *Was America Founded?*, 50. Eisenhower is sometimes ridiculed for his assertion: "Our form of government has no sense unless it is founded in a deeply felt religious faith[,] and *I don't care what it is*." Quoted in Paul Horwitz, "Religion and American Politics: Three Views of the Cathedral," *University of Memphis Law Review* 39 (2009): 978 (emphasis added). In fact, the statement cogently conveys the protean character of American providentialism.

124. See Brian Burrell, *The Words We Live By: The Creeds, Mottoes, and Pledges That Have Shaped America* (New York: Free Press, 1997), 188–92.

125. Holy Trinity Church v. United States, 143 U.S. 457, 471 (1892).

126. Zorach v. Clauson, 343 U.S. 306, 312 (1952).

127. Will Herberg, *Protestant-Catholic-Jew* (Chicago: University of Chicago Press, 1983; original 1955), 87. Herberg interpreted the American religion, however, as reflecting a need for belonging more than a genuine faith in providence.

Providentialism in America

to the generation of the Revolution. A discernible secularization separated mid-twentieth-century Americans from their distant predecessors. Thus, sociologist Christian Smith explains how in higher education, psychology, sociology, and law, the theistic assumptions and vocabulary of earlier periods were over time being displaced by a more secular perspective.[128] Writing in the year of Eisenhower's election, prominent theologian Reinhold Niebuhr already was regretfully describing the providential outlook as a thing of the past (although Niebuhr himself continued to interpret American history in providentialist terms).[129]

Even so, many Americans and especially American leaders continued to embrace providentialist thinking, or at least providentialist rhetoric. John F. Kennedy's powerful inaugural address sounded clear providentialist themes. "With a good conscience our only sure reward, with history the final judge of our deeds," Kennedy proclaimed, "let us go forth to lead the land we love, asking His blessing and His help, but knowing that here on earth God's work must truly be our own."[130]

And of course, this underlying providential faith was vital to one of the most important reform campaigns ever to shape the country—the civil rights movement most prominently led by the Reverend Dr. Martin Luther King Jr. and supported by other religious figures. Confident that "the arc of the moral universe is long, but it bends toward justice,"[131] King gave prophetic speeches that were thoroughly biblical and providentialist in character, as was his celebrated "Letter from a Birmingham Jail." As John

---

128. Christian Smith, "Introduction: Rethinking the Secularization of American Public Life," in *The Secular Revolution: Power, Interests, and Conflict in the Secularization of American Public Life*, ed. Christian Smith (Berkeley: University of California Press, 2003), 1.

129. Reinhold Niebuhr, *The Irony of American History* (New York: Charles Scribner's Sons, 1952), 4 ("Modern man's confidence in his power over historical destiny prompted the rejection of every older conception of an overruling providence in history").

130. Quoted in Robert N. Bellah, *Beyond Belief: Essays on Religion in a Post-Traditionalist World* (Berkeley: University of California Press, 1970), 169.

131. The statement was written by nineteenth-century Unitarian minister Theodore Parker, but it was a favorite of both Dr. King and Barack Obama. See Nathan S. Chapman, "'The Arc of the Moral Universe': Christian Eschatology and U.S. Constitutionalism," *Notre Dame Law Review* 98 (2023).

PART 2: THE PROVIDENTIAL REPUBLIC AND ITS (OFFICIAL) DEMISE

Fea observes, "Most historians now agree that this powerful social movement in American life was driven by the Christian faith of its proponents. As historian David Chappel has recently argued, the story of the civil rights movement is less about the triumph of progressive and liberal ideals and more about the revival of an Old Testament prophetic tradition that led African Americans to hold their nation accountable for the decidedly unchristian behavior it showed to so many of its citizens."[132]

So, the question should not be whether providentialism survived the Civil War: it did. The harder question is what happened to public providentialism after the period of the civil rights movement. We will begin to address that question in chapter 5.

First, though, we should consider the relation between American providentialism and two other possibly related phenomena that have received considerable attention in recent years and decades: "civil religion," and something often described as "Christian nationalism." And in doing so we can also take note of the darker side of providentialism, and of the criticisms that it often provokes.

---

132. Fea, *Was America Founded?*, 52. See also Noll, *America's Book*, 671 (acknowledging that the civil rights movement was "the most effective reprisal of the nineteenth century's aspirational Bible civilization").

CHAPTER 4

Civil Religion and Its Discontents

In the 1960s, Berkeley sociologist Robert Bellah began to write about something he described as "American civil religion,"[1] and his work broke the ground for what became a subject of serious and ongoing scholarly interest. Bellah did not invent the idea of "civil religion"—Rousseau and Tocqueville, among others, had written extensively and insightfully on the subject, as had Will Herberg in the 1950s[2]—but Bellah's much-discussed writings drew attention to the matter in modern American scholarship. More recently, scholars and others have both associated civil religion with and distinguished it from something often described as "Christian nationalism"[3]—a cultural phenomenon that not only scholars but also pundits, politicians, commentators, and citizens generally have often excoriated but occasionally defended.

So then, is "civil religion" the same thing as the "providentialism" we considered in the previous chapter? How are civil religion and providentialism related to Christian nationalism? And what do the criticisms of

---

1. Robert N. Bellah, *The Broken Covenant: American Civil Religion in Time of Trial*, 2nd ed. (Chicago: University of Chicago Press, 1992); Robert N. Bellah, *Beyond Belief: Essays on Religion in a Post-Traditionalist World* (Berkeley: University of California Press, 1970).

2. Will Herberg, *Protestant-Catholic-Jew* (Chicago: University of Chicago Press, 1983; original 1955), 87.

3. See, e.g., Andrew L. Whitehead and Samuel L. Perry, *Taking America Back for God: Christian Nationalism in the United States*, updated ed. (New York: Oxford University Press, 2022); Paul D. Miller, *The Religion of American Greatness* (Downers Grove, IL: InterVarsity Press, 2022), 200–227.

PART 2: THE PROVIDENTIAL REPUBLIC AND ITS (OFFICIAL) DEMISE

civil religion and Christian nationalism tell us about providentialism as a paradigm for American self-understanding?

Providentialism and "Civil Religion"

"By civil religion," Bellah explained, "I refer to that religious dimension, found I think in the life of every people, through which it interprets its historical experience in the light of transcendent reality."[4] Thus defined, civil religion seems to be, if not exactly the same thing, at least in the same neighborhood as providentialism. Moreover, in support of his descriptions of civil religion in America, Bellah referred to some of the same kinds of historical facts that we considered in the previous chapter.

Citing the appeals to deity in the Declaration of Independence, Bellah argued that "it is significant that the reference to a suprapolitical sovereignty, to a God who stands above the nation and whose ends are standards by which to judge the nation and indeed only in terms of which the nation's existence is justified, becomes a permanent feature of American political life ever after."[5] Americans, Bellah argued, "saw themselves as being a 'people' in the classical and biblical sense of the word."[6] And "the American republic, which has neither an established church nor a classic civil religion, is, after all, a Christian republic, or I should say a biblical republic, in which biblical religion is indeed the civil religion."[7] Bellah's observations sound very much like the interpretation of America's aspiration to be a "Bible civilization" that Mark Noll has recently documented at great length.[8]

Like other faiths, Bellah explained, American civil religion had its sacred or quasi-sacred texts (the Declaration of Independence, the Constitution), its prophets (Washington, Jefferson, Lincoln), its martyrs (Lincoln, later, Martin Luther King Jr.), its theologians (Lincoln again),[9] its holy days

---

4. Bellah, *The Broken Covenant*, 3.
5. Bellah, *The Broken Covenant*, 174.
6. Bellah, *The Broken Covenant*, 2.
7. Bellah, *The Broken Covenant*, 168.
8. Mark A. Noll, *America's Book: The Rise and Decline of a Bible Civilization, 1789–1911* (New York: Oxford University Press, 2022).
9. See Bellah, *The Broken Covenant*, 179 (describing Lincoln as "our greatest, perhaps our only, civil theologian").

(Independence Day, Memorial Day, Veterans Day), its rituals (presidential inaugurations, the State of the Union address, Fourth of July parades and fireworks). And "behind the civil religion at every point," Bellah observed, "lie biblical archetypes: Exodus, Chosen People, Promised Land, New Jerusalem, and Sacrificial Death and Rebirth."[10]

Bellah's analysis thus seems in key respects to support the thesis of the preceding chapter. So then, is the civil religion described by Bellah identical to the providentialism of that chapter?

Not quite. One can imagine a society of religious people who believe that God guides their nation but do not manifest that belief by creating a civil religion embodied in quasi-sacred public texts or holidays or rituals. Indeed, devout believers are sometimes highly critical of civil religion, viewing it as a form of idolatry or a corruption of true Christianity: we will return to the point.[11] And the reverse is also true: a nation conceivably might celebrate itself in quasi-religious ceremonies (lavish presidential inaugurations, reverently observed holidays, parades, and such) without actually believing in any God who guides and blesses the nation or punishes it for its injustices and transgressions. The pompous and ceremonial aspects of overtly antireligious Communist regimes would be a clear instance, but (as we will see) the description may also apply to many patriotic Americans today.

Even so, "civil religion" and providentialism seem closely related. Perhaps the best way to conceive of that relation is to say that, much as in

---

10. Bellah, *Beyond Belief*, 186. Compare Conrad Cherry, introduction to *God's New Israel: Religious Interpretations of American Destiny*, ed. Conrad Cherry (Chapel Hill: University of North Carolina Press, 1998), 11: "Documents like the Declaration of Independence and the Gettysburg Address function as scriptures that interpret these events and hence preserve the traditions of the civil religion. Washington becomes both Moses and Joshua, both the deliverer of the American people out of bondage and the leader of the chosen people into the Promised Land of independence. Lincoln assumes the role of a Christ figure in the national memory: one who tragically dedicated himself to the destiny of a united nation and whose death summed up the sacrifices that redeemed the nation for that destiny."

11. See Cherry, introduction to *God's New Israel*, 15–16. See also Frederick Gedicks, "American Civil Religion: An Idea Whose Time Is Past," *George Washington International Law Review* 41 (2010): 898 (arguing that "civil religion's tendency to devolve into state idolatry makes it normatively unattractive").

PART 2: THE PROVIDENTIAL REPUBLIC AND ITS (OFFICIAL) DEMISE

a theistic religion basic beliefs are typically embodied and expressed in Scripture and ritual, so in America, civil religion—the quasi-sacred public texts and ceremonies and prophetic figures—has developed as a manifestation or implementation of the providentialist understanding of the nation, its history, and its putative destiny. Civil religion, in other words, seems to be, or at least to have been, a sort of embodied or institutionalized providentialism.

When he began writing about civil religion in the 1960s, Bellah believed that "American civil religion [was] still very much alive."[12] Later, disillusioned, he came to see American civil religion as moribund—as "an empty and broken shell."[13] Other scholars, however (including Yale sociologist Philip Gorski, who was a student of Bellah's), have recently argued that American civil religion endures to the present day.[14] It has persisted both in a healthy form as represented, Gorski thinks, by leaders such as Bill Clinton and Barack Obama,[15] and in a corrupted offshoot that he and others describe as "Christian nationalism" manifest in figures like Ronald Reagan, George W. Bush, and especially Donald Trump.[16]

We will return to consider the relation between civil religion and Christian nationalism. For now, we might note that drawing a distinction between the two, as Gorski does, is a way of acknowledging that providentialism and civil religion have their happy and their unhappy features and consequences. Gorski's distinction is one way of recognizing this fact—but perhaps not the most helpful way. Casting all of the bad features onto a scapegoat and calling it "Christian nationalism" might leave civil religion itself looking pure and undefiled. But in fact, the core phenomenon itself, whether we regard it as providentialism or civil religion, does have its troublesome aspects, and it is important to recognize and consider these.

12. Bellah, *Beyond Belief*, 181.
13. Bellah, *The Broken Covenant*, 77.
14. See Philip Gorski, *American Covenant: A History of Civil Religion from the Puritans to the Present* (Princeton: Princeton University Press, 2017).
15. Gorski, *American Covenant*, 190–200.
16. Gorski, *American Covenant*, 175–90. Trump had not emerged as a political leader when Gorski's book was written, but he has become the central villain in later treatments of Christian nationalism. See, e.g., Whitehead and Perry, *Taking America Back for God*; Miller, *Religion of American Greatness*, 200–227.

The Perversions of Providence

The discussion of providentialism in the previous chapter could convey the impression that this feature of the American tradition has been wholly benign: providentialism has endowed Americans with a sense of purpose, supported a discourse in which they could debate important matters (occasionally on a profound level), and indeed helped Americans to think of themselves as a united community. The picture would be incomplete, however, without noting that these features—and providentialism in general, including when it is embodied in civil religion—have had their dark side as well. Without pretending to comprehensiveness, let us consider and assess some of the more conspicuous aspects.

Alienation

Contemporary culture and political thought place great emphasis on acceptance and inclusivity (as in the ubiquitous mantra of DEI—diversity, equity, and inclusion). This emphasis is apparent in modern constitutional jurisprudence, and specifically in the "no endorsement" doctrine, to be discussed in the following chapter, that from the mid-1980s until the Supreme Court's recent decision in *Kennedy v. Bremerton School District*[17] purported to forbid any governmental expressions or actions that send a message endorsing religion.[18] The primary rationale offered for this prohibition has been that any such endorsement will be exclusionary and alienating. Religious endorsements will divide Americans who agree with the government's religious message from those who do not, and will cause the dissenters to feel like "outsiders" and "lesser members of the political community."[19] So, did the providentialism that prevailed during much of the country's history, and did so unapologetically, have similar exclusionary effects?

---

17. 597 U.S. (2022).
18. Lynch v. Donnelly, 465 U.S. 668, 687–94 (1984) (O'Connor, J., concurring). As formulated, the doctrine also prohibited messages that disapprove of religion, but in practice this part of the doctrine received far less attention and emphasis than the "endorsement" part.
19. *Lynch*, 688.

No doubt it did, to some extent.[20] How serious this alienation was in earlier periods is difficult to assess. We have seen that American providentialism has exhibited a flexible and protean character. In the nation's early decades it was predominantly a Protestant affair, and yet even in that earlier period its most prominent and profound spokesmen—Thomas Jefferson and, later, Abraham Lincoln—were distinctly heterodox, as well as utterly different from each other. In the twentieth century, American providentialism expanded to encompass Will Herberg's three-faith model—Protestant, Catholic, Jew—but the dictum for which President Eisenhower has so often been unfairly ridiculed was even more ecumenical: "Our form of government has no sense unless it is founded in a deeply felt religious faith[,] and *I don't care what it is.*"[21] The malleable and expansive character of American providentialism would seem to have softened the perspective's exclusionary effects, because usually and especially in earlier periods, almost all Americans, despite their differences, could embrace or at least respect a providentialism of one kind or another.

Or at least, so argued Robert Bellah. Bellah noted that in the American civil religion, "there is no orthodox interpreter, no government-supported school of civil theology, no censor with power to forbid what does not conform. The meaning, the inner meaning, is left to private interpretation, to the speech of any man—preacher, politician, or poet—who has the power to persuade. The result [has not been] consensus—there have always been sharp cleavages as to the deepest meaning of America—but not anarchy either."[22]

To be sure, at any given time there have been Americans who did not share the dominant religious opinions; and these differences have sometimes been the source of conflict, exclusion, and persecution. Catholics,

---

20. This consequence is emphasized in David Sehat, *The Myth of American Religious Freedom* (New York: Oxford University Press, 2011). Sehat self-consciously presents American history from the standpoint of "the experience of the dissenters" (9). In Sehat's presentation, these dissenters include basically all Americans who were not part of the dominant Protestant "moral establishment," as he calls it, including non-Protestant Christians such as Catholics and Mormons, non-Christians such as Jews, and nonbelievers—the atheists and agnostics.

21. Quoted in Paul Horwitz, "Religion and American Politics: Three Views of the Cathedral," *University of Memphis Law Review* 39 (2009): 978 (emphasis added).

22. Bellah, *The Broken Covenant*, 46.

Mormons, Jews, Jehovah's Witnesses, and others have from time to time been the targets of such persecution. Strictly speaking, however, these religious minorities have been at odds not with providentialism per se, but rather with the specific religious positions that have dominated at particular times and in particular places. Indeed, religious minorities may have had their own providentialist interpretations of the nation—including of its intermittent tendencies to religious intolerance.[23]

However encompassing providentialism may be, though, there is one group that presumably would not fit within its big tent—namely, those who do not believe in a deity or providence of any sort. In other words, atheists, and atheistically leaning agnostics.[24] In the republic's early decades, however, this group seems to have been vanishingly small. A writer taking the name of "Elihu" observed during the debate on the Constitution that "it is almost the only thing that all universally are agreed in; everybody believes there is a God; not a man of common sense in the United States denies or disbelieves it."[25] In a book devoted to the question, historian James Turner contends that "if one disregards the expatriate [Joel] Barlow just before 1800, America does not seem to have harbored a single individual before the nineteenth century who disbelieved in God.... For disbelief in God remained scarcely more plausible than disbelief in gravity."[26]

Such claims may provoke suspicions. How could any historian, or for that matter any contemporary observer like "Elihu," know that everyone in America believed in God? Might there not have been people who, as Tocqueville surmised, "profess Christian dogmas because . . . they are afraid to look as though they did not believe in them"?[27] And as Turner's

---

23. See, e.g., The Book of Mormon, 1 Nephi 13:20–29.

24. Compare Cherry, introduction to *God's New Israel*, 17–18 ("Within the national boundaries, however [the civil religion] has found no way of embracing atheist or agnostic elements").

25. Essay by Elihu, *The American Mercury*, February 18, 1788, reprinted in *The Sacred Rights of Conscience*, ed. Daniel L. Dreisbach and Mark David Hall (Indianapolis: Liberty Fund, Inc., 2009), 352.

26. James Turner, *Without God, without Creed* (Baltimore: Johns Hopkins University Press, 1985), 44.

27. Alexis de Tocqueville, *Democracy in America*, trans. George Lawrence (New York: Harper & Row, 1988), 292.

PART 2: THE PROVIDENTIAL REPUBLIC AND ITS (OFFICIAL) DEMISE

description itself implies, atheism or at least "freethinking" became a more common phenomenon in the nineteenth century: Robert Ingersoll, for example, achieved fame as a tireless campaigner against Christianity and for freethinking.[28]

Even so, through much of American history, the exclusionary effect of providentialism per se does not seem to have been severe. As late as the 1960s, in praising the providentialist element of John Kennedy's inaugural address but as part of a broader and generally favorable discussion of civil religion, Bellah noted that Kennedy's "only reference was to the concept of God, a word that almost all Americans can accept but that means so many different things to so many different people that it is almost an empty sign."[29] Supreme Court decisions dealing with conscientious exemption to military service during this same period proved that the term "Supreme Being" could even be interpreted to include the beliefs of atheists or agnostics.[30] Citing the theologian Paul Tillich, the Court declared that "God" could be understood to refer to any person's "ultimate concern,"[31] whatever it might be.

So, although it seems inevitable that providentialism and civil religion must have been alienating to some, it is hard to know how extensive such alienation may have been in past periods.[32]

In addition, it is necessary to ask whether whatever alienation was experienced should be attributed to providentialism per se as opposed to being inherent in the pluralism of modern liberal democracy. As an analogy, suppose that a set of speakers degenerates into the frequent utterance of

28. Sehat, *Myth of American Religious Freedom*, 173–76.

29. Bellah, *Beyond Belief*, 170.

30. See Welsh v. United States, 398 U.S. 333 (1970); Seeger v. United States, 380 U.S. 163 (1965).

31. *Seeger*, 380 U.S. at 187.

32. Frederick Gedicks argues that whether or not civil religion served as a unifying force in the past, it cannot perform that function today. Discussing an array of demographic trends, Gedicks concludes that "the national identity defined by contemporary American civil religion now excludes between one-quarter and one-third of all Americans; that is, between one-quarter and one-third of all Americans cannot subscribe to the national identity that American civil religion ascribes to Americans, or to the historical narrative that the civil religion creates for the United States." Gedicks, "American Civil Religion," 900.

profanities, vulgarities, and insults; and suppose also that these speakers express themselves in English. All the objectionable utterances would be inseparably associated with English: even so, it would be a mistake to regard their offensiveness as a product or fault of the English language. In an analogous way, it is arguable that any alienation sometimes suffered by atheists or others, though perhaps associated with the prevailing providentialism, is more accurately attributable to democratic pluralism.

Thus, in a large and pluralistic community there will inevitably be marginal or politically powerless minorities or individuals, who may accordingly feel like "outsiders" or "lesser members of the political community." This sort of alienation, if that is what it is, is simply unavoidable. In one context it will be atheists who will feel—and in a real sense will *be*—out of sync with the dominant culture. In another context it will be socialists, or monarchists, . . . or fundamentalist Christians, or Jehovah's Witnesses, or orthodox Jews.

The basic and lamentable phenomenon—namely, of insider and outsider status and feelings—is arguably an inevitable feature of life in a pluralistic community. If the phenomenon does not arise in connection with providentialism, will it not simply develop on some other basis? Public providentialism will likely be alienating to some citizens. Conversely, the systematic eschewal of public providentialism that, as we will see, modern constitutional jurisprudence has mandated will be alienating to others—to citizens who believe, along with Washington, Lincoln, and many others, that such providentialism is a sacred obligation of nations.

Self-Righteousness

Another and perhaps more severe or at least more unseemly consequence of American providentialism is that it could, and can, promote a kind of shallow self-assurance or smug self-righteousness—what Mark Noll calls "the hubris of the elect."[33] In his history of America's God, Noll observes

33. Mark A. Noll, *America's God: From Jonathan Edwards to Abraham Lincoln* (New York: Oxford University Press, 2005), 21. Compare Cherry, introduction to *God's New Israel*, 21 ("Above all, the belief in America as God's New Israel has come to support America's arrogant self-righteousness").

PART 2: THE PROVIDENTIAL REPUBLIC AND ITS (OFFICIAL) DEMISE

how in the nineteenth century many Americans, including leading theologians and other intellectual and political leaders (with the notable exception, Noll thinks, of Lincoln), seem to have confidently supposed that they could readily discern the designs of Providence and that their cause was God's own. This confidence was characteristic of the Protestant leaders of the time, but it was also true of more heterodox figures like Ralph Waldo Emerson. In an essay in the *Atlantic*, Emerson confidently hailed Lincoln as a chosen instrument of divine Providence,[34] and on that assumption he wrote to the parents of a fallen soldier offering the dubious consolation that "one whole generation might consent to perish, if by their fall, political liberty & clean & just life could be made sure to the generations that follow."[35] When one looks back with benefit of hindsight at the various pronouncements made by American political, religious, and intellectual leaders in the events leading up to and during the Civil War, it is hard not to feel embarrassment at the presumptuous foolishness that was so self-confidently dispensed by thinkers of all sorts.[36]

Nor was such religiously cloaked self-assurance limited to the Civil War period. On the contrary. In his classic *The Kingdom of God in America*, H. Richard Niebuhr observed that "the old idea of American Christians who had been called to a special task was turned into the notion of a chosen nation especially favored. . . . As the nineteenth century went on the note of divine favoritism was increasingly sounded. Christianity, democracy, Americanism, the English language and culture, the growth of industry and science, American institutions—these are all confounded and confused. The contemplation of their own righteousness filled Americans with such lofty and enthusiastic sentiments that they readily identified it with the righteousness of God."[37]

However objectionable such flimsy self-assurance may be, however, it is again unclear to what extent it is attributable to a providentialist perspective specifically, as opposed to a more universal human pretentiousness.

---

34. George M. Frederickson, *The Inner Civil War: Northern Intellectuals and the Crisis of the Union* (New York: Harper & Row, 1965), 120.

35. Frederickson, *The Inner Civil War*, 81.

36. Such statements abound in Frederickson's history of the period.

37. H. Richard Niebuhr, *The Kingdom of God in America* (Middleton, CT: Wesleyan University Press, 1988; original 1937), 179.

Are instances of smug complacency or political or nationalistic arrogance limited to people or societies who believe in God? What about all the statements and justifications made by "the best and the brightest" during the Vietnam War?[38] And might not similar instances of overweening self-assurance be found in, say, Marxist regimes? Or even, heaven forbid, in contemporary secular progressivism?

Such shortcomings may seem particularly conspicuous and offensive, to be sure, when they occur in the context of biblical religion: that is because they contrast so starkly with a central theme of such religion, which repeatedly seeks to convict believers of their failings and to remind them that "every man at his best state is altogether vanity."[39] Which points to another pertinent observation, however: often providentialist premises have been employed in American society not to exalt audiences, or to cause them to feel complacent or self-righteous, but rather precisely to humble audiences by reminding them of these shortcomings.[40] Thus, in a sermon delivered to the Continental Congress in 1775, the Reverend Jacob Duche spoke for his country in asserting that the present crisis "hath arisen from our unnumbered sins and rebellions against [God]. . . . We have neglected to improve under [God's] past corrections. We have shamefully slighted [God's] past loving-kindnesses."[41]

In a similar vein, in the middle of World War II the Protestant theologian Reinhold Niebuhr cautiously commended the "Anglo-American alliance" as a providentially ordained arrangement for combating the evils of Nazism and Fascism. "Only those with no sense of the profundities of history would deny," Niebuhr asserted, "that various nations and classes, various social groups and races are at various times placed in such a position that a special measure of the divine mission in history falls upon them. In that sense God

---

38. Compare David Halberstam, *The Best and the Brightest* (New York: Modern Library, 2001).

39. Ps. 39:5.

40. Compare Stephen H. Webb, *American Providence: A Nation with a Mission* (New York: Continuum, 2004), 34 ("What kept this idealization of America in check was the jeremiad tradition").

41. Jacob Duche, "Sermon," reprinted in *The Founding Fathers and the Debate over Religion in Revolutionary America*, ed. Matthew L. Harris and Thomas S. Kidd (New York: Oxford University Press, 2012), 27.

has chosen us in this fateful period of history." And yet Niebuhr emphatically cautioned against a "too simple identification of the nation's purposes with God's will," and he lamented the tendency for "the sense of destiny [to] become[] purely a vehicle of pride." Religion ought to guard a people against such pride, he said, so that "a contrite recognition of [their] own sins destroys the illusion of eminence through virtue"; but he doubted that the Americans and English would be able to avoid this spiritual peril. "We may be fairly certain that the Anglo-Saxon world will not be good enough or sufficiently contrite to fulfill its historical mission with complete success."[42]

Providentialism, in other words, can and more properly does promote humility, not hubris. And yet such hubris is a real phenomenon, and often enough it *is* associated with providentialism. Duche and Niebuhr offered their exhortations to humility, after all, because they perceived that such exhortations were desperately needed. Thus, misguided or not, nationalistic hubris should be counted as a possible evil—or, in Niebuhr's view, an almost inevitable evil—of providentialism.

Legitimating Oppression

Self-righteousness may be a contemptible quality in itself, but it is most troublesome when it supports the hubristic elect (elect in their own eyes, anyway) in the oppression of others. This is perhaps the most lamentable feature of providentialism, in America or elsewhere: it can be used to rationalize and promote injustice and oppression.[43]

The most obvious instance, probably, is the practice of Southern apologists in using biblical religion to justify slavery.[44] Another conspicuous instance is the way the idea of a special American mission or destiny served to justify brutal and oppressive treatment of Native American tribes[45]—

42. Reinhold Niebuhr, "Anglo-Saxon Destiny and Responsibility," in Cherry, *God's New Israel*, 296–300.

43. Compare Webb, *American Providence*, 29 (observing that "Americans are also very adept at using the rhetoric of providence to serve their own purposes").

44. See Noll, *America's God*, 386–402.

45. See Conrad Cherry, "Westward the Course of Destiny," in Cherry, *God's New Israel*, 117. "No people in the West suffered more from the effects of an aggressively pursued Manifest Destiny than the area's Native Americans. Driven from their hunting

what Bellah described as "the primal crime on which American society is based."[46] Nicholas Guyatt, in his history of American providentialism, dwells at length on what he views as the tragic consequences of the providentialist outlook in matters of race.[47]

Guyatt is discussing the antebellum period, but if we were to look forward to the late nineteenth and early twentieth century, we would find a familiar connection between providentialist thinking and racial segregation, and also with the "Manifest Destiny" rhetoric and colonialist policies toward the Philippines and elsewhere. Senator Albert Beveridge notoriously justified such conquests on the ground that "God marked the American people as His chosen nation to finally lead in the regeneration of the world."[48] As Bellah pointed out, "the issue of Anglo-Saxon superiority and American imperial destiny came to full public consciousness at the time of the Spanish-American War, especially in the great debate over the annexation of the Philippines. Many, like Senator Beveridge, argued that it was our obligation as a chosen people to bring our blessings to the Filipinos by annexing them."[49]

As with the other evils sometimes associated with providentialism, of course, we can again ask whether it is fair to attribute such oppressiveness to providentialism per se. From the beginning of history, arguably, human beings have oppressed other human beings; and usually the oppressors have sought to rationalize or legitimate such oppression using whatever normative theory or language was at hand. In a thoroughly providentialist community, such as nineteenth-century America, whatever oppression occurs will predictably be legitimated in a providentialist vocabulary. In a Communist country, injustices (committed against, say, the kulaks, or the Uighurs) will be described and rationalized in a Marxist vocabulary. It is difficult to say to what extent such injustices should be attributable to the

---

and farming grounds, herded onto reservations consisting of undesirable land, subjected to the diseases of their white conquerors, and defrauded by unfavorable—and broken—treaties, Native Americans were tragic victims of the doctrine of 'geographical predestination.'"

46. Bellah, *The Broken Covenant*, 37.

47. See Nicholas Guyatt, *Providence and the Invention of the United States, 1607–1876* (New York: Cambridge University Press, 2007), 173–258.

48. Quoted in Cherry, "Westward the Course of Destiny," 120.

49. Bellah, *The Broken Covenant*, 59.

PART 2: THE PROVIDENTIAL REPUBLIC AND ITS (OFFICIAL) DEMISE

philosophy or creed that provides the legitimating vocabulary, as opposed to a lamentable human propensity to oppress.

On Balance . . .

Providentialism and civil religion, we have seen, have served to support American community and political discourse, and to endow Americans with a sense of mission that has included the promotion of freedom, rights, and rule of law. In more modern times, similarly inspired rhetoric was crucial to the campaign for racial equality led by the Reverend Martin Luther King Jr. But providentialism has also been enlisted to support some of the more shameful failures of the American political experience. Whether on balance providentialism has been a net positive for America, and for the world, is surely debatable. Attribution is difficult, as we have seen, and quantification is probably impossible.

So, how to perform the balance? In his writings on American civil religion, Robert Bellah spent more pages soberly discussing civil religion's failures and associated injustices than its successes. He pondered the connection of civil religion to the subjugation of Native Americans, to slavery and racism, to American imperialism, to the moral failures and shallowness that he associated with capitalism. "The story of America is a somber one," Bellah observed, "filled with great achievements and great crimes."[50] Americans "hoped they were a people of God. They often found themselves to be a people of the devil."[51] And both the achievements and crimes were related to the nation's civil religion. "Most of what is good and most of what is bad in our history is rooted in our public theology. Every movement to make America more fully realize its professed values has grown out of some form of public theology, from the abolitionists to the social gospel and early socialist party to the civil rights movement under Martin Luther King and the farm workers movement under [Cesar] Chavez. But so has every expansionist war and every form of oppression of racial minorities and immigrant groups."[52]

---

50. Bellah, *The Broken Covenant*, xxii.
51. Bellah, *The Broken Covenant*, 2.
52. Bellah, *The Broken Covenant*, 179.

Nonetheless, Bellah regarded civil religion as a net blessing.[53] He lamented what he saw as its unraveling in the 1960s and 1970s, and he urged that the best hope for America lay in a reaffirmation of the country's historic faith.[54] Without that faith, "we have lost our sense of direction";[55] and the alternative, he feared, was a drift into "authoritarianism if not fascism."[56] Those who focused only on civil religion's failures and injustices, Bellah thought, were being tragically shortsighted. "The meaning of the American experience will remain forever opaque to those who, once they have seen through the most simple-minded version of American idealism, can find only violence and self-interest in its stead."[57]

Others of course would—many others today *do*—offer a different judgment.[58] Or do these more severe critics serve as confirmations of Bellah's more nuanced assessment?

CIVIL RELIGION AND CHRISTIAN NATIONALISM

The evils associated with civil religion—exclusion, hubris, legitimation of injustice—have ensured that it has always had its critics. But in recent years, and especially since the election of Donald Trump, the critics have proliferated, and have become more vehement in honing in on something they call "Christian nationalism" or, often, "white Christian nationalism."[59] Christian nationalism has been linked, as two scholarly observers note,

---

53. "The American civil religion," he observed, "is not the worship of the American nation but rather an understanding of the American experience in the light of ultimate and universal reality." "At its best, it has neither been so general that it has lacked incisive relevance to the American scene nor so particular that it has placed American society above universal human values." Bellah, *Beyond Belief*, 186, 180.

54. Bellah, *The Broken Covenant*, 151.

55. Bellah, *The Broken Covenant*, 153.

56. Bellah, *The Broken Covenant*, 159. Bellah added, on the same page, that "those who would criticize all the accepted conventions of our society—all the inherited obligations to family, friends, work and country—as 'bourgeois' may be sowing bitter seeds."

57. Bellah, *The Broken Covenant*, 49.

58. See, e.g., Gedicks, "American Civil Religion."

59. See, e.g., Whitehead and Perry, *Taking America Back for God*; Miller, *Religion of American Greatness*.

PART 2: THE PROVIDENTIAL REPUBLIC AND ITS (OFFICIAL) DEMISE

to "white supremacy, patriarchy, xenophobia, heteronormativity, authoritarianism, militarism, rejection of science, small-government libertarianism, antiglobalist populism, antidemocratic tendencies, social conservatism, Islamophobia, protofascism, and orientations toward cultural dominance."[60]

So, what if anything do the perceived evils of Christian nationalism tell us about civil religion and providentialism in general?

A first and obvious question is whether "civil religion" and "Christian nationalism" are different labels for the same thing, or whether they can be distinguished. The scholars and critics of Christian nationalism typically say that they *can* be distinguished—that "civil religion" has been and can be a wholesome political influence while "Christian nationalism" is shameful and pernicious.[61] But the question is difficult to answer decisively, for several reasons.

First, the terms are often used loosely and in inconsistent ways. In a later writing, Bellah lamented that the term "civil religion" was being used in multiple ways and that it had "spread far beyond any coherent concept thereof."[62] Likewise, "the concept of Christian nationalism has become highly elastic, first in that it encompasses a growing range of components and second in that it has been stretched to support a variety of arguments about what Christian nationalism is and does, while offering few criteria by which to evaluate those arguments."[63]

But the slipperiness in the terminology is exceeded by the complexity of the real-world phenomena that the terms attempt to describe. A term

60. Jesse Smith and Gary J. Adler Jr., "What Isn't Christian Nationalism? A Call for Conceptual and Empirical Splitting," *Socius: Sociological Research for a Dynamic World*, September 20, 2022, https://tinyurl.com/4azrt55b (citations omitted).

61. See Whitehead and Perry, *Taking America Back for God*, 11 (noting "critical distinctions between Christian nationalism and what has traditionally been thought of as America's 'civil religion'"); Gorski, *American Covenant*, 16–23. Critics point out that in his later denunciations of Christian nationalism, Gorski seems less attentive to this distinction. See Smith and Adler, "What Isn't Christian Nationalism?"

62. Bellah, *The Broken Covenant*, 164.

63. Smith and Adler, "What Isn't Christian Nationalism?" For a more recent and detailed analysis taking account of further research, see Jesse Smith, "Old Wine in New Wineskins: Christian Nationalism, Authoritarianism, and the Problem of Essentialism in Explanations of Religiopolitical Conflict," *Sociological Forum*, July 22, 2024, https://tinyurl.com/3m3mde9r.

like "Christian nationalism," for example, is frequently applied today to millions upon millions of Americans, most of whom do not describe themselves as "Christian nationalists" and whose beliefs, motivations, purposes, and understandings surely differ from person to person, place to place, and time to time. Former *Newsweek* religion editor Kenneth Woodward observes that "White Christian nationalism is not an identity you can assert; it's an identity that's applied *to* you."[64] Reviewing the evidence that the opponents of Christian nationalism have relied on, Woodward concludes that white Christian nationalism is a "myth."

In a similar vein, sociologists Jesse Smith and Gary Adler Jr. argue that the very concept of "Christian nationalism" is both conceptually amorphous and empirically dubious.[65] They point out that scholars and critics of Christian nationalism (and the two sets mostly overlap—the scholars are almost invariably critics) typically assign subjects to the category based on the subjects' responses to six survey propositions that were designed not to identify Christian nationalism but rather to measure attitudes toward the separation of church and state. Among these six propositions are the following: "The federal government should advocate Christian values" and "The federal government should allow the displays of religious symbols in public spaces." But might not a respondent think that equality and human dignity are "Christian values," or that traditional religious displays (nativity scenes and so forth) are acceptable, without thereby indicating any proclivity for the features ascribed to "Christian nationalism," such as white supremacy or authoritarianism?[66]

---

64. Kenneth L. Woodward, "The Myth of White Christian Nationalism," *First Things*, May 2024, https://tinyurl.com/47dnvahm. Woodward notes that "according to a 2022 survey by the Pew Research Center, 54 percent of Americans have never heard of Christian nationalism. . . . And of the 45 percent who have heard at least a little about it, only 5 percent viewed the label favorably."

65. See Smith and Adler, "What Isn't Christian Nationalism?"

66. See also Woodward, "The Myth of White Christian Nationalism": "Believing that the government should promote Christian values like justice, honesty, truthfulness, and charity—virtues shared by people of other faiths and people of no faith—hardly makes a respondent a 'nationalist' or even a Christian. Again, all sorts of people support the display of religious symbols in public parks, even in New York City. Are they incipient WCNs? And what is the meaning of 'strict' separation of church and state? How can any of these questions unearth Americans who support what the authors see as an implicit theocratic threat to the country?"

PART 2: THE PROVIDENTIAL REPUBLIC AND ITS (OFFICIAL) DEMISE

Ruiqian Li and Paul Froese, similarly, analyze the survey data and show that critics of "Christian nationalism" have conflated what Li and Froese call "religious traditionalism" and "Christian statism."[67] These positions have different and even opposite political and social implications and tendencies. The racism, nativism, and exclusivism that critics ascribe to so-called Christian nationalists are mostly associated with the latter position; conversely, religious traditionalists tend to be inclusive and trusting.

Perhaps the most damning criticism of Christian nationalism is that the movement seeks to preserve or reestablish "white supremacy."[68] In the current climate of political opinion, that is a charge that resonates; in some quarters it is the kind of claim that may be viewed as almost axiomatically true. And yet it seems highly unlikely that more than a tiny fraction of the Americans described by outsiders (not by themselves) as "Christian nationalists" would consciously avow "white supremacy" as a goal. The critics of "Christian nationalism" are thus attempting to peer into the subconscious character of subjects to whom they are profoundly unsympathetic—always a hazardous enterprise. Jesse Smith observes that "it is doubtful that a single living soul adheres to the deep story [of white Christian nationalism] as [Professors Gorski and Whitehead] have written it. Most of those to whom it is being attributed would angrily object to the inclusion of the parenthetical 'white' and its implications. (A few might keep it but protest its demotion to parentheses.)"[69]

Paul Miller, while criticizing what he perceives as racist elements in Christian nationalism, acknowledges that conscious or overt racism is largely absent. "American nationalism until the mid-twentieth century was overtly racist and sectarian, advocating for White supremacy and Protes-

---

67. Ruiqian Li and Paul Froese, "The Duality of American Christian Nationalism: Religious Traditionalism versus Christian Statism," *Journal for the Scientific Study of Religion* 62, no. 4 (August 2, 2023), https://tinyurl.com/396ec9jp. Cf. Ruth Braunstein, "The 'Right' History: Religion, Race, and Nostalgic Stories of Christian America," *Religions* 12, no. 2 (2021): 95, https://tinyurl.com/5xxdbre2 (distinguishing between two versions of the Christian nation narrative: the white Christian nation version and the colorblind Judeo-Christian nation version).

68. See, e.g., Whitehead and Perry, *Taking America Back for God*, 99–106.

69. Jesse Smith, "Sociology in the Age of Trump: The Clash of Deep Stories on the Left and Right," *Public Discourse*, April 4, 2024, https://tinyurl.com/3k33xmmh.

tant dominance. The [contemporary] Christian Right's articulated ideology does neither. The change is due in part to a sincere change in heart.... Members of the Christian Right disclaim discrimination against non-Whites and non-Christians."[70] Nonetheless, Miller contends that Christian nationalists "have a blind spot for the realities of inherited, intergenerational racial inequality."[71] They are insufficiently cognizant, he thinks, of structural or systemic racism. Let us say that Miller is right: Would such a shortcoming justify the charge that those assigned to the category of "Christian nationalists" are set on promoting "white supremacy"?

The polarized and politicized context in which such discussions are unavoidably carried on today is another reason why it is difficult soberly to assess the relationship between civil religion and Christian nationalism. Given the nebulous quality of the criteria of distinction, there is a conspicuously tendentious quality in the work of scholars like Gorski who regularly assign political figures on the left (Bill Clinton, Barack Obama) to the "good" category of "civil religion" while consigning figures on the right (Ronald Reagan, George W. Bush) to the "bad" category of "Christian nationalism."

Given these difficulties, rather than draw any definite conclusion, we might try to articulate two basic but fundamentally different interpretations, while conceding that there may be no across-the-board answer to the question of which is the more accurate interpretation: the answer might vary from time to time and from person to person.

One interpretation is that the complex phenomenon described by scholars and critics as "Christian nationalism" (assuming it is a real and meaningful phenomenon at all) *is* indeed a form of civil religion, and of providentialism—albeit a markedly reactionary form. Providentialism once again is the belief, as Nicholas Guyatt put it, that "God controls everything that happens on earth"[72]—including the destinies of nations and specifically of the American nation. As we saw in the previous chapter, however, although that basic belief has often taken a Christian form in the American tradition, some of its leading representatives, including Jeffer-

---

70. Miller, *Religion of American Greatness*, 163.
71. Miller, *Religion of American Greatness*, 181.
72. Guyatt, *Providence and the Invention*, 5.

son and Lincoln, were not Christian in any orthodox sense. And although American providentialism was predominantly Protestant in the nineteenth century, over time it became much more ecumenical and inclusive. If a specifically sectarian and Christian providentialism has reappeared in the twenty-first century, therefore, that would be a notably regressive version of the general orientation.

A very different interpretation would emphasize the "nationalism" in Christian nationalism while subordinating or instrumentalizing the "Christian" component. It is apparent that not just in America but in many parts of the world—England, France, Italy, and India are obvious examples—a resurgent nationalism, or a commitment to or veneration of what are taken to be a nation's distinctive culture, traditions, and values, has become a powerful movement in the twenty-first century. Brexit, MAGA, Hindutva, right-wing nationalist parties in France, Germany, and Italy: these are all manifestations of this revivified nationalism. In emphasizing national traditions and culture, proponents of such movements may seize upon a particular religion as a sort of source or symbol of the nation's distinctiveness. But in this usage, it is not the actual beliefs or faith or sacraments taught by the religion that are embraced and valued. The religion is championed, rather, for the historical and cultural features that it is thought to represent.

A recent comparative study by Tobias Cremer provides persuasive support for this interpretation.[73] Cremer perceives in much of the Western world a troubling identity crisis in which, as a result of secularization, modernization, and globalism, growing numbers of people feel disoriented and unsure of how to understand and identify themselves; and many of these people seek belonging and identity in a resurgent nationalism. The Alternative für Deutschland party in Germany, the Rassemblement National party in France, and Trumpish MAGA populism in the United States are all manifestations of this nationalist resurgence, Cremer argues. Often the leaders of these movements purport to adopt the Christian religion as a symbol of and marker for this renewed nationalism. And yet these

---

73. Tobias Cremer, *The Godless Crusade: Religion, Populism, and Right-Wing Identity Politics in the West* (Cambridge: Cambridge University Press, 2023). Hereafter, page references from this work will be given in parentheses in the text.

same leaders are usually not serious Christians; indeed, they are often skeptical or even disdainful of the theological core of the religion. And genuinely faithful believers who join up with such movements often find themselves marginalized or discriminated against within the movements (149, 218–19).

The central point was clearly expressed by Alexander Gauland, president of Germany's nationalistic and aggressively (if only nominally) Christian party, Alternative für Deutschland. "We do not seek to defend Christianity in any religious sense," Gauland asserts, "but as a traditional way of life in Germany, as a traditional sense of home. Christianity is only a metaphor for the customs inherited from our fathers" (62).

On this interpretation, Cremer explains,

> the PEGIDA [Patriotic Europeans against the Islamisation of the Occident] demonstrators carrying crosses in Dresden may not have believed in the Christian doctrine.... The RN [Rassemblement National] protestors gathered around the statue of Joan of Arc in Paris might have had little love for the bishops and archbishops of the church that had made her a saint. And participants in the pro-Trump protests at the steps of the US Capitol might have been unbothered by their hero's public rejection of Christian public ethics and America's civil religion. Yet, they all saw such Christian symbols as remnants of an identity, community and home that they had lost through the processes of secularisation, globalisation and individualism. (267)

This resurgent nationalism has taken different paths in different settings. In Germany, Cremer argues, actively religious citizens have generally shunned the professedly Christian nationalist party; a major reason is that these citizens have the option of supporting the more centrist Christian Democratic Union and Christian Social Union parties (94–99). In France, similarly, devout citizens supported the nationalistic and ostensibly Christian parties at *lower* than average rates until the centrist and Christian-friendly alternative—the Les Republicans—collapsed after about 2017 (156–69).

In the United States, actual churchgoing evangelicals mostly declined to support the nationalistic Donald Trump in the 2016 primaries; but after

Trump emerged as the Republican nominee, lacking what they perceived as any viable alternative, evangelicals turned to Trump in what many of them described as a kind of Faustian bargain (45, 208–39). Trump and the Republicans attempted to secure this support in part by rhetoric and the occasional staged photo-op; even so, the genuinely religious element is often treated dismissively within Trump's nationalistic movement (216–19). Trump's support has been strongest among "cultural evangelicals" who rarely go to church—much lower among actual churchgoing evangelicals (230–32).[74]

Overall, Cremer argues, this ostensibly religious or Christian nationalism is not a manifestation of resurgent religion at all, as many observers have supposed. On the contrary: it amounts to what Cremer describes as "the godless crusade."

Interpreted in this way, Christian nationalism would *not* be an instance or version of providentialism; on the contrary, it would be almost the opposite of a genuine faith that God rules over the destinies of nations, including America. From a more sincerely Christian perspective, the "Christian" in Christian nationalism is subordinated to the "nationalism," which itself amounts to a sort of idolatry in which God is displaced by the "nation."

So then, which of these interpretations is more plausible? Is Christian nationalism a form of providentialism, albeit a markedly regressive and sectarian form, reflecting a sincere if misdirected manifestation of the traditional belief that God governs the affairs of nations? Or is it rather an idolatrous perversion of faith in which religious language is appropriated to further nonreligious goals and values?

But the answer to those questions is almost surely . . . yes. Nor is it just that among the people classified (usually by outsiders, again) as Christian nationalists, some are sincere religious believers while others are using religion instrumentally to further nationalistic or personal ambitions. We may be moderately confident in placing some figures on one or the other side of that divide. But in fact, the opposition between genuine faith and idolatry runs through the souls of most religious believers, and has done

---

74. The analysis by Li and Froese similarly shows that "while Trump captured the hearts and minds of the less religiously active Christian Nationalists (those who attend church infrequently), his nativist positions were less popular with the most religiously active Christian Nationalists."

so for as long as "religions" have formed around the effort to worship God; and most believers find that the struggle to live on the faithful side of the line is a lifelong quest, not an accomplished fact or once-and-for-all achievement.

Some theologians have in fact been hostile to "religion" as itself intrinsically a form of idolatry. But the more common view, probably, has been that religion in the form of rituals and creeds and institutions is a project aimed at inculcating, expressing, and practicing genuine faith, although that effort is for most religious people a fitful affair characterized by occasional successes, failures or lapses into worldliness and idolatry, and (hopefully) recoveries and repentance. This is, it seems, the human condition; and in America, as elsewhere, providentialism, civil religion, and religious nationalism are all mixed up in that confounding condition.

CHAPTER 5

Providence Banished

For the first century and a half or so of their republic's existence, Americans tended to understand their country in providentialist terms—as a nation "under God" (in a serious and not merely ceremonial sense of that phrase). This understanding was not peripheral but essential and (unofficially) constitutive; it provided national purpose, guided discourse, and underlay Americans' conception of themselves as a nation. As we have seen, American providentialism was always protean in its forms. From the outset, leading spokespersons like Thomas Jefferson and, later, Abraham Lincoln articulated versions that were quite different from each other and also heterodox relative to the prevailing Protestantism. And the providentialist understanding became increasingly ecumenical as the decades passed and the religious makeup of the country became more complex. This understanding arguably reached its high point in the 1950s, in the age of "piety on the Potomac."

During all of this period, Americans generally seemed to suppose that the official practice of providentialism, or "civil religion," was fully compatible with the American Constitution. And the Supreme Court seemed to share this supposition. Americans were, as the Court said in 1952, "a religious people whose institutions presuppose[d] a Supreme Being."[1]

And then everything changed—quite suddenly, actually, and at least partly as the result of a new constitutional jurisprudence elaborated and imposed by the Court. "Almost overnight, it seemed," political scientists

---

1. Zorach v. Clauson, 343 U.S. 306, 312 (1952).

Robert Putnam and David Campbell report, "America had turned from God's country to a godless one."[2]

The justices now said that the Constitution required government to be "neutral" in matters of religion, and that this mandate of neutrality meant that government had to confine itself—in its reasons, purposes, and expressions—to the domain of the secular. Thomas Jefferson's legendary "wall of separation between *church and state*"—in itself a salutary constraint preventing government and *churches* from asserting authority over each other[3]—was now reconstrued or reconstructed to be a wall of separation between *government and religion*. Although most of the justices may not have perceived the far-reaching implications of this new doctrine (but Justice William O. Douglas surely did!), the doctrine logically entailed that all of the entrenched and cherished features and incidents of public providentialism were now, at least in principle, out-of-constitutional-bounds.

Did the new orthodoxy amount in substance to, as John Courtney Murray had put it with reference to the secularist regimes of Eastern Europe, "atheism as the public philosophy, established by law"? The claim was occasionally made—Senator Sam Ervin of North Carolina complained imprecisely, for example, that "the Supreme Court has held that God is unconstitutional"[4]—but such assertions tended to provoke protest and derision, at least among the learned classes. Which was hardly surprising. The justices were not infidels, or sinister conspirators plotting to subvert the American religious tradition. On the contrary, they professed to be respectful of and concerned about religion, and there is no reason to doubt their sincerity.

And yet . . . there is an important sense in which, wittingly or not, the Court's decisions did establish atheism, if not as *the* public philosophy, exactly, then as a key component of or constraint on whatever public phi-

---

2. Robert D. Putnam and David E. Campbell, *American Grace: How Religion Divides and Unites Us* (New York: Simon & Schuster, 2010), 100.

3. Compare Samuel Calhoun, "Getting the Framers Wrong: A Response to Professor Geoffrey Stone," *UCLA Law Review Discourse* 5 (2009): 11 ("Jefferson's Danbury letter spoke of a 'wall' between church and state, not religion and the state. Using 'church,' rather than 'religion,' . . . emphasized that the constitutional separation was between ecclesiastical *institutions* and the civil state").

4. Quoted in Justin Driver, "Three Hail Marys: Carson, Kennedy, and the Fractured Detente over Religion and Education," *Harvard Law Review* 136 (2022): 219.

losophy or public policy might prevail.[5] Indeed, that constraint is by now hardly even controversial among respectable jurists, lawyers, and scholars. On the contrary, it is the orthodox view, and is typically taken as axiomatic and obviously correct—by liberals and conservatives alike.

In this situation, the present chapter finds itself in an awkward position. It might seem as if the main burden of the chapter would be to show that however extravagant the claim may seem on first presentment, modern establishment clause jurisprudence actually did establish atheism as the public philosophy, or at least as an essential part of or constraint on any public philosophy. But in fact, the argument for that conclusion will be relatively simple and straightforward; it is scarcely an argument at all, but merely an exercise in looking past cosmetic presentations or euphemisms in order to observe and candidly acknowledge what the new doctrine actually said and did. The more complicated challenge, to which much of the chapter will be devoted, will be to consider the features of this new orthodoxy that have permitted the justices, the legal profession, and much of the educated public to overlook, deny, or dismiss the jurisprudence's atheistic entailments.

One further mitigating observation might be offered at the outset. The claim that the Supreme Court imposed atheism as a component of the public philosophy is potentially misleading in giving the justices too much blame, or too much credit, for this development. The claim could be read to imply that the Supreme Court was an independent, originating agent in reconstructing the Constitution along atheistic lines, and then in imposing its atheistic construction on American society. That implication *might* be right—but probably not. As a general rule, people who get appointed to the Supreme Court are capable, ambitious, politically connected, mostly conventional lawyers. They are not original, visionary thinkers or radical activists; if they were, they would not find themselves on the nation's

---

5. It seems more accurate to say that the doctrine established atheism as a *part* of public philosophy, among other reasons, because just in itself atheism (here understood, basically, as the denial of the existence of God) constitutes a specific claim but hardly a complete philosophy. Moreover, atheism comes in a number of versions and varieties. The atheistic philosopher John Gray distinguishes among seven different types of atheism, some of which he finds much more plausible and attractive than others. See John Gray, *Seven Types of Atheism* (New York: Farrar, Straus & Giroux, 2018).

Providence Banished

highest judicial tribunal. The justices sometimes interpret the Constitution in novel ways, yes; but in doing so they are mostly just channeling cultural and intellectual currents or trends that they have absorbed, probably without any profound critical reflection, and projecting those trends onto constitutional law. In this way, the Court *reflects* social changes as much as or more than it *initiates* or *causes* those changes.[6]

Which is not to say that the Supreme Court is merely a passive or innocuous agent mirroring developments that were already foreordained to happen in the way they did. Even if it is not so much initiating cultural and intellectual movements as reflecting them, nonetheless by reading such developments into the Constitution the Court serves as a powerful force to ratify, entrench, and implement those movements.

Thus, the Supreme Court surely did not single-handedly bring about the civil rights revolution of the 1950s and 1960s. *Brown v. Board of Education* and the rejection of official racial segregation would not have happened if political and cultural and intellectual changes had not prepared Americans—or at least many well-placed Americans—for that revolution. Martin Luther King Jr. did far more to advance the cause of racial equality than Earl Warren and company did. Even so, *Brown* and related judicial decisions ratified and endorsed that cause, and provided the authority for the forcible imposition of the change upon a sometimes recalcitrant society. Considered retrospectively, how much of what subsequently happened is attributable to the judiciary and how much would have happened anyway, with court decisions merely echoing or channeling changes already in process, is impossible to measure.[7]

The implication of these observations for our subject is that although Supreme Court decisions construed, or reconstrued, or misconstrued the Constitution into a charter for public atheism, and although this construction had transformative consequences for America, it would be a mistake to suppose that this transformation was something that just sprang out of

---

6. For a recent, valuable study of this process, see Jack M. Balkin, *Memory and Authority: The Uses of History in Constitutional Interpretation* (New Haven: Yale University Press, 2024).

7. For a skeptical assessment of the Court's power to bring about major social change, see Gerald N. Rosenberg, *The Hollow Hope: Can Courts Bring about Social Change?* (Chicago: University of Chicago Press, 1991).

the fertile or furtive brains of Hugo Black or William Brennan and their brethren. The justices were importing into constitutional law changes in the broader culture—in the culture not just of America but of the West— that were already well under way, and indeed that had been in progress for decades and even centuries. A full account of what happened would need to consider these broader changes—changes that are familiar to those who have taken classes in what used to be called "Western Civ" under labels like humanism, secularism, and naturalism.[8] If the Court interpreted the Constitution to establish atheism as a public philosophy, that is partly because atheism was already unofficially but in an important sense established as a sort of ambient philosophy among the influential classes—a fact that would hardly have come as a surprise to someone like Friedrich Nietzsche[9] or John Dewey[10] (or, for that matter, Cardinal Joseph Ratzinger).[11] And that is one reason why the atheistic implications of the Court's decisions were largely invisible to much of the more educated public; the implications were things that this more elite public already largely took for granted anyway.

8. A full account would also need to consider the relation between the Court's decisions and doctrines addressing the relation between religion and governance and other constitutional developments. Jeff Pojanowski points out to me the possibility that as more and more political or public matters were brought into the constitutional domain and decided as a matter of constitutional law, it was likely more difficult for the Constitution to continue to be treated as a benignly detached or agnostic legal instrument. Professor Pojanowski also suggests that the loss of a public commitment to and reliance on providentialism might have been a reason why the Constitution itself came to be the focal point and ostensible source of many of our public policies and decisions. It is an intriguing and plausible suggestion that I do not attempt to pursue here.

9. For an insightful discussion of the far-reaching implications of Nietzsche's assessment of the implications of the modern "death of God," see Bruce Ledewitz, *The Universe Is on Our Side* (New York: Oxford University Press, 2021).

10. Dewey was a signatory of Humanist Manifesto I, which asserted that "the time has passed for theism, deism, modernism, and the several varieties of 'new thought'" (sixth article), and concluded by asserting that "man is at last becoming aware that he alone is responsible for the realization of the world of his dreams, that he has within himself the power for its achievement. He must set intelligence and will to the task." https://tinyurl.com/yy4kfs8a.

11. See Joseph Ratzinger, "The New Pagans and the Church" (1958 lecture), trans. Kenneth Baker, SJ, *Homiletic and Pastoral Review*, January 30, 2017, https://tinyurl.com/3fs4s6by.

Any survey of these broader developments would go well beyond the scope of this chapter and this book, however.[12] In this chapter, therefore, and conceding that our inspection considers only one dimension of a more complex social and even civilizational change, we will briefly review how the Supreme Court construed the Constitution to establish atheism as part of the public philosophy. And we will consider how the atheistic implications of the Court's new construction managed to stay mostly under the radar of public attention, at least by the professional elite.

The Coming of the New Orthodoxy

The decisions that announced and elaborated the new constitutional doctrines have been described and dissected in numerous books and articles, but for our purposes we need not dwell on the details. As a descriptive matter, most commentators treat *Everson v. Board of Education* (1947)[13] as the seminal modern case from which the rest of the jurisprudence has evolved.[14] In *Everson*, while narrowly upholding a New Jersey program for reimbursing parents for the costs of transporting their children to school (including to religious schools), the Court uttered strong separationist language and commended Jefferson's "wall of separation" as "high and impregnable."[15] *Everson* was surely an important case; but it has also been argued

---

12. For studies of such developments in this country, see Christian Smith, ed., *The Secular Revolution: Power, Interests, and Conflict in the Secularization of American Public Life* (Berkeley: University of California Press, 2003). For particularly insightful scholarly surveys of the broader developments, see, e.g., Charles Taylor, *A Secular Age* (Cambridge, MA: Harvard University Press, 2007); Remi Brague, *The Kingdom of Man: Genesis and Failure of the Modern Project* (Notre Dame: University of Notre Dame Press, 2018). See also Owen Chadwick, *The Secularization of the European Mind in the Nineteenth Century* (Cambridge: Cambridge University Press, 1976).

13. 330 U.S. 1 (1947).

14. See, e.g., Nathan S. Chapman and Michael W. McConnell, *Agreeing to Disagree: How the Establishment Clause Protects Religious Diversity and Freedom of Conscience* (New York: Oxford University Press, 2023), 129. Compare Frank J. Sorauf, *The Wall of Separation: The Constitutional Politics of Church and State* (Princeton: Princeton University Press, 1976), 19 ("The modern constitutional law of separation begins with *Everson*").

15. 330 U.S. at 18.

PART 2: THE PROVIDENTIAL REPUBLIC AND ITS (OFFICIAL) DEMISE

that the real watershed was not *Everson* but rather the decisions invalidating classroom prayer and devotional Bible reading in the public schools—*Engel v. Vitale*[16] and *Abington Township v. Schempp*[17]—of the early 1960s.[18] Certainly it was the prayer decisions that were perceived by the public as profoundly disruptive of traditional practices and understandings.[19]

But no matter: either way, it is clear enough that by the second prayer decision, *Schempp*, the Court had settled on the central doctrine that would govern judicial decisions for the rest of the twentieth century and well into the twenty-first. More specifically, the Court declared that under the establishment clause, laws and governmental actions must satisfy two requirements: they must have a "secular purpose," and they must have a "primary effect that neither advances nor inhibits religion."[20]

These requirements—the "secular purpose and effect requirements"— were derived from the seemingly more basic proposition that the Constitution requires government to be "neutral" in matters of religion—a proposition that the Court reaffirmed in case after case over the next decades[21] (and indeed that the Court continues to affirm, even amid recent doctrinal upheaval).[22] This requirement of neutrality was "absolute," the justices sometimes said,[23] and also comprehensive: governments both national

---

16. 370 U.S. 421 (1962).

17. 374 U.S. 203 (1963).

18. See Steven D. Smith, *The Rise and Decline of American Religious Freedom* (Cambridge, MA: Harvard University Press, 2014), 113–15. Gerard V. Bradley carefully reviews judicial developments between *Everson* and *Engel* and concludes that *Engel* was the transformative decision. See Gerard V. Bradley, "The Judicial Experiment with Privatizing Religion," *Liberty University Law Review* 1 (2006): 17.

19. Chapman and McConnell, *Agreeing to Disagree*, 144 (explaining that "much of the country exploded in anger" at the Court's invalidation of school prayer).

20. 374 U.S. at 222.

21. E.g., Van Orden v. Perry, 545 U.S. 677, 684 (2005); McCreary County v. ACLU, 545 U.S. 844, 860 (2005); Board of Education of Kiryas Joel v. Grumet, 512 U.S. 687, 696–97 (1994); Committee for Public Education v. Nyquist, 413 U.S. 756, 788 (1973); Walz v. Tax Commission, 397 U.S. 664, 669–70 (1970).

22. E.g., Carson v. Makin, 596 U.S. 767 (2021); Espinoza v. Montana Dept. of Revenue, 591 U.S. __ (2020); American Legion v. American Humanist Association, 588 U.S. __ (2019); Zelman v. Simmons-Harris, 536 U.S. 639, 652–53 (2002).

23. Larson v. Valente, 456 U.S. 228, 246 (1982); Epperson v. Arkansas, 393 U.S. 97, 106 (1968). See also Trump v. Hawaii, 585 U.S. __ (2018) (Sotomayor, J., dissenting).

and state must be neutral both among religions and as between religion and what the justices sometimes described as "nonreligion."[24] And governments could and must satisfy the neutrality requirement, the Court declared, by confining themselves to the domain of the "secular."

Later, in 1971, the Court added a third requirement—that laws or public programs must avoid "excessive entanglement" between government and religion—and the three-part composite came to be known as the "*Lemon* test*,*" after *Lemon v. Kurtzman*, the case in which the test was assembled.[25] But the Court never seemed quite sure just what the "no excessive entanglement" requirement meant—was the evil to be avoided administrative entanglement? political divisiveness? something else?[26]—and so, although it figured significantly in a few cases,[27] the third prong was never as important as the first two.

Then, a decade and a half after *Lemon*, the Court articulated what may already have been implicit in the doctrine and decisions—namely, that governments are constitutionally forbidden to do or say things that *communicate a message* of "endorsement" of religion. Justice Sandra Day O'Connor presented this idea as an interpretation of the *Lemon* test;[28] other scholars or jurists regarded it more as an additional test or doctrine. Either way, the jurisprudential orthodoxy was that American governments should be separated from religion and should stay within the realm of the secular, not just in the reasons they act on and the purposes they pursue, but also in their utterances, or in what governments intentionally or unintentionally communicate.

These were the basic developments: the details—which justices joined which other justices, concurring or dissenting, in which decisions, and so forth—are not of importance to us here. Our concern will be with the doctrine itself or, perhaps more accurately, with the basic idea animating that doctrine or doctrines—namely, that the Constitution erects a wall not just between the institutions of church and state but between governance

---

24. *Van Orden*, 545 at 698; Lee v. Weisman, 505 U.S. 577, 611 (1992) (Souter, J., concurring); Schempp, 374 U.S. at 305 (Goldberg, J., concurring).

25. 403 U.S. 602, 612–13 (1971).

26. See Chapman and McConnell, *Agreeing to Disagree*, 90.

27. Grand Rapids School District v. Ball, 473 U.S. 373 (1985); Aguilar v. Felton 473 U.S. 402 (1985).

28. Lynch v. Donnelly, 465 U.S. 668, 687–94 (1984) (O'Connor, J., concurring).

PART 2: THE PROVIDENTIAL REPUBLIC AND ITS (OFFICIAL) DEMISE

and religion, and that American governments at all levels are accordingly required to remain within the domain of the "secular." "Secular" not in the classical sense of "relating to this age or this world" but in the conventional modern sense of "not religious."[29]

The (Official) End of Providentialism

The new constitutional doctrine requiring governments to be religiously neutral and to confine themselves to the domain of the secular was fundamentally if *sub silentio* at war with the providentialist position that had characterized American governments through much of the nation's history. The providentialist perspective, as we have seen, had prescribed that not only individual citizens but communities and their governments should affirmatively acknowledge and seek the assistance of deity. "It is the *duty of nations as well as of men*," as Abraham Lincoln had asserted in a presidential proclamation, "to own dependence upon the overruling power of God, to confess their sins and transgressions, in humble sorrow, yet with assured hope that genuine repentance will lead to mercy and pardon."[30] Presidents from Washington to Adams to Jefferson to Madison to Lincoln had accordingly discharged this duty, officially and unapologetically, in their inaugural addresses, in official declarations of prayer and thanksgiving, and in other ways.

And yet, any such actions or expressions by government would clearly violate the doctrine requiring government to confine itself to the realm of the secular and to forgo any expressions that would be perceived as endorsing religion. And indeed, this implication was recognized by candid observers (although it was somehow *not* perceived—or at least not

---

29. Compare John Ayto, *Dictionary of Word Origins* (London: A&C Black, 1990): "secular Latin *saeculum*, a word of uncertain origin, meant 'generation, age.' It was used in early Christian texts for the 'temporal world' (as opposed to the 'spiritual world').... The more familiar modern English meaning 'non-religious' emerged in the 16th century." For discussion of the changing senses of the term "secular," see Steven D. Smith, *The Disintegrating Conscience and the Decline of Modernity* (Notre Dame: University of Notre Dame Press, 2023), 160–61.

30. Quoted in Mark A. Noll, *One Nation under God? Christian Faith and Political Action in America* (New York: HarperCollins, 1988), 98.

acknowledged—by the Court itself or its mainstream defenders) almost as soon as the new orthodoxy was announced.

In a concurring opinion in the first prayer case, *Engel v. Vitale*, Justice William O. Douglas exuberantly listed other measures now eligible for invalidation: the opening invocation at Supreme Court sessions ("God save the United States and this honorable Court"), the national motto (In God We Trust), the words "under God" in the Pledge of Allegiance, legislative and military chaplains, presidential religious proclamations, the use of the Bible in administering official oaths, and perhaps even official recognition of the Christmas holiday.[31] Likewise, although less enthusiastically, a *Wall Street Journal* editorial opined that the decision "must logically require the excision of all those other countless official references to God—such as in the Declaration of Independence, the Pledge of Allegiance, the Star Spangled Banner, the words used to inaugurate the President, open the Congress and convoke the Supreme Court itself."[32]

The general public similarly seems to have perceived the radical implications of the prayer cases. Justin Driver observes that "it would be virtually impossible to exaggerate the vehement disapproval that *Engel* generated across the nation."[33] Historian Bruce Dierenfield reports that the decision provoked "the greatest outcry against a U.S. Supreme Court decision in a century"[34]—a century that had included *Brown v. Board of*

---

31. *Engel*, 370 U.S. at 437 n. 1, 440 n. 5, 442 n. 8 (Douglas, J., concurring).

32. Editorial, reprinted in *Religious Liberty and the Supreme Court*, ed. Terry Eastland (Washington, DC: Ethics and Public Policy Center, 1993), 138.

33. Driver, "Three Hail Marys," 218. See also Robert S. Alley, *Without a Prayer: Religious Expression in Public Schools* (Buffalo, NY: Prometheus, 1996), 28, 230 (*Engel* "sent shock waves through large portions of the citizenry" and "caused an enormous uproar against the Supreme Court"); Julia C. Loren, *Engel v. Vitale: Prayer in the Public Schools* (n.p.: Cengage Gale, 2001), 7, 61 (observing that "the public outcry against the Court's ruling was swift and loud" and that "newspaper editorials across the country denounced the ruling"). Lucas Powe notes that "*Engel* produced more mail to the Court than any previous case (and few write to say what a good job the justices are doing)." Lucas A. Powe, *The Supreme Court and the American Elite, 1789–2008* (Cambridge, MA: Harvard University Press, 2009), 260.

34. Bruce C. Dierenfield, *The Battle over School Prayer* (Lawrence: University Press of Kansas, 2007), 72. Writing at the time, Philip Kurland observed that "the immediate reaction to *Engel* was violent and gross." Philip B. Kurland, "The School Prayer Cases,"

Education. At a Conference of State Governors, every governor except New York's Nelson Rockefeller denounced *Engel* and urged enactment of a constitutional amendment to overturn the decision.[35]

In ensuing years, conservative politicians such as Ronald Reagan would continue to call for such an amendment. Conversely, supportive advocates and scholars would often call for the Court to "walk the walk"—to follow through on its professed commitments by invalidating the numerous vestiges of religion in governance.[36] Activists like Michael Newdow and the Freedom from Religion Foundation[37] have vigorously promoted such a program.

In fact, no such thoroughgoing purge of religion from politics and governance has occurred. Implementation of the secularism doctrine has been erratic, perhaps because the Court never fully grasped the implications of its doctrine, or perhaps because in the face of popular opposition the Court has not wanted to acknowledge and enforce those implications. Official rationalizations for this spotty enforcement (which we will notice shortly) were often palpably unbelievable, and the consequence was that among a family of constitutional doctrines that are often elusive or unevenly applied, establishment clause jurisprudence gained a reputation for being distinctively incoherent.[38] For now, the important point is that the Court's unwillingness fully to enforce its doctrine does not mean that both the avid proponents and the critics of that doctrine were mistaken in their understanding of what the logic of the doctrine entailed. If government is supposed to be confined in its purposes, considerations, and expressions to the secular, and if "secular" is given its conventional modern meaning

---

in *The Wall between Church and State*, ed. Dallin H. Oaks (Chicago: University of Chicago Press, 1963), 142.

35. Dierenfield, *The Battle over School Prayer*, 146.

36. E.g., Steven B. Epstein, "Rethinking the Constitutionality of Ceremonial Deism," *Columbia Law Review* 96 (1996): 2083.

37. See, e.g., Elk Grove School District v. Newdow, 542 U.S. 1 (2004).

38. Mary Anne Case reports that "most well-informed observers, from the Justices of the Supreme Court themselves to the lower court judges, litigators, legislators, academics, and commentators who closely follow their work in this area, agree that the Court's Establishment Clause jurisprudence is, and for some time has been, a shambles." Mary Anne Case, "Who Conquers with This Sign? The Significance of the Bladensburg Cross," *Roger Williams University Law Review* 26 (2021): 345.

Providence Banished

of "not religious," then it is hard to see how there would be any place for providence—or for appeals to providence, or reliance on providence—in the law or in the processes of governance.

The Establishment of Atheism?

So then, did the new doctrine amount to, as John Courtney Murray had put it, "the establishment of atheism as the public philosophy"?[39] But the answer to that question seems clear enough, so long as we respect the qualifier—"atheism *as the public philosophy.*" Atheism has not been a popular position in the American tradition, and so it is understandable that the justices and their supporters would not want to *call* their doctrine atheistic, or even to think of it as atheistic. And indeed, the justices clearly did not want to impose atheism in the way that position had been imposed in, for example, the Communist regimes; the Court was not intent on eliminating God from American society or on expunging religion from the private sphere. On the contrary, the justices were solicitous of religion as a private matter, as was evident in the doctrine that evolved in this same period purporting to protect the free exercise of religion.[40] But whatever label they or their supporters used, the fact is that by excluding God from the public sphere, the justices did in substance render that sphere atheistic, or a-theistic, in character. Officially, at least.

This conclusion was already foreshadowed in chapter 1's discussion of agnosticism. We considered in that discussion William James's contention that there are "forced choices" in which neutrality is impossible and any answer other than a yes is for all practical purposes equivalent to a no. *Do you accept our invitation to accompany us on our expedition to the North Pole?* (This was James's example.) *Will you marry me? Do you want to buy the house on Second and Main that is up for sale? Will you take a job at our company? Will you accept the Hugger-Mugger Fellowship to attend graduate*

---

39. Murray's contention and its meaning are discussed in the prologue.
40. See, e.g., Sherbert v. Verner, 374 U.S. 398 (1963). I say that the doctrine "purported" to protect the free exercise of religion because, as has been widely recognized, the courts' actual decisions never did provide the strong protection that the formal doctrine appeared to promise.

school in philology beginning next fall? These questions appear to present forced choices in which it is impossible simply to remain undecided.

You might feel ambivalent or indecisive in any of these situations. Your sincere response might be, "I'm not sure. I can't decide. I *refuse* to decide." In your mind, your mental state is not the same as that of someone who says, emphatically, "No! Of course not. I categorically reject your proposal." In short, you might ardently wish to remain neutral with respect to any of these questions. And yet in practice, or for all practical purposes, your ambivalent, indecisive answer—or your ostensible neutrality—has the same consequences as a straightforward rejection. In practice, neutrality in such matters means no—and no is not neutral.

Do you believe and trust in God? Is this another forced choice? If the question is taken at face value and in the abstract, it does not seem to compel a choice—at least as to the part about *believing* in God. Surely it is possible to be undecided on the question—to withhold judgment. To remain agnostic. This undecided or neutral stance is possible, as we saw in chapter 1, on a detached level; and it no doubt reflects the position that many thoughtful people sincerely hold. But insofar as the theistic proposition or question comes with demands and consequences—with promises of attendant blessings or deprivations—agnosticism disappears as a practical option. As the part about "trusting in God" already implies. If you do not decide in favor of the theistic proposal, or at least do not choose to live in accordance with the theistic proposal, you are in the same position as someone who simply and outright rejects that proposal. "He that is not with me is against me,"[41] as Jesus said.

But what is true for an individual is in this respect true for a government as well. If (as Washington and Lincoln and so, so many others have supposed) a theistic position has implications or entailments for how a government should speak and act, then a government that declines to accept the position and its entailments has in effect rejected it. The government through its authoritative officials or spokespersons might protest, "No, we're not rejecting the theistic proposition; we are simply remaining neutral toward it." The protestation might be sincere enough: maybe the government really, really would prefer to avoid taking sides on the

---

41. Matt. 12:30.

question. Understandably so. But the practical effect will be the same. The government might in some sense not *be* atheistic, exactly; but it is acting *as if* it were atheistic. It is speaking and deciding and acting in the same way that it would, in other words, if it were atheistic. And for governments as for individuals, actual and "as if" atheism amount for practical purposes to pretty much the same thing.

Here is another way to approach the question. The new constitutional doctrine explicitly mandated that governments must remain within the domain of the "secular." In its conventional modern meaning and usage, "secular" *means* "not religious." "Religious" is an amorphous term, to be sure, but whatever religion is thought to mean, belief in and commitment to God is the core and quintessential instance (and hence the reference point for debates about whether other more doubtful or borderline cases are or are not religious).[42] Consequently, no one will doubt that belief in or commitment to God is a "religious" belief or commitment. And if a sphere of activity (such as government) is supposed to be "secular," meaning "not religious," then it follows that invocation of or reliance on God is out of place in that sphere.[43]

To remain secular in this sense is not necessarily to reject God in any general or categorical way. And yet to say that some area of life—business, higher education, science—is or should be "secular" in the modern sense of "not religious" *is* to say, at least by clear implication, that God is not

---

42. See, e.g., Kent Greenawalt, "Religion as a Concept in Constitutional Law," *California Law Review* 72 (1984): 753.

43. From a detached perspective, it is true, "religion" (including theistic religion) can be viewed as just one important kind of thing or fact in the world, in the same way that communism or populism or nationalism are important facts in the world. Religion, in other words, has its secular and sociological dimension. So it is no violation of secular norms to say something like "Religion is a powerful force in the United States." Indeed, one might even say that "*God* is a powerful force in American life" so long as "God" is understood to refer to the sociological fact of belief in God. Nor would it violate secular norms for a person, or a government, to *take account of* religion viewed as such—as a fact in the world to be reckoned with. Atheists can and, unless they are into self-deception, should acknowledge such facts about "God" and religion. But as soon as someone treats God as an actual reality and as some kind of normative authority who must be respected, such treatment is "religion" in the sense that is foreign to the modern meaning of "secular."

relevant for and is not to be invoked within that area. In that sense, secularism is atheistic, or a-theistic, not necessarily in general but for the areas it comes to cover. People working in those areas are not supposed to invoke God. Rather, they are supposed to talk and live "as if" there is no God, or as if God does not matter. As if they were atheists.

This is perhaps an "as if" atheism, or a "methodological atheism" akin to the "methodological naturalism" that is sometimes said to prevail in science. For practical purposes, though, there is little difference between an out-and-out atheism and an "as if" or methodological atheism. Under either heading, people will think and speak and act like atheists.

This analysis applies equally to government and political deliberation insofar as those domains are subjected to a "secularism" requirement. Such a requirement is not *semantically* equivalent to an imposition of atheism. Nor, once again, does the requirement forbid people to be religious believers for personal purposes or in other domains of life. The justices were friendly to religion in this sense; they supposed, as Gerard Bradley has put it, that "religion can be a nice thing in the private lives of individuals."[44] This is a crucial distinction between the modern American doctrine and, say, the Communist regimes that have actively sought to repress religion. And yet, insofar as it is actually recognized and enforced, the secularism requirement *does* mandate that people acting in the domain of government and political deliberation will act as if they are atheists.

In that crucial sense, the modern constitutional doctrine did indeed amount to "the establishment of atheism as the *public* philosophy."

A Demure Atheism

This was to be sure a bashful, not a boisterous, atheism; it was an atheism that for understandable reasons preferred to remain anonymous, or to go under other names and labels. And the new orthodoxy was protected by a variety of covers that served to obscure its character *as* atheism. In seeking to understand what happened on the Court and in America, we should notice some of these covers.

---

44. Gerard V. Bradley, "Dogmatomachy—a 'Privatization' Theory of the Religious Clause Cases," *St. Louis University Law Journal* 30 (1986): 300.

Actually, we have already noticed two of the major reasons for overlooking the atheistic implications of the new doctrine. One reason is that the requirement of secularism applied only to governance and public decision making; it did not apply to the private sphere. It thus did not look like the truculently atheistic ideology of Communist regimes, which *did* attempt to root out religion even from the private domain. One way to put the point would be that the Court's secularism doctrine had the effect of establishing atheism only as "the *public* philosophy," to borrow Murray's phrase; it was not a totalistic atheistic philosophy, as under Marxism. This was an important difference, surely. And yet the public sphere, to indulge in gross understatement, is not unimportant. An atheistic public philosophy had major and transformative implications for politics and society.[45]

A second reason why the doctrine's atheistic implications could be overlooked, once again, is that the doctrine was presented under the heading not of atheism but rather of religious "neutrality." And yet this was a very religiously unneutral neutrality: it was a "neutrality" that regularly and logically ruled in favor of purely secularist views of government and against the providentialist views that so many Americans had favored. As our discussion of "forced choices" has already suggested, there are situations in which a plea of neutrality amounts to rejection of one position and acceptance of the alternative. If the alternatives are (a) "for public purposes we should act on both pertinent secular and pertinent religious considerations" (which was basically the old, providentialist view) and (b) "we should act exclusively on secular reasons" (which was the new orthodoxy), the response that "we are religiously neutral, and therefore we should act exclusively on secular reasons" is not meaningfully neutral between those alternatives; it is nothing less than an embrace of one of the competing positions and rejection of the other.

In some instances the spuriousness of this claim to neutrality was almost impossible to ignore (and yet even in these cases the justices seemingly managed the impossible). In *Epperson v. Arkansas*, for example, the Court struck down an Arkansas law that prohibited the teaching of evolution in public schools. The Court reasoned that under the constitutional

---

45. The effect of the new doctrine, as Gerard Bradley says, was "the imprisonment of religion in a nonpublic ghetto." Bradley, "Dogmatomachy," 280.

requirement of religious neutrality, "the State may not adopt programs or practices in its public schools or colleges which 'aid or oppose' any religion. This prohibition is absolute."[46] Arkansas had prohibited the teaching of evolution, the Court surmised, because evolution was contradictory to religious teachings. In passing that prohibition, therefore, the state had acted to protect religion, thereby violating the constitutional requirement of religious neutrality.

As Justice Hugo Black pointed out in a concurring opinion, however, the Court's reasoning contradicted itself.[47] If the schools are absolutely prohibited from either "aid(ing) or oppos(ing) any religion" (as the Court said they are), and if evolution contradicts and opposes some religious beliefs (as the Court said it did), the logical conclusion would be that the schools are constitutionally and absolutely forbidden to teach evolution. Black's logic seems compelling; and if one finds the majority's reasoning persuasive as well, the obvious conclusion is that in this context there simply is no "neutral" position.

And that conclusion might be generalized, arguably, to every situation in which a genuine controversy exists. The very fact of a controversy suggests a conflict between secular and religious (or providentialist) perspectives. And in consistently siding with the secular and against the religious or providentialist position, a court necessarily and ipso facto rejects the religious perspective and its accompanying or supporting religious beliefs. How can such an outcome possibly be presented with a straight face as religiously "neutral"?[48]

And yet the justices *did* make that claim, over and over again; and it seems possible and even likely that they believed what they said. How was that possible? The question prompts a closer reflection on how the ideal of "neutrality"—of "secular neutrality"—could have gained such a mystifying, obfuscating hold on the nation's judicial and other elites.

---

46. *Epperson*, 393 U.S. at 106.

47. 393 U.S. at 109 (Black, J., concurring).

48. I develop this point at greater length in Steven D. Smith, "The Paralyzing Paradox of Religious Neutrality," *San Diego Legal Studies* (August 17, 2011), paper no. 11-060, https://tinyurl.com/yut6r42e. See also Steven D. Smith, *Rise and Decline*, 130–38.

Providence Banished

NEUTRALITY AND OBFUSCATION

So, once again, how could the justices have convinced themselves that in requiring government to limit itself to the domain of the secular, they were merely implementing a commitment to "neutrality"—to neutrality both among religious positions and between religion and "nonreligion"? Any answer to the question will necessarily be speculative. Part of the answer may be that academic theorists came to the aid of the neutrality project by elaborating sophisticated or sophistical versions of neutrality that worked to obfuscate the plain and nonneutral implications of the ideal.[49] And yet it seems unlikely that the justices themselves, or the general public, paid much attention to the abstruse scholarly formulations (the most impressive of which were devised well after that Court had already been proclaiming the neutrality requirement for decades).

It is more likely that the justices and the supportive part of the public were influenced by two other powerful considerations. The first of these was, basically, necessity: the justices and their supporters could make themselves believe that neutrality was possible because they really, really

---

49. See especially Andrew Koppelman, *Defending American Religious Neutrality* (Cambridge, MA: Harvard University Press, 2013). And see also Douglas Laycock, "Formal, Substantive, and Disaggregated Neutrality toward Religion," *DePaul Law Review* 39 (1990): 993; Douglas Laycock, "Substantive Neutrality Revisited," *West Virginia Law Review* 110 (2007): 51. The basic idea animating the academic defenses of neutrality of Koppelman and others is that neutrality presupposes some baseline, and that a particular law or policy can be adjudged to be "neutral" only relative to that baseline. If the "baseline" is said to be, say, "no aid that might advance religion," for example, then a refusal to give aid that might advance religion will be deemed religiously "neutral"—even if all manner of comparable nonreligious causes and interests *do* receive aid and religious causes and interests are thereby disadvantaged relative to others. If the baseline is "strict governmental secularism," then secular government will be religiously neutral—by definition, and relative to that baseline—even if all sorts of religious claims and interests are thereby rejected or disadvantaged. Baseline neutrality, however, only pushes the problem back one level. Now the problem is how to formulate a "neutral" baseline. Moreover, there is no obvious reason why the "baseline" might not be something like "what we have traditionally done in the past." Relative to that baseline, the providentialist practices that the Court struck down were in fact neutral—by definition—and it was the Court that was deviating from the course of neutrality.

wanted and even *needed* it to be possible. The second was the idea that religion is—inherently?—a purely private phenomenon.

Consider first how powerfully attractive—even irresistible—the idea of neutrality can be. In any context in which conflicting sides dispute passionately or even violently, it is tempting (for an individual person, for a court, for a nation) to adopt a stance of neutrality. Anything other than neutrality will bring one into the fray, with all the unpleasantness and fractiousness and risk that such involvement inevitably entails, and with all the potential for offense that one would understandably want to avoid. Better just to observe from a distance—to stay neutrally detached.

Such detachment may seem especially appealing if the constitutional jurisprudence of church and state, like modern liberal government generally, is seen (as it has been, plausibly enough, by John Rawls and many others) as a response to the chaos and violence that ensued with the breakup of Christendom and the horrific "wars of religion." For decades after the breakup, we recall, Catholics and Protestants fought bloody wars in Europe to establish their own position as the dominant orthodoxy. The French civil wars of 1562–1598 (and the notorious St. Bartholomew's Day massacre). The Thirty Years' War, which devastated much of central Europe. The English civil war of 1640–1660.[50] And even after the so-called Peace of Westphalia established a fragile peace on the principle of *cuius regio, eius religio*, interreligious strife continued—in England, in France, in New England and Virginia, and elsewhere. A commitment to governmental neutrality in religious matters may seem like the obvious and welcome answer to all this strife and chaos.

In addition, the neutrality principle seems consistent with, or possibly even identical with, the sacrosanct American commitment to equality. The logic can seem irresistible. All people are to be treated equally, or with "equal concern and respect": that is axiomatic. Right? Therefore, all people are to be treated equally regardless of their religion (or lack thereof). Therefore, governments cannot discriminate among *people* on the basis of their religion. Therefore, governments cannot discriminate among *religions* by preferring one religion—or one religious position or

---

50. See generally Richard S. Dunn, *The Age of Religious Wars, 1559–1715*, 2nd ed. (New York: Norton, 1979).

belief—over others. Therefore, government must be . . . religiously neutral. QED. Where in this train of seemingly inexorable reasoning is it even possible to get off?

It is thus understandable that the principle of religious neutrality would command support across the political and jurisprudential spectrum. And it did—pretty much. The ideal has been as central to the Roberts Court as it was to the Warren-Brennan Court; it is as strongly embraced by conservative scholars and jurists as by liberals.[51] Neutrality is the sort of ideal that, from a certain point of view, we really, really need to be viable. And so it is perhaps not surprising that highly placed people would convince themselves that the ideal *is* viable—even when it quite plainly is not.

But beyond the power of necessity, or perceived necessity, neutrality could also seem to be possible and even natural, and could seem to avoid the kinds of criticisms noted above, on one crucial assumption—namely, that "religion" is the kind of thing that is somehow or inherently a purely private matter and concern. Suppose that religion were a private avocation that some people choose to engage in—something like, say, golf or, as Stephen Carter has suggested, building model airplanes.[52] On that assumption, religion, like golf and model building, would have no apparent relevance to or implications for the broad run of public actions and exercises and policies:[53] and governmental neutrality toward that avocation would be the obviously correct stance.

---

51. Thus, while cogently criticizing a great deal in modern establishment clause jurisprudence and persuasively explaining how the modern decisions misunderstand what the founders did, Nathan Chapman and Michael McConnell are nonetheless steadfast in arguing that the establishment clause mandates religious neutrality on the part of government. And in praising the Supreme Court for moving away from the *Lemon* test in favor of "context-specific rules," Chapman and McConnell explain that "the rules differ somewhat depending on the context, but they all are an effort to implement the principles underlying the historical understanding of the Establishment Clause, ensuring the government maintains religious neutrality." Chapman and McConnell, *Agreeing to Disagree*, 188.

52. Stephen L. Carter, "Evolutionism, Creationism, and Treating Religion as a Hobby," *Duke Law Journal* 1987 (1987): 978. To be clear, Carter does not contend that religion *is* like building model airplanes; he merely observes that modern legal discourse often treats religion *as if* it were a sort of hobby like building model airplanes.

53. Compare Douglas Laycock, "Religious Liberty as Liberty," reprinted in *Religious Liberty: Overviews and History*, vol. 1 (Grand Rapids: Eerdmans, 2010), 59 (asserting

PART 2: THE PROVIDENTIAL REPUBLIC AND ITS (OFFICIAL) DEMISE

As a comparison, take golf. Some people like golf, passionately. Some people don't; they find golf to be boring and pointless—a bunch of grown men and women hitting a little white ball with sticks and trying to knock it into a small hole. There is no apparent reason for government to take sides between these groups. And golf is just golf: it has no apparent implications for the broad run of issues—taxes, regulations, foreign policy, and such—that government addresses. So government can, and would be well advised to, remain benignly neutral between the golf-lovers and the golf-haters (and the golf-indifferentists). And any person or group that might demand governmental endorsement of and support for golf—for golf relative to, say, bowling, or gardening—would in effect be officiously and gratuitously asking the government to intervene in a domain where government does not have any legitimate business.

The same is true for religion—or at least it would be true if religion were a purely private concern or avocation like golf.

And it seems virtually certain that the Supreme Court's insistence on religious neutrality reflected just such an assumption—namely, that religion is a purely private sort of thing. Indeed, the Court said as much, repeatedly: "The Constitution decrees that religion must be a private matter for the individual, the family, and the institutions of private choice."[54] What Walter Dellinger said of Justice Sandra Day O'Connor was largely true of the Court as a whole: Dellinger approved of O'Connor's establishment clause opinions, he said, because "of her consistent voting on a very simple principle: government religion, bad; private religion, good. Her view of religion was robust private choice."[55]

The problem is that the proposition is demonstrably false: religion is *not* by its nature a purely private concern or avocation. On the contrary, unlike golf, religion in its basic beliefs and commitments has a vast range of

---

that "beliefs at the heart of religion—beliefs about theology, liturgy, and church governance—are of little importance to the civil government").

54. The statement was made in Lemon v. Kurtzman, 403 U.S. 602, 625 (1971), and was repeatedly affirmed thereafter. See Larkin v. Grendel's Den, 459 U.S. 116, 126 (1982); *Grand Rapids*, 473 U.S. at 398; Marsh v. Chambers, 463 U.S. 783, 802 (1983) (Brennan, J., dissenting).

55. Walter E. Dellinger III, "Showcase Panel IV: The Role of Government in Defining Our Culture," *Northwestern University Law Review* 102 (2008): 479.

implications for government. The whole history of religion in the West, the whole tradition of providentialism in America, ought to have made that fact overwhelmingly clear. Nor is religion's political or public relevance in any sense unique to the Christianity that has prevailed in the West and in America (or to the biblical or Judeo-Christian tradition, as it is often called). On the contrary: if we consider the "pagan" religions that preceded Christianity in ancient Greece and Rome, the public character of religion is even starker. Indeed, it might be said that in antiquity religion was almost entirely a public and political phenomenon:[56] the private or more interior dimension of religion has been largely a Christian or Christian and Jewish contribution.[57]

And yet, in the face of such overwhelming evidence, the modern Supreme Court declared, over and over again, that religion is a private matter, or that it belongs in the private domain. These pronouncements were offered as if the justices were merely observing something that was inherently or obviously or axiomatically true. And on this (manifestly false) assumption, the Court's claims to neutrality seemed plausible, as they would if the government professed to be neutral with respect to golf.

But did the justices really believe that religion is a purely private matter? How could they believe such a thing when the proposition was belied by the whole history of religion in America—by the very practices (such as school prayer) that the Court was acting to invalidate based on, ironically, an ostensible commitment to religious neutrality? Any answer to that question will be, once again, speculative. Part of the answer, again, is probably that the justices declared religion to be purely private because they really, really wanted and needed it to be private—so that government could assume a stance of neutrality toward it. Another part of the answer, however, may be that for some people religion *is* a purely private concern; and it seems likely that the justices themselves—some or most or possibly all of them—belonged to that class of people. They could say with a straight

56. See Steven D. Smith, *Pagans and Christians in the City: Culture Wars from the Tiber to the Potomac* (Grand Rapids: Eerdmans, 2018), 62–70.
57. Compare Guy Strousma, *The End of Sacrifice: Religious Transformations in Late Antiquity*, trans. Susan Emanuel (Chicago: University of Chicago Press, 2009), 2 ("If one has to specify in a single word the nature of this change [from paganism to Christianity], I would accept the Hegelian analysis that stresses the *interiorization* of religion").

face that religion is a purely private concern because just *for them*—for them personally—that proposition seemed to be true.

The proposition might be true in either of two ways, or for two kinds of people. Suppose a particular justice—there would have been several candidates on the Court in the 1960s—is "not a religious person." He may or may not be a self-conscious atheist or agnostic; but in either case he doesn't go to church, read the Bible, pray, or give much thought to God or sin or the afterlife. He knows, of course, that other people (possibly even including some of his family or friends) *are* "religious," and while perhaps finding their motives, reasons, and tastes inconvenient or puzzling, he nonetheless respects their choice to embrace religion. And yet he will naturally regard their religion as a matter of personal choice or lifestyle. Some people garden, some golf, and some go to church. Takes all kinds. It's all a matter of personal predilection.

Religion, so viewed, is or at least appears to be an inherently private affair—one about which government might sensibly remain neutral.

A different kind of justice—Justice Brennan, perhaps—*is* a religious person (though perhaps not a particularly fervent one).[58] But the religion in which he was raised—Catholicism—is a minority faith that still provokes a certain degree of distrust in a generally WASP-ish professional environment. And so in attending a public high school, a private secular college (the University of Pennsylvania), and a private secular law school (Harvard), and later working for a private law firm and socializing at an exclusive country club, this justice has long learned to quarantine his Catholic faith in a private compartment in his life.[59] He mostly avoids speaking about religion with non-Catholic classmates or colleagues. He talks and decides and acts—lives his life—on pretty much the same terms and criteria as his non-Catholic or nonreligious associates. And he observes the rule of etiquette that says it is impolite to talk about religion in public settings. This justice is religious, sort of, but his religion is relegated to a purely private role in his life.

58. As a boy, Brennan was required by his parents to attend Mass, but he recalled this requirement as "an agony we went through every Sunday whether you liked it or not." Seth Stern and Stephen Wermeil, *Justice Brennan: Liberal Champion* (Boston: Houghton Mifflin Harcourt, 2010), 13. His own sons would later recall their father often dropping them off for Sunday Mass on his way to the golf course (165).

59. See Stern and Wermeil, *Justice Brennan*, 16–44.

Providence Banished

For either of these justices, it will be easy to say that religion is a purely private matter—because *for him*, that is an accurate description. And once it comes to be assumed that religion is a purely private affair, the idea that government can and should be neutral toward religion and that government can be religiously neutral simply by confining itself to the (secular) public domain seems to make sense. The idea basically just means that government should stick to its proper business and not intrude into private matters that are none of its affair anyway. Justice Brennan was probably the leading architect on the Court of the new "secular neutrality" doctrine, and it seems entirely plausible that he believed all the things he said about religion belonging in the personal or private realm. He was merely reading into the Constitution a position that he had already and long ago adopted for purposes of his own life and career.[60]

The problem once again is that even if religion is a purely private affair for some people, for many others—and historically and intrinsically—religion is *not* a purely private matter. The whole history of American providentialism, the history of Western religion, the history of religion in antiquity: these histories all attest to that fact. The recurring controversies over religion today—in America and throughout the globe—likewise attest to the fact. And the Court (largely composed, probably, of justices who were either "not religious" or who, like Brennan, had learned to quarantine their own religion) was in fact rejecting the religious beliefs and commitments of millions upon millions of Americans—while purporting, ironically, to follow a path of scrupulous religious neutrality.

To be sure, a less parochial and more cognizant jurist might acknowledge all of this, off the record, so to speak, and yet insist on the neutrality jurisprudence nonetheless—not because religion actually *is* a private matter or because genuine neutrality is actually possible, but rather as part of a deliberate project of remaking or reshaping religion so as to domesticate it or render it politically innocuous. Religion is not inherently private, perhaps; but in the interest of civil peace and democracy, it can and should be *made to be* private. In this vein, the political philosopher J. Judd Owen argues that a host of modern political thinkers from Hobbes and Locke to Tocqueville have engaged in a self-conscious effort to tame and denature

---

60. For elaboration, see Steven D. Smith, *Disintegrating Conscience*, 131–75.

PART 2: THE PROVIDENTIAL REPUBLIC AND ITS (OFFICIAL) DEMISE

religion—to "make religion safe for democracy," as Owen puts it.[61] In a similar spirit, the Princeton political philosopher Stephen Macedo has argued that for the good of civil peace the government ought to deliberately cultivate "wishy-washy religion."[62]

From a certain point of view, these might be rationally defensible projects. But they emphatically could not honestly claim to be "religiously neutral." On the contrary, they deliberately and aggressively disfavor and attempt to suppress some kinds of religion while favoring and promoting tamer kinds of religion or "nonreligion."

ERRATIC ENFORCEMENT

Another reason why the new constitutional doctrine did not appear to establish "atheism as the public philosophy" is that, as noted, the doctrine was never rigorously implemented or enforced by the Court anyway. Consequently, although many incidents of the traditional providentialism were invalidated, other and sometimes even more conspicuous features were passed over. And so a critic who contends (as this chapter does) that the Court has imposed public atheism on the country can be met with what appear to be stark counterexamples. What about the national motto—In God We Trust—which continues to appear on every dollar bill? What about the words "under God" in the Pledge of Allegiance? (The Ninth Circuit did at one point rule that these words were unconstitutional, at least as recited by public school children;[63] but the Supreme Court promptly reversed the ruling—not on the merits but on a technical and procedural ground.)[64] How can a nation that features such expressions be said to be atheistic—even in the public realm?

As an official matter, to be sure, all these vestiges of past providentialism have escaped invalidation because they are *not* actually religious. Not anymore. That has been the Court's official position. Yes, a proposition

61. J. Judd Owen, *Making Religion Safe for Democracy: Transformation from Hobbes to Tocqueville* (New York: Cambridge University Press, 2015).
62. Stephen Macedo, "Transformative Constitutionalism and the Case of Religion," *Political Theory* 26 (1998): 61–63.
63. Newdow v. U.S. Congress, 313 F. 3d 500, 502 (9th Cir. 2002).
64. *Elk Grove School District*, 542 U.S. 1.

like In God We Trust might *seem* religious to a naive observer; and at one time, the proposition probably *was* actually religious. But over time those words have lost their religious significance[65]—at least for a "reasonable observer"—and they now serve the more ceremonial and secular functions of "solemnizing public occasions, expressing confidence in the future, and encouraging the recognition of what is worthy of appreciation in society."[66] So said the justices, in any case; and for anyone who actually believes such rationalizations, the removal of God from the public sphere has in fact been achieved. Public atheism, or governmental atheism, is a *fait accompli.*

For those who find such rationalizations incredible, by contrast (which is to say for nearly everyone),[67] God continues to play at least a peripheral or ceremonial role in American public life. But it is a role covered with camouflage, denial, and hypocrisy.

THE CONSEQUENCES OF PUBLIC ATHEISM

Officially, as we have seen, the providentialism that was central to the American self-understanding for over a century and a half was banished in the 1960s. So what? A skeptic might say that the change has been mostly cosmetic. An occasional Christmas display or Ten Commandments marker or graduation prayer will be ruled out of bounds. But presidential inaugurations continue to be rife with religious expressions and prayers. And even the most prominent theistic expressions—in the national motto and the Pledge of Allegiance—have been spared, albeit under a sort of shabby subterfuge. So, how much difference has the Court's modern secularism doctrine actually made? Seriously?

---

65. Compare Mayle v. U.S., 891 F.d 680, 684 (7th Cir. 2018) (ruling that "the motto has no theological import.... The original religious significance of 'In God We Trust' has dissipated and the motto is now secular").

66. *Lynch*, 465 U.S. at 693 (O'Connor, J., concurring).

67. See, e.g., Steven H. Shiffrin, "The Pluralistic Foundations of the Religion Clauses," *Cornell Law Review* 90 (2004): 70–71. Compare Chapman and McConnell, *Agreeing to Disagree*, 158 ("No one is satisfied. Secularists believe any public religious symbol demeans the citizenship of nonbelievers. Believers think the cases trivialize and threaten traditional religion. Commentators of all stripes find them inconsistent and incoherent").

PART 2: THE PROVIDENTIAL REPUBLIC AND ITS (OFFICIAL) DEMISE

There is no way to answer such a question with precision. And yet it seems that the change has been of quiet but extraordinary significance. Thus, through much of the nation's history, millions and millions of schoolchildren were exposed to daily prayer and Bible reading. The prayers were brief and theologically innocuous, and the Scripture readings were succinct. Probably they did little to instill genuine piety. Even so, these exercises imparted a smattering of biblical knowledge, and, more importantly, they conveyed the conception that the nation is presided over by a supervising deity. For several generations, now, the millions of citizens whose formation has occurred in public schools have gone without this influence and instruction. Has the change made a difference?

Once again, there is no way to be certain. The nation does seem to be more secular today than it was. And biblical literacy appears to be far lower than it once was—even among self-identifying Christians. Recent survey evidence reported that 60 percent of those surveyed could not name even five of the ten commandments; 50 percent believed Sodom and Gomorrah were a married couple; and 12 percent thought that Joan of Arc was Noah's wife.[68] (Fans of the game show *Jeopardy!* will have seen evidence of this diminishment: contestants regularly demonstrate remarkable familiarity with all sorts of subjects—rap artists, movies and TV shows, sometimes history or geography—but these same contestants will often stare blankly when even the most elementary Bible questions are asked.)

To be sure, these changes cannot automatically be attributed to an altered constitutional jurisprudence. As we noted at the outset of this chapter, that jurisprudence to some extent simply copied or incorporated historical and cultural changes that were happening anyway. And yet it seems certain that the elimination of Bible reading and prayer from the public schools would be a contributor to such trends.

Within law, it is arguable that the most important effects of the Supreme Court's constitutional reconstruction have appeared not in the cases that explicitly present establishment clause issues—cases about crosses or Ten Commandments monuments, for example—but rather in cases where laws and practices grounded in Christian premises or traditions have been

---

68. Benjamin Hawkins, "Nation's Biblical Illiteracy at Root a Matter of the Heart," *Pathway*, January 12, 2023, https://tinyurl.com/y25xcdpe.

challenged under provisions such as the Fourteenth Amendment's due process and equal protection clauses. In these cases, the secular conception imposed by the Court has been powerfully influential *sub silentio*. Religious considerations that might otherwise be important or even decisive have been conspicuous by their absence—much like the dog that was crucial in the Sherlock Holmes story because it *didn't* bark.

The leading instance, probably, concerns laws regulating matters of procreation and marriage. Traditionally these laws had reflected the nation's Christian heritage[69]—a fact that for decades had seemed constitutionally unproblematic. Indeed, even after the Court recognized a right to contraception (initially only for married couples, but later extended to unmarried people as well) and then a right to abortion, traditional marriage laws had seemed to raise no constitutional problem. While celebrating the Court's implementation of the sexual revolution in constitutional law, Professor Geoffrey Stone acknowledges that many of the Court's pathbreaking decisions would have been unimaginable in any earlier era of American history.[70] As the years passed, however, challenges became more common. And increasingly the assumption seemed to be that insofar as such laws were grounded in Christian or religious beliefs, they were no longer legitimate. Reasons that once would have supported laws now became causes for invalidation.

Usually the legal cases did not on their face present establishment clause issues; rather, they were adjudicated under the Fourteenth Amendment's due process and equal protection clauses. Under Fourteenth Amendment doctrines, however, a state could defend its laws against such challenges only by showing that the laws served some important and legitimate state interest. And in accordance with the secular neutrality conception, it came to be assumed that if the reason for a law or the interest served by it was "religious," that reason or interest could not count as a basis for upholding the law.[71] This assumption meant that states or other parties defending the

---

69. See Robert E. Rodes Jr., *On Law and Chastity* (Durham, NC: Carolina Academic Press, 2006).

70. Geoffrey R. Stone, *Sex and the Constitution: Sex, Religion, and Law from America's Origins to the Twenty-First Century* (New York: Liveright, 2017), 534–35.

71. In *Cruzan v. Missouri Dept. of Health*, 497 U.S. 261, 350 (1990) (Stevens, J., dissenting), for example, Justice Stevens argued that the state's asserted interest in preserving the life of a person who did not wish to continue living was religious in nature

laws had to forgo any justifications that might sound or be construed as "religious."[72]

Indeed, courts might sometimes say that a law was unconstitutional because even though a state had tried to justify it on purely secular grounds, the "everyone knows" reality was that the law was actually based on religious values or beliefs. From which it seemed to follow that the law was accordingly unconstitutional.[73]

Sex and marriage are hardly peripheral aspects of life. Changes in sexual norms and marriage patterns have thus amounted to a profound change in American society. Moreover, these changes arguably reflect a more general transformation in the way Americans understand themselves, their world, and their country.

How did these changes come about? Questions of historical causation are complex, to be sure, and beyond scientific measurement. Many influences converge to produce such changes. But it is fair to say that among those influences has been the Court-imposed transformation of America from a nation that is providentialist in its self-understanding into . . . something else.

Just what America has been transformed into is far from clear, and is currently fiercely contested. Which is a segue into part 3 of this book.

---

and therefore constitutionally illegitimate: "As I already suggested, it would be possible to hypothesize such an interest on the basis of theological or philosophical conjecture. But even to posit such a basis for the State's action is to condemn it. It is not within the province of secular government to circumscribe the liberties of the people by regulations designed wholly for the purpose of establishing a sectarian definition of life." Although Stevens's position was asserted in dissent, the majority did not disagree with Stevens's view that a religiously based interest was constitutionally illegitimate; rather, the majority denied that the state's interest in preserving life was religious in character.

72. For an elaboration and extended defense of this position, see Edward Rubin, "Assisted Suicide, Morality, and Law: Why Prohibiting Assisted Suicide Violates the Establishment Clause," *Vanderbilt Law Review* 63 (2010): 763.

73. Perry v. Schwarzenegger, 704 F. Supp.d 921, 930, 952 (N.D. Cal. 2010); Varnum v. Brien, 763 N.W.d 862, 897–904 (Iowa 2009).

Part 3

Providentialism and the Travails of Liberalism

According to what Nicholas Guyatt describes as "historical providentialism,"[1] or what we have called "special mission" providentialism, America was to have a distinctive role in history and a distinctive contribution to make to humankind. And what was that distinctive contribution supposed to be? Answers have varied. But probably the most common answers have converged on... liberalism. Not on the *word* "liberalism," which would have been used rarely and in different senses in some earlier periods.[2] And not on liberalism in the more partisan sense in which "liberal" and "conservative" are traditional antagonists. But liberalism in the broader sense in which the term is understood to encompass a cluster of associated political commitments[3]—to individual liberty, rights

---

1. Nicholas Guyatt, *Providence and the Invention of the United States, 1607–1876* (New York: Cambridge University Press, 2007), 5–6.
2. Compare Helena Rosenblatt, *The Lost History of Liberalism* (Princeton: Princeton University Press, 2018), 23 (observing that "no one spoke of liberalism during the eighteenth century. The word and concept had not yet been conceived"). Rosenblatt argues that "America took possession of liberalism only in the early twentieth century, and only then did it become an American political tradition") (3).
3. Compare Cass R. Sunstein, "Why I Am a Liberal," *New York Times*, November 20, 2023, https://tinyurl.com/wcmkx5nn (contending that "liberals believe in six things: freedom, human rights, pluralism, security, the rule of law and democracy"). For further discussion of the core of "the liberal project," see Steven D. Smith, "Christians and/as Liberals," *Notre Dame Law Review* 98 (2023): 1500–1504.

(especially including the freedoms of speech and religion), equality, rule of law, and representative government (the term "liberal democracy" having become almost a redundancy).[4] Liberalism in this broad sense was to be—and arguably has been—America's gift to the world.

This is a proposition that was endorsed at the founding (again, not typically under the *label* of "liberalism"); and even without any assumption of providential backing, it is widely endorsed today—in, for example, American foreign policy. And there are surely continuities in what was then and is still being endorsed. At least in the abstract, all of the things mentioned above—liberty, rights, equality, rule of law, representative government—were valued then and are widely valued now. And yet there are also important cleavages, and one of the most fundamental has to do with providentialism.

In the founding period and for many decades thereafter, providentialism and liberalism were intimate allies. Or so it seemed. America was destined to bring the blessings of liberty to the world because the providential plan had so foreordained: it was for this purpose that providence had brought colonists to this land and supported them in their quest for independence and nationhood.

Moreover, the justifications for the various commitments that made up the cluster of liberalism were themselves rooted in the providential plan. Despite their manifest differences, humans were equal, as the Declaration of Independence asserted, because they had been made so by "their creator." They were equal in the sense that they had been endowed *by their creator* with certain "unalienable rights." Rights and law were not merely human constructions that could be crafted and recrafted, or curtailed or abolished, as humans might see fit; they were derivations from and reflections of the providential plan, which was beyond the power of mortals to construct or deconstruct. Religious freedom was a right justified by reference to, as Jefferson put it, "the plan of the holy author of our religion."[5]

---

4. See Rosenblatt, *Lost History of Liberalism*, 52 ("Today we are so used to speaking of 'liberal democracy' that it is easy to conflate the two terms").

5. "A Bill for Establishing Religious Freedom," reprinted in *The Sacred Rights of Conscience*, ed. Daniel L. Dreisbach and Mark David Hall (Indianapolis: Liberty Fund, 2009), 250.

Providentialism and the Travails of Liberalism

This intimacy between religion and the political ideals that we describe as "liberal" was a kind of unprecedented experiment, and its apparent success was an unanticipated revelation. It had long been supposed—as it is by many again today—that religion and egalitarian democracy are intrinsically antagonistic. And yet, as Tocqueville explained to a skeptical world, in America the marriage seemed to work. And what was happening in America, Tocqueville believed, was a harbinger for the rest of humanity.[6]

In modern times, by contrast, this reliance on a providentialist foundation and framework has not merely dropped out of mainstream thinking about liberal commitments; in respectable contexts—Supreme Court jurisprudence, for example, or Rawlsian political philosophy—it has been affirmatively renounced. Even forbidden, at least for public purposes. Liberalism, of course, leaves people free, as individuals, to believe in providence if they so choose: the Court and also Rawls would admit—indeed, would insist on—that much. But some people will believe in providence while others will not; consequently, any *public* or governmental reliance on or endorsement of providence would violate the requirement of religious neutrality and would fail to treat citizens with the equal respect that liberalism promises. The believers would become "insiders," as modern constitutional jurisprudence puts it, while the nonbelievers would be rendered "outsiders."[7] Consequently, the *public* embrace of providentialism, far from being a necessary support for liberalism, would ipso facto constitute a violation of liberal ideals.

So runs the dominant thread of respectable thought today. The overall trajectory, it seems, has been from a deeply providentialist liberalism to a self-consciously secularist—and thus nonprovidentialist, nonreligious—liberalism.

---

6. See generally Alexis de Tocqueville, *Democracy in America*, trans. George Lawrence (New York: Harper & Row, 1988). However, it was not only in America that liberalism was deemed to depend on religion. Helena Rosenblatt points out that in France, Benjamin Constant, one of the important early theorizers and proponents of liberalism, "also spoke eloquently about religion. He articulated a point that he would emphasize throughout his career: a liberal government could not survive without religion." Rosenblatt, *Lost History of Liberalism*, 66.

7. See Lynch v. Donnelly, 465 U.S. 668, 688 (1984) (O'Connor, J., concurring).

So, how should we regard this trajectory? Is it a path of progress? Or of degeneration? (Or perhaps a bit of both?)

Blackstone famously declared that the common law "works itself pure,"[8] and perhaps the same is true for liberalism? Liberalism began as a rough-hewn construction mixed up with inherited preliberal elements (including public religion), perhaps, but over time it became more fully and purely itself. More untaintedly liberal.

Offered today, this interpretation has for us a pleasantly self-congratulatory quality, and it resonates nicely with narratives of progress that have characterized the modern world. Science has advanced; technology has advanced; democracy has advanced—so why not liberalism? Thus, at a time when religious thinking was still pervasive, it is perhaps not surprising that incipient commitments to freedom, equality, democracy, and rule of law were thoroughly enmeshed in religious and providentialist ideas, and that proponents of these new liberal commitments did not yet discern the tensions between such commitments and the publicly sponsored religiosity that people of the time took for granted. But as the nation and its people became more at home with liberal principles and had time to reflect upon them (not just in the abstract but in often painful and conflicted practical experience), these tensions became more conspicuous. And so while continuing to respect its citizens' religious liberty, the nation naturally undertook to extricate its liberal commitments from the religious entanglements of their infancy and adolescence. The development of a more secular liberalism thus reflects a process of purification and maturation.

Indeed, secularized liberalism is not merely an improved form of the basic product; once the implications of liberalism have come to be better understood, this is just what liberalism comes to mean, and to be. Or so it may seem. So even to talk about "secular liberalism" is to commit a sort of redundancy—like "round sphere" or "flat plane." Political philosophers Charles Taylor and Jocelyn Maclure thus report that "there is a broad consensus that 'secularism' is an essential component of any liberal democracy composed of citizens who adhere to a plurality of conceptions of the world

---

8. Quoted in William D. Popkin, *Evolution of the Judicial Opinion* (New York: New York University Press, 2007), 172.

Providentialism and the Travails of Liberalism

and the good"[9] (and are there any liberal democracies that do *not* harbor such a plurality?).

On some such premise, legal scholars Richard Schragger and Micah Schwartzman discuss, in alarmed tones, the resurgence of what they call "religious antiliberalism."[10] Schragger and Schwartzman do not show that the exceedingly diverse movements and thinkers they lump together for condemnation under this label actually oppose traditional liberal commitments; and indeed, at least some of these "antiliberals" appear to be at least as supportive of freedom of speech, freedom of religion, and representative democracy as Schragger and Schwartzman themselves are. But Schragger and Schwartzman basically equate liberalism with the modern orthodoxy of secular government as reflected in the philosophy of John Rawls and in Supreme Court decisions of the late twentieth century. Anyone who deviates from that orthodoxy and separationist jurisprudence is ipso facto "antiliberal."

The view that modern liberalism is the result of purification gains powerful support from the fact that in important respects, nearly everyone will agree that modern liberal governance *has* more fully honored at least some liberal commitments that were only very imperfectly respected in earlier periods. American liberalism means "government of the people, by the people, and for the people," as Lincoln put it; but popular governance has surely been enhanced by the extension of the franchise to women and racial minorities. Equality is a central liberal commitment, but that commitment was notoriously and egregiously violated by the institutions of slavery and Jim Crow segregation. These violations have been corrected, at least to a significant extent, in more recent times.

The interpretation of liberalism's course as one of progress and purification thus has obvious appeal. But it also encounters a serious problem—namely, that in today's world, the perfected or purified or mature modern liberalism is arguably in deep trouble. It seems to be increasingly beleaguered from both the right and the left, and both in theory and in practice.

---

9. Charles Taylor and Jocelyn Maclure, *Secularism and Freedom of Conscience*, trans. Jean Marie Todd (Cambridge, MA: Harvard University Press, 2011), 2.

10. Richard Schragger and Micah Schwartzman, "Religious Antiliberalism and the First Amendment," *Minnesota Law Review* 104 (2020): 1341.

Self-proclaimed conservatives attack liberalism in favor of "nationalism."[11] Or they criticize liberalism for undermining traditional gender and sexual norms and traditional institutions like the family.[12] A prominent if controversial rightward-leaning Harvard law professor relentlessly disparages liberalism as a "hideous insect."[13] Elsewhere, more left-leaning theorists and actors increasingly embrace a "progressivism" that looks distinctly illiberal in its attitudes to matters like freedom of speech and religion. Communitarians write much-discussed books with titles like *Why Liberalism Failed*.[14] Cass Sunstein, in the course of a vigorous defense of liberalism, acknowledges that "more than at any other time since World War II, liberalism is under siege. On the left, some people insist that liberalism is exhausted and dying and unable to handle the problems posed by entrenched inequalities, corporate power and environmental degradation. On the right, some people think that liberalism is responsible for the collapse of traditional values, rampant criminality, disrespect for authority and widespread immorality."[15]

Three decades ago, a theorist like Francis Fukuyama could contentedly announce an "end of history" in which, after centuries of tumult and conflict, the nations and cultures of the world were at last converging on an enduring liberal democratic answer to the challenges of political association.[16] Today, a manifestly embattled Fukuyama writes spirited defenses of liberalism against foes on all sides and of various sorts (including self-proclaimed liberals of the "neoliberal" variety).[17] One of the wisest

---

11. E.g., Yoram Hazony, *Conservatism: A Rediscovery* (New York: Simon & Schuster, 2022).

12. E.g., Scott Yenor, "On Preserving a Political Community in Revolutionary Times," *Journal of Contemporary Legal Issues* 24 (2023): 165. Helena Rosenblatt reports that "critics accuse [liberalism] of a long list of sins. They say that it destroys religion, the family, the community." Rosenblatt, *Lost History of Liberalism*, 1.

13. Adrian Vermeule, "A Christian Strategy," *First Things*, November 2017, https://tinyurl.com/2xhs54bw.

14. Patrick J. Deneen, *Why Liberalism Failed* (New Haven: Yale University Press, 2019).

15. Sunstein, "Why I Am a Liberal."

16. Francis Fukuyama, *The End of History and the Last Man* (New York: Simon & Schuster, 1992).

17. Francis Fukuyama, *Liberalism and Its Discontents* (New York: Farrar, Straus & Giroux, 2022).

and most influential liberal philosophers, William Galston, pleads for the defense of liberalism against antiliberal tendencies on both the progressive left and the conservative or reactionary right.[18]

Much of this criticism and defense is academic or theoretical in character. But in the practical world outside the academy, American liberalism (if that is what the modern American political system represents) seems similarly traumatized. Political scientists report that "dislike, even at times hatred, of the opposing party and its leaders reflects a growing divide between Democrats and Republicans over a wide range of economic and social issues. But it also reflects a growing divide over race, religion and values—a chasm that could become dangerous as partisans come to see each other not just as political adversaries, but as enemies."[19] One observer explains that the "level of hatred—which political scientists call 'negative partisanship'—has reached levels that are not just bad for democracy, but are potentially destructive." Such mutual hatred is "a prelude to democratic collapse."[20] David French perceives an America composed of "two different communities who glare at each other from across a vast cultural and ideological divide, with little understanding of opposing views."[21]

If modern secular liberalism is the purified product, in short, that product is arguably exhibiting some sort of self-destructive design defect. Liberalism seems vulnerable, besieged—even, at times, suicidal.[22] Schragger and Schwartzman observe that "it is now common to hear the claim that

---

18. See, e.g., William Galston, "Contemporary Conservative Thought: The View from San Diego," *Journal of Contemporary Legal Issues* 24 (2023): 177.

19. Alan Abramowitz and Steven Webster, "'Negative Partisanship' Explains Everything," *Politico*, September/October 2017, https://tinyurl.com/ypufcnst.

20. Lee Drutman, "How Hatred Came to Dominate American Politics," FiveThirtyEight, October 5, 2020, https://tinyurl.com/mpmurrte. See also Adam K. Raymond, "How Close Is the U.S. to Civil War? About Two-Thirds of the Way, Americans Say," *New York Intelligencer*, October 24, 2019, https://tinyurl.com/bd3uscp5.

21. David French, *Divided We Fall: America's Secession Threat and How to Restore Our Nation* (New York: St. Martin's, 2020), 89. For a more recent, thoroughgoing assessment of the currently perilous state of American liberal democracy (albeit one that I did not come across until this book was well advanced in the editing process), see James Davison Hunter, *Democracy and Solidarity: On the Cultural Roots of America's Political Crisis* (New Haven: Yale University Press, 2024).

22. See, e.g., Douglas Murray, *The War on the West* (New York: Broadside Books, 2022).

liberalism is in crisis, that it has failed, or that it is collapsing into some other regime type, usually authoritarianism of a socialist or fascist variety."[23] Noting "the omnipresent foreboding of our time," Mary Eberstadt reports that "premonitions of social and political catastrophe abound."[24] An Axios-Ipsos survey discovered that "four-fifths of Americans—both Republicans and Democrats—say America is falling apart."[25]

In an analogous vein, in a book called *Liberalism against Itself*, political philosopher Samuel Moyn has recently argued that the dominant modern strand of liberalism—Moyn calls it "Cold War liberalism"—departed dramatically from earlier versions (although Moyn emphasizes not the providentialist dimension of earlier liberalism but rather its progressivism and perfectionism). And Moyn argues that "Cold War liberalism has failed. Every day, more and more, we see that its approach bred as much opposition as it overcame, and created the conditions not for universal freedom and equality but for the waves of enemies such liberals keep finding at the gates."[26]

Indeed, it is often matter-of-factly stated that liberalism is a thing of the past—that we live today in a "postliberal" world.[27]

From the providentialist perspective, the currently imperiled state of

---

23. Schragger and Schwartzman, "Religious Antiliberalism," 1356.

24. Mary Eberstadt, *Primal Screams: How the Sexual Revolution Created Identity Politics* (West Conshohocken, PA: Templeton, 2019), 6, 5. For a similar if somewhat tamer assessment, see Ross Douthat, *The Decadent Society: America before and after the Pandemic* (New York: Simon & Schuster, 2018). See also Kim Parker, Rich Morin, and Juliana Menasce Horowitz, "Looking to the Future, Public Sees an America in Decline on Many Fronts," Pew Research Center, March 21, 2019, https://tinyurl.com/yteuxbcw. Compare Deneen, *Why Liberalism Failed*, 2 ("Today, some 70 percent of Americans believe that their country is moving in the wrong direction, and half the country thinks its best days are behind it").

25. Mike Allen, "Republicans and Democrats Agree—the Country Is Falling Apart," *Axios*, January 14, 2021, https://tinyurl.com/4fkxdnzb.

26. Samuel Moyn, *Liberalism against Itself: Cold War Intellectuals and the Making of Our Times* (New Haven: Yale University Press, 2023), 14.

27. See, e.g., M. T. Steiner, "Post-Liberal Politics—Left, Right, and Center," *Quillette*, July 2, 2019, https://tinyurl.com/2tnz6e8x; Joel Harrison, *Post-Liberal Religious Liberty: Forming Communities of Charity* (Cambridge: Cambridge University Press, 2020).

Providentialism and the Travails of Liberalism

American liberalism would not be surprising. We saw in chapter 3 that the providentialist perspective that prevailed in America for decades served to provide a sense of national purpose and to inform a discourse in which Americans could debate challenging issues like union and slavery. Indeed, the idea that the nation had a special purpose in the larger providential scheme was crucial in permitting Americans, despite their conflicting views and interests, to think of themselves—to "imagine" themselves—as a community at all. Take away the providential perspective and what would replace it to support these vital functions? Would *anything* satisfactorily replace it? *Has* anything replaced it?

In a recent, lengthy historical and sociological analysis, James Davison Hunter argues that nothing has. Americans, Hunter contends, are "unable to tell a common story about ourselves except the story that ours is now a fragmented and polarized society." And he asks: "when there is no common story a people can tell themselves, and no common means by which a people might sort these things out, what else is there to order collective life?"[28]

John Courtney Murray, with whose interpretation of America this book began, anticipated the kind of condition that we seem to be experiencing, and his prognosis was not optimistic. Murray, as we saw, believed that America was grounded in a "public consensus" based on the "self-evident" truths set forth in the Declaration of Independence, including the "first truth" asserting "the sovereignty of God over nations as well as over individual men."[29] But the consensus around these truths was vulnerable to the "incessant thieveries of forgetfulness."[30] And what would happen if the founding truths were forgotten, or renounced?

> What is at stake is America's understanding of itself. Self-understanding is the necessary condition of a sense of self-identity and self-confidence, whether in the case of an individual or in the case of a people. If the American people can no longer base this sense

---

28. Hunter, *Democracy and Solidarity*, 408, 430.
29. John Courtney Murray, SJ, *We Hold These Truths: Catholic Reflections on the American Proposition* (New York: Sheed & Ward, 1960), 28.
30. Murray, *We Hold These Truths*, 11.

on naive assumptions of self-evidence, it is imperative that they find other more reasoned grounds for their essential affirmation that they are uniquely a people, uniquely a free society. Otherwise the peril is great. *The complete loss of one's identity is, with all propriety of theological definition, hell. In diminished forms it is insanity.* And it would not be well for the American giant to go lumbering about the world today, lost and mad.[31]

If Murray was right, and if critics like Hunter are also right, it would seem to follow that America's current condition is, "with all propriety of theological definition, hell."

In this context, we might consider a different narrative, perhaps as a replacement for or perhaps as a needed supplement to the story of liberal progress or self-purification. Perhaps the course from providential liberalism to secularized liberalism has been one not of progress and purification at all—or at least not *only* of progress and purification—but rather or also of decline and enfeeblement.[32]

These are large questions, hardly to be answered in a couple of short chapters in a book like this one. Nonetheless, the following chapters take up selective aspects of the question. Chapter 5 considers the consequences of the loss of the providentialist foundation for liberal commitments to rights, equality, and justice. Chapter 6 reflects on the effect of the Supreme Court's repudiation of the providentialist self-understanding for Americans' ability to conceive of themselves as a nation.

---

31. Murray, *We Hold These Truths*, 5–6 (emphasis added).

32. Compare Kevin E. Stuart, "Liberalism Is Failing Because It Rejected Orthodox Christianity," *Public Discourse*, May 28, 2019, https://tinyurl.com/45rbhmsh.

CHAPTER 6

Liberalism without Foundations

At the founding and for much of the nation's history, providentialism provided a foundation for liberal commitments to rights, equality, and representative government. People were equal, despite their manifest differences in ability and virtue, in that they had been equally endowed by the Creator with rights. And the advancement of liberalism—or of rights, equality, and representative government—was part of the providential plan. The cosmos itself, and world history itself in its providentialist character, thus backed up or underwrote liberal claims. Or at least so Americans commonly assumed, and asserted.

Contemporary secular liberalism, by contrast, attempts to get by without any such providentialist foundation; more generally, it usually tries to get by without foundations at all. In this respect, modern liberal thinking follows the "antifoundational" path of much modern theorizing about knowledge and ethics.[1]

It is not that there is no overall dominant worldview. Today the educated person typically still operates with an at least implicit view about how the world and the universe are constituted—a view that is likely shaped, directly or through a kind of tacit absorption, by scientific naturalism and Darwinism in particular.[2] But liberal commitments are not grounded in that worldview in the

---

1. For a general discussion, see Mark Bevir and R. A. W. Rhodes, *The State as Cultural Practice* (Oxford: Oxford University Press, 2010), chapter 3, https://tinyurl.com/3e56u4ju.

2. John Searle has described the worldview that, he says, is not optional but rather "a condition of your being an educated person in our era":

PART 3: PROVIDENTIALISM AND THE TRAVAILS OF LIBERALISM

way they were once grounded in the providentialist worldview. Liberal commitments today, rather, are "freestanding," to borrow a term from John Rawls.[3]

To be sure, liberal thinkers may sometimes assert that commitments to human equality and human rights are grounded in the idea of "human dignity."[4] But what is the grounding or foundation for *that* idea? As a historical matter, the commitment to human dignity is traceable to the biblical concept of the *imago Dei*: humans were created by God, and in the image of God.[5] Secular liberalism is estopped to give that answer. Moreover, the secular and Darwinian worldview subverts more than it supports the idea that human beings have some distinctive and sacrosanct "dignity."[6] Thus, once again, the assertion of human dignity today seems to be a more freestanding claim—one that does not purport to be derived from any deeper or more encompassing scientific or philosophical truth.

> The world consists entirely of entities that we find it convenient, though not entirely accurately, to describe as particles. These particles exist in fields of force, and are organized into systems.... Examples of systems are mountains, planets, H2O molecules, rivers, crystals, and babies. Some of these systems are living systems; and on our little earth, the living systems contain a lot of carbon-based molecules, and make a very heavy use of hydrogen, nitrogen, and oxygen. Types of living systems evolve through natural selection, and some of them have evolved certain sorts of cellular structures, specifically nervous systems capable of causing and sustaining consciousness. Consciousness is a biological, and therefore physical, though of course also mental feature of certain higher-level nervous systems, such as human brains.
>
> John Searle, *The Social Construction of Reality* (New York: Simon & Schuster, 1995), 6.

3. See, e.g., John Rawls, *Political Liberalism* (New York: Columbia University Press, 1996), 10.

4. This was a favorite theme, for instance, of Justice William Brennan. See Seth Stern and Stephen Wermeil, *Justice Brennan: Liberal Champion* (Boston: Houghton Mifflin Harcourt, 2010), 418.

5. See Kyle Harper, "Christianity and the Roots of Human Dignity in Late Antiquity," in *Christianity and Freedom*, vol. 1, *Historical Perspectives*, ed. Timothy Samuel Shah and Allen D. Hertzke (Cambridge: Cambridge University Press, 2016), 123, 127, 130.

6. See John Gray, *Straw Dogs: Thoughts on Humans and Other Animals* (New York: Farrar, Straus & Giroux, 2002), 31 ("Darwin's theory shows the truth of naturalism: we are animals like any other").

Liberalism without Foundations

The antifoundational character of modern liberalism is manifest in two of liberalism's more prominent modern academic defenders—John Rawls and Richard Rorty. For Rawls, attempting to ground liberal commitments in a religious foundation (or for that matter, in any other "comprehensive doctrine") would itself be incompatible with liberalism. After all, there is no consensus today about any such religious or comprehensive doctrine; so tying liberalism to such a (contested) doctrine would render it vulnerable—and would at least implicitly treat the nonadherents to the preferred doctrine with less than equal respect. For Rorty, America's liberal prospects require "forgetting about eternity"—letting go of attachments to any religious or metaphysical or "theoretical frame of reference" and replacing such attachments with hope for a future built strictly by human beings not beholden to any "nonhuman authority."[7] "We are the first thoroughgoing experiment in national self-creation: the first nation-state with nobody but itself to please—not even God. We are the greatest poem because we put ourselves in place of God: our essence is our existence, and our existence is in the future. Other nations thought of themselves as hymns to the glory of God. We redefine God as our future selves."[8]

Here then it seems that we have a fundamental difference between providential and modern secular liberalism: the first claims that liberalism needs—and has—a foundation in the basic ontology and history of the world, while the second forgoes and indeed eschews any such foundation. So, which interpretation is more viable? Is the transition from a foundational to an antifoundational liberalism one of progress? Or of decline—even, perhaps, of collapse?

Are Foundations Necessary?

Each answer has its appeal. The foundational approach can claim support in ordinary experience and common sense, which may seem to teach that things—skyscrapers, dams, geometry, belief systems, civilizations—are built on foundations, and that when these foundations are eroded or removed, things fall down and fall apart.

---

7. Richard Rorty, *Achieving Our Country: Leftist Thought in Twentieth-Century America* (Cambridge, MA: Harvard University Press, 1998), 15–24, 18, 20, 18.
8. Rorty, *Achieving Our Country*, 22.

PART 3: PROVIDENTIALISM AND THE TRAVAILS OF LIBERALISM

A familiar parable of Jesus makes the point. A wise man builds his house upon a rock, and when storms come the house stands solid. A foolish man forgoes any solid foundation—he builds upon sand—and when the rain and wind come the man's house falls down, "and great [is] the fall of it."[9] The current travails of foundation-free liberalism are a contemporary illustration of Jesus's point; or so it may seem.

But perhaps the image of the house built upon foundations is the wrong image or analogy. A different comparison might be to, say, an airplane. A plane when it is being built rests on the ground, of course, and it continues to rest on the ground before it is actually flown. But once in flight, the plane leaves the ground behind. So long as it is flying, no foundation is needed—no grounding. Indeed, grounding is not only unnecessary but potentially fatal: renewed contact with the ground would indicate that the flight is over; and any sudden grounding would be disastrous. In a similar vein, perhaps providentialism was a necessary foundation for liberalism as the American project was first getting going. It was a new and audacious experiment, and some sort of supposed providential underwriting may have been required. But the project has now been proceeding for many decades, and it no longer needs its primitive foundations. Or so the "progress" narrative would suggest.

So then, which analogy better illuminates the career and the current condition of liberalism? Are foundations needed or not?

Let us consider that question by reflecting on two of liberalism's defining commitments—to rights, and to equality.

Rights—Grounded or Freestanding?

Consider first the commitment to rights—a commitment that is arguably at liberalism's essential core. As we have seen, for Thomas Jefferson and the signers of the Declaration of Independence, humans enjoy those rights with which they are "endowed by their creator." "The word 'right' was always a signpost pointing back to the divine plan of the Creation," as Daniel Boorstin explained, and "no claims [of right] could be validated except by

---

9. Matt. 7:24–27.

the Creator's plan."[10] (For Jefferson and many of his contemporaries, this validation was mediated through a hypothetical "social contract," but we need not concern ourselves with those complications here.)[11] Moreover, it was of the utmost importance that people should understand this point. "And can the liberties of a nation be thought secure," Jefferson asked, "when we have removed their only firm basis, a conviction in the minds of the people that these liberties are the gift of God?"[12]

But *why* should it be so imperative that people understand rights and liberties in this way? Let us suppose for purposes of argument that rights did or do in some sense come from providence: Even on that supposition, why should it be necessary that "the people" continue to regard them as such? Take some other blessing that a religious believer might likewise regard as a gift of God—say, the gift of sight. The believer may maintain that God gave us the precious capacity of vision; were it not for God's benevolence, the world would be dark to us. Suppose that the believer is right. Even so, the atheist who rejects this explanation can still appreciate and make use of the gift of sight. It is not as if atheists have to go around with their eyes shut: surely even the most dogmatic believer can concede that much.

Indeed, the same might be said for the world as a whole. That world, says the religious believer, is God's creation; without God nothing that we describe as the world, including ourselves, would even exist. But whether or not this claim is correct, the world plainly *does* exist, and so do we; and we can live exuberantly in the world whether or not we understand or believe in the world's and our own divine origin and foundation.

Might not the same be true of rights? Whether or not Jefferson was correct that rights are in some sense the gift of God—that we have the rights with which we are "endowed by our Creator"—still, we can appreciate, assert,

---

10. Daniel J. Boorstin, *The Lost World of Thomas Jefferson* (Chicago: University of Chicago Press, 1993), 194–95.

11. For a detailed explanation of how many of the founders processed natural law through social contract thinking, see Vincent Phillip Munoz, *Religious Liberty and the American Founding: Natural Rights and the Original Meaning of the First Amendment Religion Clauses* (Chicago: University of Chicago Press, 2022), 42–82.

12. Thomas Jefferson, *Notes on the State of Virginia*, ed. Frank C. Shuffleton (New York: Penguin Books, 1999; original 1785), 169.

and exercise rights without making any reference to God. Can't we? We've seen it done, haven't we? Rights, like vision and like the world itself, do not go away just because we fail to acknowledge a divine basis for them.

So we should take a closer look at the idea of and the commitment to rights. In what sense might this commitment depend on a providentialist foundation, as Jefferson suggested it does? In what way might rights be jeopardized if we fail to recognize a divine basis for them?

The First Step: Rights as Dependent on Law

When we argue about rights, we are usually arguing about which rights we do or do not have.[13] Is there a right to abortion? To same-sex marriage? To a subsistence-level income? And so on, and so on. Or we may be arguing about what a particular right includes or entails. Does the right to free speech entail that a person can, say, issue vague threats against the mayor—or the president?[14] And so forth. But let us set aside for now the usual questions about what rights we have and begin instead with the prior question: What *is* a right? What does it even *mean* to say that someone has a "right to X"?

Although the term is surely used in different senses, probably the most familiar and useful answer is that a "right" is a legally protected interest. Human beings have a myriad of *interests*—things we need or want or find gratifying. But it would be quite pointless and self-defeating to describe all of these needs and wants—all of these interests—as *"rights."* If everybody has a right to everything they want, no one has a real right to anything. (Because many of us will surely want some of the same things, so what then?) The concept of rights serves to distinguish and prioritize among the various interests that people have: some of our interests are matters of "rights," while others are not. You may *want* to be free to speak your mind, and you may want to have a princely salary and a charming spouse, and you may want your colleagues and peers to hold you in high esteem; but

---

13. The analysis in this section is developed at greater length in Steven D. Smith, "Nonsense and Natural Law," in Paul F. Campos et al., *Against the Law* (Durham, NC: Duke University Press, 1996), 100.

14. Compare *Watts v. United States*, 394 U.S. 704 (1969).

at least in the American legal system, you have a *right* only with respect to the first of these wants.

So then, how is the distinction to be drawn? What is the criterion for distinguishing between interests that enjoy the status of being "rights" and those that do not? Again, probably the most useful and conventional answer asserts that some interests but not others are protected by laws. Many of the things people want—most of them, probably—are not legally protected or ensured. Those things are just interests, but there is no "right" to them. Conversely, other interests *are* legally protected. It makes sense to say that we have "rights" to those things.

And indeed, this is the common and received sense of the term "rights." If I buy and obtain legal title to a car or a house, then my interest in that car or house is recognized and protected by law; and we accordingly say that I have a "right" to possess the car or to live in the house. You may own a car or a house that is much better than mine, and that I would very much like to drive and to live in. Maybe your car has features—excellent gas mileage, perhaps, or superb safety features—so that I could even plausibly claim to *need* your car or one like it (for my long daily commute on treacherous freeways, perhaps). But the law does not recognize or protect any interest of mine in *your* car or house; consequently, I have no "right" to those things.

There might be other ways of trying to distinguish among interests. We might try to distinguish based on intensity of desire: there are things that I vaguely want, and things that I really, really want. Or we might try to distinguish between mere wants and actual needs. And we *could* try to use the term "rights" to mark these distinctions. So I would have a right to something if I really, really want it, or if I don't merely want but actually need it. But defining rights in one of these ways would present intractable practical and theoretical problems, and in any case would depart from the common understanding of what it means for something to be a right. "I need you"; "I need your love"; "I can't live without your love": these are familiar refrains in a host of popular songs. The assertions might be heartfelt, or possibly even true; and yet we know that the lyricist or singer has no *right* to that love—and indeed will probably have to do without it. (Which is what gives the songs their poignancy.) So the more useful and common understanding, once again, is to think of a "right" as a legally protected or legally ensured interest.

PART 3: PROVIDENTIALISM AND THE TRAVAILS OF LIBERALISM

So understood, rights presuppose and depend on the existence of some background body of laws that protect or ensure some interests but not others. Without some such body of laws, it makes no sense to talk about "rights."

STEP TWO: RIGHTS AND THE PROVIDENTIAL PLAN

The assumption that rights depend on a background body of law works well enough—and indeed it is probably taken for granted—so long as we are talking about positive legal rights. Does Jones have a right to X—to property, or free speech, or abortion, or whatever? We look for an answer by examining the positive law of the jurisdiction where Jones resides to see whether that law protects X. If it does, then Jones has a right to X; otherwise not.

In the American and liberal tradition, however, the term "rights" is not limited to positive legal rights. Indeed, it is of the essence of liberalism to insist that human beings have rights that are "unalienable," as the Declaration of Independence says, or "natural," or "human," and that these rights exist whether governments and legal systems recognize them or not. That is the essential point of natural or human rights: they serve as criteria or standards for prescribing what governments should and should not do, and for criticizing governments that fail to recognize and respect these rights. We want to be able to say that the government of some jurisdiction is acting unjustly—maybe even that the government itself is illegitimate—because it is not respecting the unalienable or natural or human rights to X, Y, or Z. Which is exactly what the Declaration of Independence did say.

But if the term "rights" means legally protected interests, and if it accordingly makes sense to talk of rights only with reference to some background body of laws that protects some interests, what is the background body of laws that makes it possible to say that humans have "natural" or "human" rights to X, Y, and Z—whether or not a particular government's laws protect those interests? Or that a government whose laws do not protect X, Y, and Z, and that accordingly infringes X, Y, and Z, is not merely behaving badly or cruelly; the government is violating its subjects' "rights"?

Here we begin to see the sense of Jefferson's view that, as Boorstin explained, "the word 'right' [is] a signpost pointing back to the divine plan of the Creation." In the classical providentialist view, the providential plan creates or amounts to a normative order constituted by a set of "natural laws" that prescribe and prohibit—not in detail, typically, but in broad strokes. In this view, God or providence is to the natural law (and thus to the corollary rights) what the king or the legislature are to positive law and positive legal rights. In a masterful study, legal historian Richard Helmholz has shown how pervasive this understanding of law and rights was in early America.[15] As Alexander Hamilton explained: "The deity ... has constituted an eternal and immutable law, which is, indispensably, obligatory upon all mankind, prior to any human institution whatever. ... This is what is called the law of nature. ... It is binding over all the globe, in all countries, and at all times. ... Upon this law, depend the natural rights of mankind."[16]

In this classical understanding, governments and positive legal systems have an essential role in specifying and implementing the broad prescriptions and prohibitions of the natural law, and the specific implementations will differ from one jurisdiction to another. So positive legal rights will likewise differ from jurisdiction to jurisdiction. The rights to freedom of speech and religion are not defined in the exact same way in America as in England or France. And yet the broad principles—the providentially ordained prescriptions and prohibitions—are of general applicability. And thus it is meaningful and coherent to say, on the assumption of a providential plan, that a particular government or enactment that disregards the natural law has violated someone's natural or inalienable right. Slavery is a violation of human rights even in a jurisdiction whose laws affirmatively recognize and protect slavery (as Americans in the early republic sometimes shamefully acknowledged).[17]

Eliminate the assumption of a background natural normative order, conversely, and the claim that someone has a natural or human right to X loses its meaning. It is as if I carried a hundred dollar bill to a barter culture devoid of currency and tried to exchange the bill for a batch of goods.

---

15. See R. M. Helmholz, *Natural Law in Court: A History of Legal Theory in Practice* (Cambridge, MA: Harvard University Press, 2015), 127–72.

16. Alexander Hamilton, "The Farmer Refuted," reprinted in *The Founding Fathers and the Debate over Religion in Revolutionary America*, ed. Matthew L. Harris and Thomas S. Kidd (New York: Oxford University Press, 2012), 29.

17. See Helmholz, *Natural Law in Court*, 161–65.

Against the backdrop of *our* economic system, the bill is money—legal tender—but in the barter culture money does not exist; so my bill is nothing but a worthless piece of paper. In our economic system it is sensible and true to say that the bill is worth a hundred dollars. In the barter culture, that same statement is not so much false as meaningless.

And so it seems that rights are not like sight, after all, or like something that can be appreciated and used whether or not we acknowledge it as a gift of God. With "rights" the situation is different. The concept of a "right" makes sense only on the assumption of a background normative order. Take away that background order and—poof!—the rights disappear.[18]

Or so it may seem, considered in the abstract. But now we come to a challenging question: Does our actual historical experience support this analysis?

Testing the Claim

At least on first look, the answer would seem to be no. Thus, the preceding analysis would seem to yield a prediction that if the providential foundation is discarded, for public purposes anyway, natural or nonpositivist human rights would disappear (at least unless the providential foundation could be replaced by one based on some other "comprehensive doctrine"—which, as noted, freestanding liberalism also eschews). Positive rights—rights conferred on us by the positive law—would still exist, of course. But the very concept of a prepositivist "natural" right would no longer make sense; and so it may seem that people would or should stop talking about such things—or such nothings. This conclusion would vindicate the pronouncement of one hard-core positivist, Jeremy Bentham, who complained that natural rights are "nonsense—nonsense on stilts."[19]

And yet if we assess that prediction of the disappearance of natural or human rights against what has actually happened, it seems that the predic-

---

18. For a recent scholarly account of how eighteenth- and nineteenth-century American lawyers understood rights and law in basically this way, see Stuart Banner, *The Decline of Natural Law: How American Lawyers Once Used Natural Law and Why They Stopped* (New York: Oxford University Press, 2021).
19. Jeremy Bentham, "Anarchical Fallacies," in *The Works of Jeremy Bentham*, ed. J. Bowring, vol. 2 (Edinburgh: Simpkin, Marshall & Co., 1843), 489, 501.

Liberalism without Foundations

tion fails. Our history has not unfolded as this analysis seems to predict. On the contrary.

Thus, as we have seen, the providentialist framework came to be repudiated in America, officially and for public purposes at least, in the latter half of the twentieth century. And yet far from disappearing, appeals to rights proliferated. The school prayer decisions solidified the new secular orthodoxy by 1963, thereby officially banishing the traditional public providentialism. And far from withdrawing from the rights business, the Supreme Court almost immediately began to articulate a whole new array of previously unrecognized rights—to contraceptives,[20] to abortion,[21] to be free from discrimination on the basis of sex and then sexual orientation,[22] to elect to die under certain situations of incapacitation and terminal illness,[23] to marry a person of the same sex or gender.[24] Americans now enjoy a panoply of rights that could scarcely have been imagined even as recently as the 1970s.[25] This all has amounted to, as Jamal Greene puts it, a "rights explosion," and to a dominant mode of thinking about political issues that Greene calls "rightsism."[26]

The judicial decisions just noted do not precisely contradict the analysis above, perhaps, because the Court purported to be recognizing positive

---

20. E.g., Griswold v. Connecticut, 381 U.S. 479 (1965).

21. Roe v. Wade, 410 U.S. 113 (1973), overruled in Dobbs v. Jackson Women's Health Organization, 597 U.S. 215 (2022).

22. E.g., Craig v. Boren, 429 U.S. 190 (1976) (sex discrimination); Romer v. Evans, 517 U.S. 620 (1996) (sexual orientation discrimination).

23. Cruzan v. Director, Missouri Dept. of Health, 497 U.S. 261 (1990).

24. Obergefell v. Hodges, 576 U.S. 644 (2015).

25. Leigh Ann Wheeler observes that "as late as 1973, few Americans could conceive of the possibility that the U.S. Constitution might protect sexual rights and provide for sexual citizenship." Leigh Ann Wheeler, *How Sex Became a Civil Liberty* (New York: Oxford University Press, 2013), 3. Geoffrey Stone, an enthusiastic proponent of the new jurisprudence of sexuality, acknowledges that "Supreme Court justices from almost any prior era in American history would be stunned to learn of the role the Supreme Court and our Constitution have come to play in our contemporary disputes ... over such issues as obscenity, contraception, abortion, sodomy, and same-sex marriage." Geoffrey R. Stone, *Sex and the Constitution: Sex, Religion, and Law from America's Origins to the Twenty-First Century* (New York: Liveright, 2017), xxvii–xxviii.

26. Jamal Greene, *How Rights Went Wrong: Why Our Obsession with Rights Is Tearing America Apart* (New York: Houghton Mifflin Harcourt, 2021), 58–86.

legal rights embedded in positive law—especially in the terse but suddenly pregnant clauses of section 1 of the Fourteenth Amendment. But since these newly declared rights could find little sustenance either in the text or the enactors' understanding of those clauses, or for that matter in the judicial precedents, it was hard not to hold the suspicion that the Court was importing what it took to be human or natural rights into the Constitution: and both admirers and critics of the Court sometimes said as much.[27] Moreover, in popular discourse claims of rights of all sorts likewise proliferated; and these supposed rights were not necessarily tied to specific legal provisions at all. The terms "rights revolution" and "rightsism" describe not just constitutional jurisprudence but popular discourse and popular thinking as well. People were claiming a right to marry a same-sex partner well before the Supreme Court constitutionalized such a right in *Obergefell v. Hodges*.

Not everyone has celebrated this development, of course; but even critics acknowledge it. Jamal Greene contends that, as his book's subtitle says, the "obsession with rights" is "tearing America apart." The country is "hurtling toward tragedy."[28] Whether or not Greene is correct, the fact remains that the renunciation of the providentialist foundation on which Americans like Jefferson had depended did not signal the end of rights talk. On the contrary.

In short, with the abandonment of the providentialist framework, rights talk did not recede, as our earlier analysis seemed to predict, but rather proliferated. It even, as some concerned observers suggested, accelerated to the point of being out of control.

27. See, e.g., Michael J. Perry, *The Constitution, the Courts, and Human Rights* (New Haven: Yale University Press, 1982). Criticism of the new rights jurisprudence as a revival of "natural law" came from dissenting justices such as Justice Hugo Black. See, e.g., *Griswold*, 381 U.S. at 511–527 (Black, J., dissenting).

28. Greene, *How Rights Went Wrong*, xxxv. Greene is not the first to make this criticism. Compare, e.g., Mary Ann Glendon, *Rights Talk: The Impoverishment of Political Discourse* (New York: Simon & Schuster, 1991), 14: "Our rights talk, in its absoluteness, promotes unrealistic expectations, heightens social conflict, and inhibits dialogue that might lead toward consensus, accommodation, at least the discovery of common ground.... In its relentless individualism, it fosters a climate that is inhospitable to society's losers, and that systematically disadvantages caretakers and dependents, young and old. In its neglect of civil society, it undermines the principal seedbeds of civic and personal virtue."

Liberalism without Foundations

This development surely complicates the analysis offered earlier, but does it actually disconfirm that analysis? Perhaps not. We need to take a closer look.

THE BUBBLING OF RIGHTS

Although the loss of the providential framework did not lead to the disappearance of rights talk, that talk *has* come to seem increasingly unmoored. People may continue to talk about "rights" that supposedly exceed or exist independent of the established positive legal rights, but it is often not clear what people mean when claiming such a "right." Are they asserting that the right is somehow implicit in the Constitution, in the way that rights to contraception or abortion were said to be? That they think a particular "right" *should be* recognized in positive law? Or is it just that an advocate thinks some particular interest is especially important and uses the vocabulary of "rights" to indicate that valuation, or to give weight to his position? Is the term "rights" by now just a sort of rhetorical exclamation mark?

Very often it seems impossible to say. People talk about "rights" more freely and urgently and often indignantly than ever before, perhaps, and they may claim more rights than they ever did in the past. And yet it is very difficult to say just what they mean by such talk.

And this observation provokes a suspicion: maybe the classic liberal commitment to rights *has* collapsed after all, albeit it in a deceptive way. Here is an analogy: we might say that a monetary system has ceased to function—has collapsed—if all the currency is removed from the system. There is no money anywhere, and hence no monetary system. But we might also say that the monetary system has collapsed if huge quantities of currency are infused into the system such that the dollars or pesos or francs lose their value. Now there is money everywhere, but it isn't worth much. Might something analogous have happened with rights?

Consider this aspect of the matter: traditionally, rights had a presumptively categorical quality.[29] Some such meaning probably persists in everyday speech. Insofar as you have a "right" to something—your car, your

---

29. Jamal Greene acknowledges this feature but criticizes it. Greene, *How Rights Went Wrong*, 110.

house, your job—I cannot take that thing from you; and neither can the government—not even if I or the government really, really want or need it. Perhaps a "right" is not absolutely categorical: it can be suspended, perhaps, when something like national survival is at stake, as during the Lincoln presidency. Even so, a "right" comes close to being a categorical protection.[30] As Ronald Dworkin, a preeminent champion of rights, used to put it: rights "trump" other interests or policies, even something like the general welfare.[31] That is what it means—or at least what it *meant*—to have a right.

Once the idea of rights as interests protected by a system of laws is replaced by a foundationless and unmoored conception of rights as . . . who knows what?, rights tend to lose this categorical quality. Insofar as claims about "rights" now have a mostly rhetorical function, that rhetorical function will come to be understood, at least tacitly; and the rhetoric of rights will thereby suffer deflation. If just about anything that people really want can now be described as a "right," it will mean less to say that something is a right.

This deflation, or this loss of force or meaning, is apparent in Jamal Greene's analysis of rights. As noted, Greene is concerned about "rightsism"—rights and rights talk, he thinks, have gotten dangerously out of

---

30. To be sure, insofar as rights refer to legally protected interests and hence are dependent on a background legal system, that system may not be simple, and the corollary rights will then not be simple either. There may for instance be various conditions of defeasability. Your property right in something means that the government cannot just take that thing. But the property right is not simple and absolute; it may be understood to mean, for example, that government *can* acquire something for public use by following a prescribed procedure and providing just compensation. That kind of controlled defeasability is built into the right. Even so, the right itself, whatever it is, has a presumptively categorical quality.

31. See, e.g., Ronald Dworkin, *Taking Rights Seriously* (Cambridge, MA: Harvard University Press, 1977), 193. Discussing "what it means to say that an individual has a right against the State," Dworkin explained that "the prospect of utilitarian gains cannot justify preventing a man to do what he has a right to do. . . . There would be no point in the boast that we respect individual rights unless that involved some sacrifice, and the sacrifice in question must be that we give up whatever marginal benefits our country would receive from overriding these rights when they prove inconvenient. So the general benefit cannot be a good ground for abridging rights."

control—but he does not favor any abandonment of such rights or such talk. Instead, he argues, we should reconceive rights in less categorical terms. To say that you have a right to something should not mean that government *must* respect or refrain from infringing that right; it merely means that in case of a conflict between your so-called right and some governmental action or policy, your "right"-protected interest should be given weight, or regarded as important. If you had no "right," government presumably could regulate or restrict you for pretty much any legitimate reason, however slight; but if you have a "right," government will need a stronger interest to support the regulation or restriction.[32]

Greene emphasizes that this understanding of rights is not idiosyncratic with him: he is merely recommending an approach to rights that is already prevalent in the "proportionality" jurisprudence practiced in Europe and indeed through much of the world.[33] And although Greene severely criticizes American courts for not adopting the proportionality approach, a similar conception is arguably already reflected in the "balancing" that American courts frequently purport to perform, in which someone's ostensible right is "balanced" against the governmental interest.[34] At least in the legal profession, this deflated concept of rights is by now virtually axiomatic.

But however desirable this approach may or may not be, it openly forfeits the presumptively categorical quality that has typically been associated with the idea of a "right." Indeed, the very nature of a "right" is fundamentally altered—and downgraded.

In this way, the simultaneous proliferation but devaluation of rights serves to illuminate one important feature of the providentialist and foundational approach that might otherwise be overlooked: if rights are thought to be based on some foundation (such as the natural law or the providential plan), that foundation may help both to ground or *support* rights and also—this is the newly noticed feature—to *limit* them. Interests of various kinds might be valuable, and valued, but if they are not protected or ensured by the foundational legal system, those interests are not

---

32. Greene, *How Rights Went Wrong*, 56–57, 110.
33. Greene, *How Rights Went Wrong*, xxii–xxiii.
34. For a classic explanation and critique, see T. Alexander Aleinikoff, "Constitutional Law in the Age of Balancing," *Yale Law Journal* 96 (1987): 943.

"rights." And both the supportive and the limiting functions are necessary to give rights meaning—to explain what it means and why it matters that something is said to be a "right."

Take away the foundation, however, and both the supportive and the limiting functions are removed. The loss of support means now that to say something is a "right" is not to say very much. And the loss of limits means that it now becomes possible, as a rhetorical matter, to describe just about any strongly favored interest as a "right," and there is now no framework within which that claim of right can be assessed and then accepted or rejected. If there is no definite or usable conception of what a right is, or of how something comes to be a "right," or of how to distinguish between those interests that are rights and those that are not, then there is no way to say that anything someone ardently desires is not a right. If we cannot explain what a right *is*, we can hardly explain what a right is *not*. And so it is perhaps paradoxical but upon reflection unsurprising that as the basis for rights is removed, rights talk can now run rampant and unrestrained.

And yet in a deeper sense this appearance of rights running out of control is deceptive, because it seems that when rights talk and rights claims become unmoored and ungrounded, "rights" will no longer be what they once were, or mean what they once meant.

Rights in the modern world thus reflect a sort of bubbling process in which rights become at the same time more expansive and yet more fragile, even illusory. Rights have been puffed up far beyond what anyone formerly conceived. But the rights are arguably hollow, in the sense that they no longer provide the categorical or near-categorical protection that was once associated with a right.

And so it may be argued that the apparent proliferation of rights in the modern world supports our earlier analysis after all. That analysis suggested that the concept of a right has meaning only against the backdrop of a legal order in which some interests are legally protected and others are not. Eliminate the background legal order, and rights would lose their meaning. And despite appearances and obfuscations, this is arguably just what has happened in the modern world. The *word* is still with us, to be sure; indeed, it is profligately deployed for whatever rhetorical force it may still carry. But the word no longer means what it once did. "Rights" are no longer rights.

Liberalism without Foundations

And we can imagine Jefferson renewing his question: "And can the liberties of a nation be thought secure, when we have removed their only firm basis, a conviction in the minds of the people that these liberties are the gift of God?"

Providence, Inequality, and Injustice

This complex development—this development in which a liberal commitment, once freed from its former foundation, is subject to both inflationary and deflationary tendencies—is not limited to rights. A similar analysis might be given for other liberal commitments—equality, liberty, rule of law, representative government.[35] But let us look beyond these specific liberal commitments and ask more generally what the loss or abandonment of the providential perspective does not just to the ideal of equality but to the sense of justice and injustice itself.

We might start by noticing what might seem to be a paradox. Modern American governments have arguably done more to promote equal justice among people—passed more laws, spent more money, adopted more programs—than earlier governments did, or even than almost any governments in human history have done. To be sure, perfect justice will never be achieved in this world: even so, one might suppose that the massive effort to promote social justice and equality would have produced a population that is relatively more contented than past populations have been.

And yet, as we look out at the world, it seems that, if anything, the opposite condition obtains. We live in a culture of by now almost universal

---

35. Americans today arguably enjoy greater liberty in the sense of more rights and freedoms than they did in earlier periods; meanwhile, Americans are arguably subject to more regulations and restrictions and exactions than at any time in the past. In 1776 Americans revolted against England because of complaints about the oppressiveness of taxes that seem negligible compared to the taxes and regulations that are routinely imposed today. Of course, the complaint at that time was not just about the taxes per se, but about the lack of representation in the lawmaking body that enacted the taxes. Today the franchise has been extended—and yet most of the actual regulations and restrictions that govern the citizens in their daily lives come from administrative agencies that are not elected and whose decrees are beyond the control or even the comprehension of the vast majority of citizens. In sum, freedoms have arguably been much extended—and greatly reduced.

grievance.[36] Remarking on "the bitterness, recrimination, and widespread discontent that have dominated the political sphere in recent years," Rachel Lu observes that "grievance has been the primary fuel of both political parties for some years now."[37]

Not every individual claims to be aggrieved, of course. But groups of all kinds—groups situated on opposite sides of some of the salient cultural and political divides—regard themselves as victims of discrimination and injustice. Racial minorities assert grievances and demands for reparations. But descendants of the European colonizers (as well as some minorities) feel aggrieved by the remedies adopted in response to racial grievances—affirmative action programs,[38] for example. Women are the victims of discrimination; so are men.[39] Liberals are discriminated against; so are conservatives.[40] Traditional Christians perceive themselves as persecuted; so do sexual and gender minorities.[41] The poor are in their view oppressed by the wealthy; the wealthy often feel that the government has become oppressive in, among other things, its taxation and wealth redistribution

---

36. Compare Mark Milke, *The Victim Cult: How the Grievance Culture Hurts Everyone and Wrecks Civilization* (n.p.: Thomas & Black, 2021), 3–4: "Now consider the 21st century's healthier and longer lives; more food than our ancestors could have imagined; more money, choices, and comforts for billions and improvements in diets, health, and lifespans even for the poorest; rights previously unknown for many with expanded choices for women and others long discriminated against. . . . Despite such flourishing conditions for many, the rise of grievances and constellations of people that obsess over them—victim cults—has proceeded apace."

37. Rachel Lu, "A Nation of Ingrates?" *Law & Liberty*, February 13, 2024, https://tinyurl.com/4w3c4y3a.

38. See, e.g., Students for Fair Admissions v. President, Harvard College, 600 U.S. 181 (2023).

39. See Dan Cassino, "Why More American Men Feel Discriminated Against," *Harvard Business Review*, September 29, 2016, https://tinyurl.com/mrcta845.

40. Compare George Hawley, "Beyond Grievance Politics," *Law & Liberty*, May 16, 2024, https://tinyurl.com/3u92fkkt ("Much of the online right in particular has clearly embraced its own version of the victimhood mentality. So many popular accounts on X (formerly Twitter) do nothing but serve, all day long, content designed to stoke outrage and a sense of resentment among conservatives").

41. These clashing perceptions of grievance manifest themselves in highly visible legal controversies. See, e.g., 303 Creative LLC v. Elenis, 600 U.S. 570 (2023); Masterpiece Cakeshop v. Colorado Civil Rights Comm'n, 584 U.S. 617 (2018).

policies.[42] And human characteristics of all sorts—race, gender, ethnicity, sexuality, religion, obesity, beauty, ability, wealth, education level, family heritage, marital status—are increasingly perceived as lines of division and as sites and sources of discrimination, oppression, and injustice.[43]

Sociologist James Davison Hunter argues that in contemporary America, "moral rage [against perceived injustices] becomes a form of capital. It is the means by which political parties and special-interest groups mobilize their supporters. It also becomes the means by which special-interest groups raise money in support of their cause." Indeed, "rage against injury and its perpetrators emerges as a source of moral authority. . . . [It] becomes the source from which any claims to grievance are made legitimate." Indeed, the self-identifying victims of injustice come to define themselves in terms of their victim status: "Outrage against a grievance caused by others . . . becomes the source of authentic identity and authentic action." Consequently, "rage, hatred, and the desire for revenge that emanates from injury become the course of meaning and purpose for those who see themselves as victims."[44]

A culture in which almost every group seems to feel resentful and aggrieved, in which rage is systematically cultivated for political and other

---

42. See Rainer Zitelmann, "Why We Should Be Concerned about Prejudice toward the Rich," Foundation for Economic Education, July 11, 2020, https://tinyurl.com/53wevema. For a general, critical presentation of libertarian philosophies that view taxation and redistribution as oppressive and sometimes as "theft," see Andrew Koppelman, *Burning Down the House: How Libertarian Philosophy Was Corrupted by Delusion and Greed* (New York: St. Martin's, 2022).

43. An illustrative though hardly exhaustive list comes from a group at Amherst College calling itself WeTheProtestors; the group demanded that the college president issue an apology to "students, alumni and former students, faculty, administration and staff who have been victims of white supremacy, colonialism, anti-black racism, anti-Latin racism, anti–Native American racism, anti–Native/indigenous racism, anti-Asian racism, anti–Middle Eastern racism, heterosexism, cis-sexism, xenophobia, anti-Semitism, ableism, mental health stigma, and classism." Milke, *The Victim Cult*, 115–16.

44. James Davison Hunter, *Democracy and Solidarity: On the Cultural Roots of America's Political Crisis* (New Haven: Yale University Press, 2024), 423–24. Hunter adds: "Identity groups become so deeply attached to their own impotence, exclusion, and subordination because they provide the premises upon which the group's existence depends. So even while the group seeks to avenge injury, it reaffirms injury as the foundation of its existence; even while it seeks to resist its subordination, it reinforces its subordination as the basis of its identity" (425).

PART 3: PROVIDENTIALISM AND THE TRAVAILS OF LIBERALISM

purposes, in which grievance becomes a source of personal identity, is hardly one in which a liberal community—or any other kind of community—can flourish. Indeed, it is doubtful that such a culture is sustainable over the long run.[45] And yet, ironically perhaps, these grievances are all traceable to and nurtured by modern liberal commitments and ideals—the ideal of "equal concern and respect," for example.[46] Modern liberal societies embraced the ideal of "equal concern and respect," and it turned out that this ideal was being violated just about everywhere someone might look. Government attempts to address one kind of injustice—formal racial discrimination, for example—and two or more other kinds of injustice seem to spring up Hydra-like in its place.

How did this happen? Well, begin with a commonplace: differences and hence inequalities among human beings are ubiquitous. People differ from each other in race and gender, obviously, and these differences can be the source of discrimination and injustice. But these often-noted differences barely begin to fill out the catalogue of human inequalities. Suppose we could somehow erase or at least equalize differences in privilege and opportunity based on race or sex, or even on wealth or family inheritance. People would still differ enormously from each other in myriad respects, and these differences would be at least as important to the actual well-being and happiness of individual human beings as those few select differences—race, gender, and such—that have traditionally been identified as sources of inequality and injustice.

Some people would still be attractive in appearance; others for no fault of their own would be unattractive; and these differences would powerfully affect people's prospects for friendship, sexual fulfillment, romance, marriage, and family. Likewise for differences in personality: some people are witty and charming, others clumsy or boring. Some people are endowed with athletic ability, in vastly varying degrees, or with musical or artistic

---

45. Compare Timothy Snyder, *Bloodlands: Europe between Hitler and Stalin*, quoted in Milke, *The Victim Cult*, 2 ("No major act of war or mass killing in the twentieth century began without the aggressors or perpetrators first claiming innocence and victimhood").

46. Compare Hunter, *Democracy and Solidarity*, 449: "And the intensity of the longing for an ideal world, then, is redirected into fury against the present, a fury channeled into the demand to purge, dismantle, deconstruct, and negate."

talent: and again these differences can be determinative of prospects that many people care about passionately. (My own dream of playing right field for the Pittsburgh Pirates was cruelly crushed when I was the only player cut from my Little League team.) People are possessed of intelligence of different kinds and in vastly different measures. In varying degrees people are tall or short, thin or obese, dark or pale, fast or slow, charming or boorish, clever or dull, energetic or lethargic, wise or foolish, disposed to virtue or inclined to vice, . . . lucky or unlucky. All of these differences—these inequalities—are undeniable; hardly any of them are freely chosen; many of them are mostly irremediable; and all of them can be influential or even decisive with respect to people's prospects, well-being, and happiness.

Thus, for every person who feels aggrieved because of discrimination based on his or her race or sex, there are probably ten people, or a thousand, who are unhappy because they are homely in appearance or awkward in conversation, and hence are thwarted in their desires for romance, friendship, and respect.

In recent decades, of course, numerous laws have been passed and vast sums have been spent in the attempt to eliminate some of the disparate effects of some differences—especially of race and gender. These laws and efforts and expenditures, for all they may have achieved, barely begin to touch the vast ocean of inequalities that make life more blessed and fulfilling for some people than for other people.

So, how should we regard all of these profound and pervasive inequalities?

Inequalities within a Providential Frame

Start by looking at the question from a providentialist perspective. If the universe has been created by God according to a providential plan, that plan provides a standpoint from which to understand and evaluate the plethora of human inequalities.

From this perspective, at least some of the inequalities will seem to be arbitrary or contrary to the providential plan—and hence unjust and hence, ideally, in need of correction. Thus, in the Roman Empire, law and culture unapologetically treated men much more favorably than women, citizens more favorably than noncitizens and slaves, Romans more favor-

PART 3: PROVIDENTIALISM AND THE TRAVAILS OF LIBERALISM

ably than non-Romans. The apostle Paul, however, declared that these distinctions were irrelevant in the kingdom of God. "There is neither Jew nor Greek, there is neither bond nor free, there is neither male nor female: for ye are all one in Christ Jesus."[47] And beginning with church fathers like Gregory of Nyssa, this more egalitarian standard became the basis of unprecedented criticism of the virtually universal systems of slavery.[48] The apostle James likewise severely condemned Christians who treated the wealthy as more honorable or meritorious than the poor.[49] Centuries later, Martin Luther King Jr. was a courageous and eloquent modern representative of this tradition of Christian opposition to oppression and injustice.

At the same time, the providential perspective in its Christian version did not prescribe the flattening of all individual differences that might confer on some people more respect and more power or privilege than others enjoyed. On the contrary, the Christian idea was that many differences are both functionally valuable and enriching to the overall body. "Just as a body, though one, has many parts, but all its many parts form one body," wrote Paul, speaking of the church, "so it is with Christ. . . . God has placed the parts in the body, every one of them, just as he wanted them to be." In this organic conception, "the eye cannot say to the hand, 'I don't need you!' And the head cannot say to the feet, 'I don't need you!' On the contrary, those parts of the body that seem to be weaker are indispensable."[50]

In a similar vein, in his well-known "city on a hill" speech, John Winthrop began by declaring that "God Almighty in his most holy and wise providence, hath soe disposed of the condition of mankind, as in all times some must be rich, some poore, some high and eminent in dignity, others mean and in submission." And Winthrop gave reasons for these inequalities. Differences ensured that "every man might have need of others, and from hence they might be all knitt more nearly together in the Bonds of brotherly affection." In addition, inequalities served to "show forth the glory of [God's] wisdom in the variety and difference of the creatures, and

---

47. Gal. 3:28.
48. See Kimberly Flint-Hamilton, "Gregory of Nyssa and the Culture of Oppression," 2010, https://tinyurl.com/crmp64xt.
49. James 2:1–11.
50. 1 Cor. 12:12, 18, 21–22 NIV.

Liberalism without Foundations

the glory of his power in ordering all these differences for the preservation and good of the whole."[51]

In this view, paradoxically, even in and because of their inequalities people can enjoy a kind of essential equality, in the sense that everyone, of high status or low, is a valuable part of the body and is needed to contribute to the welfare of the whole. More broadly, many of the differences that can be described as inequalities are valuable and necessary as part of the encompassing providential plan, which is beneficent to all. In this respect, such inequalities are *not* undesirable or unjust—much in the way that inequalities among the players of different positions on a football team or among musicians in a symphony orchestra are not injustices to be corrected, but rather differences to be preserved and appreciated and used to good advantage.

Even after these valuable inequalities have been explained and justified, however, a (likely very large) residuum of unjustified inequalities will remain; and these are the subject of justified grievances—and of efforts to correct such injustices. And yet (as both believers and nonbelievers might well agree), it is unlikely that most of these injustices will be fully or even approximately corrected within the lifetimes of most of the victims of such injustices. At this point, at least the Christian version of providentialism offers a redemptive promise. Although injustices will persist in this fallen world, the ultimate condition will be one of justice. The meek may be oppressed at present, but ultimately they will inherit the earth. "Every valley shall be exalted, and every mountain and hill shall be made low."[52] Borrowing from an earlier Christian thinker a metaphor that was a favorite of Martin Luther King Jr. and Barack Obama: "The arc of the moral universe is long, but it bends toward justice."[53] In this way, the providential perspective, at least in its Christian version, offers a kind of consolation for those injustices that will inevitably persist in this fallen world. (Revolutionary

---

51. John Winthrop, "A Modell of Christian Charitie," reprinted in *The Sacred Rights of Conscience*, ed. Daniel L. Dreisbach and Mark David Hall (Indianapolis: Liberty Fund, 2009), 123–31.

52. Isa. 40:4; cf. Luke 3:5.

53. See Nathan S. Chapman, "'The Arc of the Moral Universe': Christian Eschatology and U.S. Constitutionalism," *Notre Dame Law Review* 98 (2023): 1439. The statement was made by the nineteenth-century Unitarian minister Theodore Parker.

reformers like Marx have of course recognized this consoling function and have been savagely critical of it, viewing it as an obstacle to revolution or to needed reforms: religion is in this sense the "opiate of the masses.")[54]

Inequalities without Providence

So much for the providentialist perspective on inequalities and injustice. Now take away the providentialist assumption. All of the inequalities—or at the very least those which individuals cannot overcome by the exercise of their agency—are now without any sort of excuse or vindication. Without a providential plan, there is no ordained organic whole of which everyone, the great and the small, are all necessary parts. No arc of the universe bending toward justice. No providentially ordained redemption. What then?

On these premises, it seems, reasoning might go in either of two pretty much contrary ways. (Or, paradoxically but unsurprisingly, it might and often does go both ways, even though the directions are opposite.) Perhaps the most logical course would be, basically, nihilistic or Thrasymachean in character. The background normative order against which many inequalities could be deemed wrong or unjust is no longer available, and so the conclusion might be that normative judgments of justice or injustice no longer have sense or meaning. Things are what they are; that is all.

The human world in this respect is like the world that we observe in nature, and in nature documentaries. There are the strong and the weak, the predators and the preyed upon. We see lions hunting down gazelles, polar bears devouring seals. But there is no basis for moral judgment or condemnation of injustices. This is just the way the universe has evolved. Animals do what they do; it would be merely sentimental to castigate the lions or the polar bears for being what they are. Of course, if the gazelles somehow devised a way to defeat or eradicate the lions, there would be nothing unjust about that either.

We might imagine arrangements in which satisfactions were increased and pains reduced—in which more animals get more of what they want. If

---

54. Karl Marx and Friedrich Engels, *Critique of Hegel's Philosophy of Right*, trans. Tim Newcomb (pub. by author, 2023; original, 1844), 21.

Liberalism without Foundations

the welfare of the animals matters to us, we might want to promote such arrangements. Even so, judgments of justice and injustice applied to the African savannah or the icy Arctic would be as out-of-place as would be the application of Miss Manners table etiquette.

On this reasoning, the loss of the background normative order has a deflationary effect on perceptions or claims of injustice—for humans as for animals.

But our reasoning might instead take a different and profoundly inflationary direction (albeit perhaps a less strictly logical one). Suppose that we are unwilling or unable to cast aside our propensity to make moral judgments—judgments of praise and blame, or of moral indignation. Now, no longer assessable against an inclusive and redemptive background normative order, all the ubiquitous inequalities among human beings—all the circumstances in which some humans have more wealth and power and opportunity than others—are instances of presumptive injustice. And so we look out on the world—a world thoroughly suffused with inequalities, most of them unchosen—and perceive a seething mass of profound injustice. And without any larger organic whole or redemptive plan, these inequalities-injustices are simply without excuse.[55]

To be sure, some inequalities might serve valuable functions—incentivizing people to work and create in socially beneficial ways in order to achieve more power and wealth, for example. We might want to put up with or even encourage these sorts of inequalities in order to reap such utilitarian benefits.[56] Even so, the resulting unequal distributions, although mutually advantageous, would still be presumptively unjust.

In prevalent thinking today, both sorts of reasoning are discernible. Thus, in much theorizing associated with thinkers like Marx, Nietzsche, and Foucault, and more generally with Darwin, the emphasis is on a struggle

---

55. Compare John Courtney Murray, SJ, *The Problem of God: Yesterday and Today* (New Haven: Yale University Press), 108 ("At the bottom of an atheism whose matrix is the problem of evil, there lies a moral absolute. It asserts not only that evil has no right to exist but that its existence is intolerable").

56. John Rawls approved a version of this tradeoff in what he called "the difference principle," which permits some inequalities if they work to the benefit of the least well-off. John Rawls, *A Theory of Justice* (Cambridge, MA: Belknap Press of Harvard University Press, 1971), 75.

for survival and power as a principal motivating force in human conduct. A Thrasymachean theme is readily discernible in this interpretation of society.[57] And yet the seemingly nihilistic implications of this view are largely overborne by the heavily judgmental and moralistic character of contemporary social justice discourse, in which indignation, assertions of grievance, and accusations of unwarranted privilege and injustice are ubiquitous. And this pervasive indignation has its own expansionary logic because, as noted, without the redemptive potential of the providential view, it can seem that all of the ubiquitous inequalities *are* manifestations of injustice.

This analysis may also help to explain why, even as over the last century human welfare has improved and a host of governmental programs and antidiscrimination laws have attempted to attack injustices and reduce inequalities, the sense of grievance and victimhood seemingly proliferates and intensifies. Every group sees itself as aggrieved. Rage (or ressentiment, as Hunter calls it, borrowing from Nietzsche) becomes the condition of our time; it becomes "a perverse ontology, a mode of being."[58] And this mentality makes a certain kind of sense. After all, a group could hardly be perceived as an identifiable group at all unless it were differentiated in some way from others outside the group; but every such point of differentiation will almost inevitably correlate with differences—some advantageous, perhaps, but others disadvantageous—in status, power, wealth, or privilege. And if all such differences are presumptively injustices, then every group *is* to that extent aggrieved.

And thus the abandonment of the providential perspective leads quite naturally to the culture of victimhood in which everyone is aggrieved. But this is a condition, as noted, in which a liberal community (or any other community) can hardly be expected to flourish. A community, once again, is an "imagined" entity. It exists if people imagine themselves to be joined together in a common project. But how are people supposed to achieve such imaginings in a world in which there is no overall plan or purpose, and no justification for the ubiquitous inequalities that afflict the residents of such a society?

---

57. See generally Helen Pluckrose and James Lindsay, *Cynical Theories: How Activist Scholarship Made Everything about Race, Gender, and Identity—and Why This Harms Everybody* (Durham, NC: Pitchstone Publishing, 2022).

58. Hunter, *Democracy and Solidarity*, 425.

Liberalism without Foundations

Liberalism Unmoored

Liberalism today is or purports to be "freestanding," as Rawls put it—not grounded in any providential or other comprehensive doctrine. "Freestanding," however, is arguably a euphemism for "unmoored." And a liberalism that is unmoored—that has no anchor or foundation—is one with nothing to support it but also (and this condition may be even more worrisome) with nothing to limit or restrain it. Whether this unsupported and uncontained project is sustainable over the long run, or even the relatively short run, seems currently very much in doubt.

CHAPTER 7

Canceling the American Past?

Assessments of Justice William O. Douglas vary wildly, but I think it is one measure of the man to say that placed alongside of Douglas, most of our current justices look just a bit tame, or timid, or perhaps small. In that gaunt company, Douglas seems almost like a force of nature—a larger-than-life figure (for better or worse). And I would suggest that his distinctive stature owes something to his somewhat precarious relationship to truth.

A recent biography indicates (and in a lecture instituted in his honor I should put this gently) that Douglas was not in 100 percent agreement with thinkers like Kant, or Saint Augustine, who taught that we are categorically required to be honest in everything we say. Douglas many have departed further from that requirement than most of us do, or find acceptable, particularly in reporting on his own life.[1]

But if Douglas sometimes took liberties with the facts, there seems to be a sort of imaginative energy and recklessness and even courage in his ostensible fabrications: we wouldn't say that Douglas was too *timid* to tell the truth, or that he refrained from saying what he believed (or ruling as he thought right) for fear of offending someone. And perhaps owing to that

---

1. Bruce Allen Murphy, *Wild Bill: The Legend and the Life of William O. Douglas* (New York: Random House, 2003).

This chapter reproduces the 2005 William O. Douglas Lecture at Gonzaga Law School, which was titled "Justice Douglas, Justice O'Connor, and George Orwell: Does the Constitution Compel Us to Disown Our Past?" It appears in print here for the first time. I have not revised or updated the lecture, except that I have completed some citations and added the postscript, "The Orwellian Rewriting of History."

same recklessness or courage, I think Douglas also had an unusual, almost oracular capacity to grasp large, momentous truths—and to proclaim them with the eloquence that their gravity called for.

Whatever you may think about the result or the legal reasoning in *Griswold v. Connecticut*, for example, and however ironic the words may seem given Douglas's own marital adventures, his paean to marriage in the case seems moving and true.[2] We can understand why some couples have incorporated Douglas's language into their wedding ceremonies. And we may even wish that some scholars currently writing in a deflationary way about marriage would grasp the sense of Douglas's pronouncement.

My theme in this lecture, however, arises out of another of Douglas's celebrated utterances—his assertion in *Zorach v. Clauson*[3] that "we are a religious people whose institutions presuppose a Supreme Being." The statement has two parts. The first is sociological in nature: "We are a religious people." This seems to be basically an empirical proposition and, granting that it is a generalization subject to significant exceptions, most research seems to confirm it:[4] there is no reason why an atheist could not accept that conclusion, regretfully perhaps, as a purely empirical matter.

Justice Douglas's second claim is more political or perhaps theoretical in nature: our institutions presuppose a Supreme Being. For convenience, let's call this "the presupposition claim." To be sure, Douglas did not elaborate on exactly *how* our institutions presuppose a Supreme Being, nor did he offer evidence or argument in support of the presupposition claim. It is not surprising that he did not do these things: that would not have been Douglas's style. He tended to proclaim, or to declaim—to issue sweeping, majestic utterances. An uncommonly intelligent man, he surely had the

---

2. Griswold v. Connecticut, 381 U.S. 479, 486 (1965): "We deal with a right of privacy older than the Bill of rights—older than our political parties, older than our school system. Marriage is a coming together for better or for worse, hopefully enduring, and intimate to the degree of being sacred. It is an association that promotes a way of life, not causes; a harmony in living, not political faiths; a bilateral loyalty, not commercial or social projects. Yet it is an association for as noble a purpose as any involved in our prior decisions."

3. 343 U.S. 306, 313 (1952).

4. See generally George Gallup Jr. and D. Michael Lindsay, *Surveying the Religious Landscape: Trends in U.S. Beliefs* (Fayetteville, NC: Morehouse Publishing, 1999).

PART 3: PROVIDENTIALISM AND THE TRAVAILS OF LIBERALISM

capacity to offer close argument for his views if so inclined, but usually he was *not* so inclined; he seemed to lack the patience, or the motivation.

In this case, though, and writing in the early 1950s—the period in which "under God" was added to the Pledge of Allegiance and Ten Commandments monuments proliferated across the country—even a more fastidious justice might have thought that argument for Douglas's claim was superfluous. Douglas was merely reciting what millions of Americans took for granted—and what authoritative, prophetic interpreters of America from Jefferson to Lincoln to the president who had appointed Douglas to the bench (FDR) had said over and over and over again. Perhaps it would have seemed frivolous to support the assertion with argument or evidence: after all, even the most obsessive law review editors typically do not demand that an author provide supporting citations for sentences reporting that George Washington was the first president or that Thomas Jefferson came from Virginia.

That was a half century ago, though, and things have changed—drastically. The proposition that our institutions presuppose a Supreme Being cannot be taken for granted *now*. On the contrary, what may be the most influential understanding of our constitutional order (at least in the academy)—namely, the sort of "political liberalism" or secularist neutrality associated in various versions with people like John Rawls, Stephen Macedo, Amy Gutman, and Bruce Ackerman—insistently *denies* that our institutions presuppose any such thing. On the Court itself, an occasional justice—Justice Scalia, perhaps, or Justice Thomas—might still affirm Douglas's claim. And other justices conceivably might *quote* Douglas for historical or rhetorical purposes. But we would be shocked to find any similar outright declaration in a current Supreme Court majority opinion.[5] The Court today tries to be assiduously inoffensive—inoffensive to the people who count, anyway[6]—and to prevent other public officials from

---

5. A quick Westlaw search indicates that Douglas's statement was last quoted by a justice in a dissenting opinion by Chief Justice Burger in *Bender v. Williamsport Area School Dist.*, 475 U.S. 534, 554 (1986). The last majority opinion to quote the statement was *Lynch v. Donnelly*, 465 U.S. 668, 675 (1984).

6. The Court has not appeared greatly concerned about the exclusionary or alienating effects of its decisions on, say, Christian fundamentalists. For a thoughtful exploration of the problem, see Nomi Maya Stolzenberg, "'He Drew a Circle That Shut Me

doing or saying things that might offend those people or cause them to feel like "outsiders";[7] and it is obvious that official statements proclaiming that "we are a religious people whose institutions presuppose a Supreme Being" might easily have those undesired effects.

Thus, a public figure who tries to stand up in a conspicuous way for the conception of America that Douglas tersely asserted should be prepared to be reviled, perhaps sued, possibly (at least if he is, say, a state court judge in Alabama and stubborn) even removed from office.[8] And a public school teacher who actively taught students—in a civics lesson, perhaps—that "we are a religious people whose institutions presuppose a Supreme Being" would risk being disciplined for violating the constitutional doctrine forbidding governmental endorsement of religion.[9]

This reversal in the constitutional climate provokes questions. How exactly should we understand Justice Douglas's presupposition claim? Is the claim plausible? And what has happened in the half century since he asserted it? Could Douglas's claim have been true and appropriate when he made it but no longer true and appropriate? If so, how does a true theoretical or historical statement become untrue? More generally, given the change from Douglas's time to ours, how should we regard our political and constitutional heritage—a heritage that until relatively recently routinely generated statements like Douglas's? Those are the questions I want not to answer, unfortunately, but at least to think about in this lecture.

How Do Our Institutions "Presuppose a Supreme Being"?

We can start by trying to understand what Douglas's assertion might mean. The presupposition claim itself is familiar enough. The Pledge of Allegiance (at least for now) affirms succinctly that we are a nation "under God," and that phrase, though formally added to the Pledge in 1954, de-

---

Out': Assimilation, Indoctrination, and the Paradoxes of Liberal Education," *Harvard Law Review* 106 (1993): 581.

7. See, e.g., Allegheny County v. ACLU, 492 U.S. at 595 (plurality opinion by Blackmun, J.); Lynch v. Donnelly, 465 U.S. at 688 (O'Connor, J., concurring).

8. See, e.g., Glassroth v. Moore, 335 F.3d 1282 (11th Cir. 2003).

9. See Williams v. Vidmar, Case No. 504-CV-4946 JW PVT (U.S. Dist. Ct. N. Dist. Cal., pending).

PART 3: PROVIDENTIALISM AND THE TRAVAILS OF LIBERALISM

rives from Lincoln's Gettysburg Address,[10] which is by consensus acknowledged as one of the classic statements of the essential meaning of America. Historians collect mountains of similar statements from Americans both famous and forgotten over the centuries.[11] But in what sense might such statements be true? Exactly *how* might our institutions "presuppose a Supreme Being"?

I think there are two different kinds of answers to that question: we might call them the "providential" and the "philosophical" answers. These answers reflect different conceptions of the Supreme Being: the providential answer appeals to the kind of God portrayed in the Bible—to the God of Abraham, Isaac, and Jacob—while the philosophical answer is more reflective of what is sometimes called the God of the philosophers. But although these conceptions of deity are different, I do not believe they are incompatible (any more than it is incompatible to say that someone is a professor and also a parent). Many people surely have believed—and continue to believe—in both.

The providential answer maintains that a mindful, personal God works actively in history to bring about his purposes—it will be most convenient here to follow traditional usage in adopting the masculine pronoun—and that he blesses and causes to prosper not only individuals but also nations who acknowledge and reverence him. This faith can sometimes support triumphalism and smugness, but it need not: it can also express and inspire hope and humility and a struggle for justice on behalf of the poor and oppressed.

The providential view has obvious scriptural roots—particularly in the Hebrew scripture that Christians call the Old Testament but also emphatically (for those who accept it) in that distinctively American scripture, The Book of Mormon—and it has been affirmed in this country from the early days of the republic to the present in millions of speeches and sermons and

---

10. For discussion, see Michael J. Perry, *Under God? Religious Faith and Liberal Democracy* (New York: Cambridge University Press, 2003), 124–25.

11. See, e.g., Michael Novak, *On Two Wings: Humble Faith and Common Sense at the American Founding* (San Francisco: Encounter Books, 2002); James H. Hutson, *Religion and the Founding of the American Republic* ([Washington, DC]: Library of Congress, 1998); Patricia Bonomi, *Under the Cope of Heaven: Religion, Society, and Politics in Colonial America* (New York: Oxford University Press, 1988).

prayers and by figures small and great, from Washington and Adams to Lincoln to the second Bush. Lincoln's stunningly powerful Second Inaugural Address, engraved on one wall of the Lincoln Memorial, is probably the most profound statement of a providential interpretation of our experience by an American political leader.[12] But as a more characteristic expression we might recall a speech given by Benjamin Franklin in the Philadelphia convention. "In this situation of this Assembly," Franklin reasoned,

> groping as it were in the dark to find political truth, and scarce able to distinguish it when presented to us, how has it happened, Sir, that we have not hitherto once thought of humbly applying to the Father of lights to illuminate our understandings? In the beginning of the Contest with G. Britain, when we were sensible of danger we had daily prayer in this room for the divine protection.—Our prayers, Sir, were heard & they were graciously answered. All of us who were engaged in the struggle must have observed frequent instances of a superintending providence in our favor. To that kind providence we owe this happy opportunity of consulting in peace on the means of establishing our future national felicity.
>
> And have we now forgotten that powerful friend? or do we imagine that we no longer need his assistance? I have lived, Sir, a long time, and the longer I live, the more convincing proofs I see of this truth—*that God Governs in the affairs of men.* And if a sparrow cannot fall to the ground without his notice, is it probable that an empire can rise without his aid? We have been assured, Sir, in the sacred writings, that "except the Lord build the House they labour in vain that build it." I firmly believe this, and I also believe that without his concurring aid we shall succeed in this political building no better, than the Builder of Babel. We shall be divided by our little partial local

---

12. See Mark A. Noll, *America's God: From Jonathan Edwards to Abraham Lincoln* (New York: Oxford University Press, 2005), 426: "None of America's respected religious leaders—as defined by contemporaries or later scholars—mustered the theological power so economically expressed in Lincoln's Second Inaugural. None probed so profoundly the ways of God or the response of humans to the divine constitution of the world. None penetrated as deeply into the nature of providence. And none described the fate of humanity before God with the humility or the sagacity of the president."

interests; our projects will be confounded; and we ourselves shall become a reproach and bye word down to future ages.[13]

The more philosophical version of Justice Douglas's presupposition claim holds that our defining constitutional commitments can be explained and justified best—perhaps *only*—on theistic premises. As the Declaration of Independence explains, our rights to liberty and equality are themselves the gifts of the Almighty: they are rights with which we are "endowed by [our] Creator." "And can the liberties of a nation be thought secure," Thomas Jefferson asked, "when we have removed their only firm basis, a conviction in the minds of the people that these liberties are the gift of God?"[14]

In recent years, scholars like Jeremy Waldron, George Fletcher, and Louis Pojman[15] have raised essentially the same question with respect to our constitutional commitment to equality. Waldron observes that "it may seem to us now that we can make do with a purely secular notion of human equality; but as a matter of ethical history, that notion has been shaped and fashioned on the basis of religion. That is where all the hard work was done." And Waldron adds, "I actually don't think it is clear we—now—can shape and defend an adequate conception of basic human equality apart from some religious foundation."[16]

In a similar vein, Michael Perry has argued that the justification for human rights is "ineliminably religious."[17] In a different way, I have argued for the same conclusion.[18]

---

13. *Notes of Debates in the Federal Convention of 1787 Reported by James Madison* (New York: Norton, 1966), 209–10.

14. Thomas Jefferson, *Notes on the State of Virginia*, ed. Frank C. Shuffleton (New York: Penguin Books, 1999; original 1785), 169.

15. See Jeremy Waldron, *God, Locke, and Equality* (Cambridge: Cambridge University Press, 2002); George Fletcher, "In God's Image: The Religious Imperative of Equality under Law," *Columbia Law Review* 99 (1999): 1608; Louis Pojman, "On Equal Human Worth: A Critique of Contemporary Egalitarianism," in *Equality: Selected Readings*, ed. Louis P. Pojman and Robert Westmoreland (Oxford: Oxford University Press, 1997), 295.

16. Waldron, *God, Locke, and Equality*, 242, 13.

17. Michael J. Perry, *The Idea of Human Rights: Four Inquiries* (New York: Oxford University Press, 1998), 11–41.

18. Steven D. Smith, "Nonsense and Natural Law," in Paul F. Campos et al., *Against the Law* (Durham, NC: Duke University Press, 1996), 100.

I have been talking about commitments to *equality* and to *rights*. But more generally, it is arguable that an even more basic and constitutive commitment—to rule of law—rests on theistic assumptions. Though that suggestion will seem exotic today, it would not have seemed especially provocative to leading figures in the Anglo-American legal tradition from Alfred to Bracton to Fortescue to Coke to Blackstone—all of whom affirmed the basic idea that human law derives from the law of God. As Coke put it, a common law decision "agrees with the judicial law of god, on which our law is in every point founded."[19] In nineteenth-century America, likewise, judges and scholars routinely recited that "Christianity is part of the common law," and in a fascinating and illuminating article Stuart Banner shows that this maxim was significant not so much for any consequences it had for specific legal cases or controversies, but rather because it expressed "not a doctrine so much as a meta-doctrine." This metadoctrine helped support a "nonpositivist" view of the common law "as having an existence independent of the statements of judges,"[20] and hence as something that was there to be "discovered," not made.

Today, of course, we have been educated to follow Holmes in rejecting this older notion—held by the best legal minds over the centuries—of law as (in Holmes's mocking description) a "brooding omnipresence in the sky."[21] Thus, for generations now lawyers and scholars have been taught and have recited that law can be and has been established quite nicely on a purely human and positivistic footing. I am skeptical: though I cannot try even to summarize the analysis here, in a recent book I argue that the modern project of freeing law from its classical metaphysical commitments has failed.[22] If I am right, it might be a permissible simplification to assert, echoing Douglas, that our *legal* institutions "presuppose a Supreme Being."

---

19. Quoted in Jonathan Rose, "Doctrinal Development: Legal History, Law, and Legal Theory," *Oxford Journal of Legal Studies* 22 (2002): 334. For a brief discussion of similar views by leading figures in the common law tradition, see Steven D. Smith, *Law's Quandary* (Cambridge, MA: Harvard University Press, 2004), 46–47.

20. Stuart Banner, "When Christianity Was Part of the Common Law," *Law & History Review* 16 (1998): 27, 61, 50, 60.

21. Southern Pacific Co. v. Jensen, 244 U.S. 205, 222 (1917) (Holmes, J., dissenting).

22. Smith, *Law's Quandary*.

PART 3: PROVIDENTIALISM AND THE TRAVAILS OF LIBERALISM

The philosophical rationale for the presupposition claim can be offered in stronger or weaker versions. In the strongest version the rationale would assert that our commitments to equality, rights, and rule of law *can* be justified on theistic assumptions and *cannot* be justified in any other way. Though in the past I have sometimes made that sort of strong claim with respect to rights, today I would be more cautious, about both the positive and negative components. The theistic arguments for rights, equality, and law are complicated and subject to criticism, I think. And it is very hard to prove a negative: you might knock down one or several nontheistic rationales for rights or equality, for example, but how can you be sure that someone will not devise a better one? So a more modest version of the philosophical claim would assert that at least plausible theistic rationales for our constitutional commitments can be and have been offered, that as a historical matter these rationales have been powerfully influential in American thinking on the subject, and that it is not at all clear that nontheistic rationales can do as well.

That modest version seems to me wholly compelling, but before moving on, it is probably necessary to say something about—who else?—Mr. Jefferson. Jefferson was and remains a controversial character; but as author of the Declaration of Independence, statesman and president, and theorist and spokesman for American democracy, in our self-understanding Jefferson deservedly counts for a lot. And it is often said that Jefferson was a secular thinker, an Enlightenment figure, that he believed in rights and equality not on religious but rather on Lockean natural rights/social contract grounds, that if he believed in God at all it was in the detached, distant god of deism, that if he sometimes included religious references in his public pronouncements (and in the Declaration of Independence itself), this was only for public consumption.[23] If this interpretation of Jefferson is right, then it is fair to say that the presupposition claim is at least somewhat undermined.

But I think it is clear that the interpretation is misleading. Jefferson was to be sure a "secular" and "Enlightenment" thinker—but not in the sense that modern secularists want those terms to carry.[24] The subject warrants

23. See Michael P. Zuckert, *The Natural Rights Republic* (Notre Dame: University of Notre Dame Press, 1996), 56–61, 87–89.
24. For a discussion of the important differences between eighteenth-century and

lengthy discussion that I have neither the time nor the competence to provide, but fortunately some able historians have already supplied it. An overwhelming case for the theistic core of Jeffersonian thought is offered in Daniel Boorstin's *The Lost World of Thomas Jefferson*.[25] Or you could look at one of the best histories of the period—Henry May's *The Enlightenment in America*.[26] Boorstin observes that "Jefferson on more than one occasion declared 'the eternal pre-existence of God, and his creation of the world,' to be the foundation of his philosophy,"[27] and his book shows how Jefferson's declaration was correct. This theistic foundation was especially essential and conspicuous in Jefferson's thinking about politics, law, and rights: "no claim [of rights] could be validated except by the Creator's plan."[28] Henry May notes that "[a] benign God, a purposeful universe, and a universal moral sense are necessary at all points to Jefferson's political system."[29]

But wasn't Jefferson a "deist," a term which today may be taken to mean something like being 99 percent of the way to agnosticism? Well, though the label seems a bit slippery, it is accurate to call Jefferson a deist. But for Jefferson and his circle, deism in the sense of rational religion was wholly compatible not only with belief in God, but with belief in a God who actively guides history—and in particular the history of this nation. Thus, Boorstin reports that Jefferson "read in the peculiar physical conditions of America the Creator's designation of a special role." He "in his own terms ascribed to the American republic a . . . providential destiny."[30] It was Jefferson, after all, who proposed that the Great Seal of the United States should depict "the Children of Israel in the Wilderness, led by a Cloud by day, and a Pillar of Fire by night."[31]

---

twentieth-century interpretations of "the Enlightenment," see Steven D. Smith, "Recovering (from) Enlightenment?" *San Diego Law Review* 41 (2004): 1263.

25. Daniel J. Boorstin, *The Lost World of Thomas Jefferson* (Chicago: University of Chicago Press, 1993).

26. Henry F. May, *The Enlightenment in America* (New York: Oxford University Press, 1976).

27. Boorstin, *The Lost World*, 30.

28. Boorstin, *The Lost World*, 196.

29. May, *The Enlightenment in America*, 302.

30. Boorstin, *The Lost World*, 223–27.

31. Timothy L. Hall, "Roger Williams and the Foundation of Religious Liberty," *Boston University Law Review* 71 (1991): 455, 524n71.

PART 3: PROVIDENTIALISM AND THE TRAVAILS OF LIBERALISM

Might Jefferson have been merely pretending to be religious for public or political purposes? That interpretation seems implausible, not only because the religious references are so pervasive in his thinking and writing but, more importantly, because theistic premises are essential to the very logic of his arguments and views.

But suppose that the darkest suspicions (or, depending on your point of view, the most sanguine hopes) somehow turned out to be vindicated: some researcher discovers decisive evidence showing that privately, deep down, Jefferson was an out-and-out, not-in-front-of the-maids atheist, and that all of his religious references—in the Declaration, in his presidential speeches, in his writings and letters to colleagues and friends in the American Philosophical Society—were purely for political and rhetorical purposes. The discovery would surely be of interest to historians and biographers, and to any of us insofar as we take an interest in Jefferson for his own sake, but how exactly would it be significant for our assessment of Justice Douglas's presupposition claim? A successful politician—and Jefferson surely was one—might be viewed as someone with a good sense of what the electorate believes, and of what the electorate will accept as a good reason for supporting the politician and his projects. Even if what the politician says is not ultimately persuasive evidence of what *he personally believes*, it is still good evidence of *the beliefs that the political community accepted and acted on*.

After all is said and done, of course, historians of the period will surely continue to research and interpret and debate.[32] But I think it would be hard for anyone to deny that the providential view or the philosophical view or both have been held by millions upon millions of Americans from the early days of the republic through the present day. And taken together, they seem more than sufficient to justify Justice Douglas's assertion that "we are a religious people whose institutions presuppose a Supreme Being."

So then, how did that understanding of America come to be the disfavored target of lawsuits and constitutional doctrines in recent decades?

---

32. For an excellent collection of competing interpretations on the issue, see Thomas S. Engman and Michael P. Zuckert, eds., *Protestantism and the American Founding* (Notre Dame: University of Notre Dame Press, 2004).

Canceling the American Past?

What has happened to change the constitutional climate since Justice Douglas made his famous assertion?

The World Turned Upside Down?

A full explanation would surely be complex, but for present purposes we can limit ourselves to changes at the level of constitutional doctrine and, more specifically, to two crucial developments in the Supreme Court's interpretation of the First Amendment's establishment clause. The first crucial event occurred in 1971 when, drawing upon language from earlier decisions, the Supreme Court codified what (collapsing for present purposes the first and second prongs of the so-called *Lemon* test) we can call a "secularity" requirement. Government would be restricted to acting for secular purposes and in ways that have primarily secular effects.

In announcing this doctrine, the Court does not seem to have thought that it was saying anything especially momentous or controversial. Does anyone doubt that government is supposed to confine itself to the realm of the secular? The Court's assumption is understandable, because "secular" is an ambiguous term, and there are senses in which hardly anyone *does* doubt that American government is supposed to be secular.[33] I am a religious believer, and I have numerous friends and acquaintances who are religious believers, both conservative and liberal, and so far as I know I am not acquainted with a single person who wants government to get into the business of promoting baptism for the purpose of saving souls.

Because the term is ambiguous, however, the secularity requirement also created the possibility of equivocation, controversy, and unanticipated extension. For example, the *Lemon* Court does not seem to have anticipated that its doctrine might have the effect of excluding religious arguments and justifications from the "public square," as we say: it was not even until a decade and a half later that the "religion in the public square" debate really got going. But it was not long before lawyers and advocates began to realize—and promote—more restrictive versions of the secularity requirement.

---

33. For further discussion, see Steven D. Smith, "Nonestablishment under God? The Nonsectarian Principle," *Villanova Law Review* 50 (2005): 1, 4–6.

PART 3: PROVIDENTIALISM AND THE TRAVAILS OF LIBERALISM

One such extension occurred in the second crucial development I need to notice here. In 1984, Justice Sandra Day O'Connor proposed that the secularity requirement be extended to government expressions by means of a doctrine prohibiting government from endorsing religion.[34] Paradoxically, O'Connor offered this proposal as a rationale for upholding the inclusion of a crèche in a municipal Christmas display. Since the objection to the crèche was precisely that it endorsed religion—Christianity in particular—this was a very odd (or at least oddly timed) proposal; the insouciance of picking the crèche case as the occasion for introducing the "no endorsement" test provokes doubts about how much thought O'Connor had actually given to her own proposal. Suspicions of confused thinking may be reinforced if we recall that it was at about this same time that Justice O'Connor briefly made headlines by appearing to endorse a "Christian nation" interpretation of the country.[35]

But, perhaps appreciating the implications of O'Connor's proposal more clearly than she herself did, her opponents who dissented in the crèche case immediately embraced her suggestion. The "no endorsement" test was beguiling to nearly all commentators as well. (Including, I blush to admit, to me: I promptly wrote up an article praising O'Connor's proposal as the remedy for our establishment clause woes, but in the providential scheme of things none of the numerous law reviews to which I submitted the article wanted to publish it. There but for the grace of God . . .) In any case, within a few years the "no endorsement" doctrine had firmly entrenched itself in First Amendment jurisprudence.

It did not take long for people to realize, however, that a prohibition on governmental endorsements of religion would jeopardize or flat-out condemn a host of long-standing practices and celebrated documents and pronouncements—the national motto (In God We Trust), the Pledge of Allegiance ("under God"), a whole host of state and municipal seals and displays and practices, maybe even the names of half of the cities in California and Texas. That last item may seem facetious, but Douglas Laycock

---

34. *Lynch*, 465 U.S. at 688 (O'Connor, J., concurring).
35. For a brief account of the incident, see Christopher E. Smith and Linda Fry, "Vigilance or Accommodation: The Changing Supreme Court and Religious Freedom," *Syracuse Law Review* 42 (1991): 937–38.

does not seem to have been joking when he asserted in a law review article that in principle the names of Los Angeles and Corpus Christi *are* unconstitutional.[36] Looking backward, we can quickly see that even if we are charitable enough to excuse Lincoln and Washington and Jefferson and the signatories of the Declaration of Independence for violating a constitutional precept that had not yet been announced, those luminaries *did* contradict and transgress the "no endorsement" principle, over and over again.

Indeed, they did so deliberately and flagrantly and on the most solemn of public occasions, such as official proclamations and presidential inaugurations. In a proclamation Washington declared that "it is the duty of all nations"—notice that the duty applies to *nations*, not just to private individuals—"to acknowledge the providence of Almighty God, to obey His will, to be grateful for His benefits, and humbly to implore His protection and favor." Washington's successor, John Adams, issued a similar proclamation declaring that "the safety and prosperity of nations ultimately and essentially depend on the protection and the blessing of Almighty God, and the national acknowledgement of this truth is an indispensable duty which the people owe to him."[37] Jefferson's second inaugural implored the favor of "that Being in whose hands we are, who led our fathers, as Israel of old, from their native land and planted them in a country flowing with all the necessaries and comforts of life, who has covered our infancy with His providence and our riper years with His wisdom and power, and to whose goodness I ask you to join in supplications with me."[38] Or consider the preamble to Jefferson's famous Virginia Bill for Religious Freedom: "Almighty God hath created the mind free," such that compulsion in matters of religion represents "a departure from the plan of the Holy Author of our religion, who being Lord both of body and mind, yet chose not to

---

36. Douglas Laycock, "Equal Access and Moments of Silence: The Equal Status of Religious Speech by Private Speakers," *Northwestern University Law Review* 81 (1986): 8.

37. Reprinted in John T. Noonan Jr. and Edward McGlynn Gaffney Jr., *Religious Freedom: History, Cases, and Other Materials on the Interaction of Law and Religion* (New York: Foundation Press, 2001), 202–3.

38. Noonan and Gaffney, *Religious Freedom*, 206.

propagate it by coercions on either, as was in his Almighty power to do."[39] Do you detect any endorsement of religion there?

Jumping ahead closer to the present, Franklin D. Roosevelt declared in his 1939 State of the Union Address that "storms from abroad directly challenge three institutions indispensable to Americans, now as always. The first is religion. It is the source of the other two—democracy and international good faith."[40] Indeed, every single president from Washington to Bush has alluded or appealed to God in an inaugural address, and every state constitution acknowledges God.[41]

Or, to return to the statement with which we started: Justice Douglas asserted that "we are a religious people whose institutions presuppose a Supreme Being." Is there any plausible way to read that statement by which it does not endorse religion, or give nonbelievers cause to feel like "outsiders" in the political community? Remember that Douglas made the statement not as a private individual, not even in one of his flamboyant dissents, but rather officially, as part of a majority opinion speaking for the highest court in the land. If the Constitution forbids endorsement of religion, then surely Douglas and the Court were violating the Constitution when they made this famous assertion.

So, how are we as citizens today to regard our pervasively tainted history—tainted, that is, under the current "no endorsement" prohibition?

Disowning Our Past?

There are several possible responses to that question, I think: all of them entail a certain disavowal of our constitutional and political heritage. The starkest response would be straightforward repudiation of the offending portions of our heritage. Just as we have done with other regrettable parts of our past—slavery, for example—we could condemn past endorsements

---

39. Reprinted in Virginia Act for Religious Freedom, reprinted in *Church and State in the Modern Age: A Documentary History*, ed. J. F. MacClear (New York: Oxford University Press, 1995), 63–64.

40. "Franklin D. Roosevelt Speeches: Message to Congress; The New Deal," Pepperdine School of Public Policy, January 4, 1939, https://tinyurl.com/3mw4vju8.

41. William J. Federer, *The Ten Commandments and Their Influence on America Law* (St. Louis: Amerisearch, 2003), 49–55.

of religion and strive to eliminate persisting vestiges of those endorsements. That is of course what the Ninth Circuit tried to do in *Newdow*, the Pledge of Allegiance case,[42] and what a number of legal scholars think we should do with the Pledge and a few other such expressions, such as the national motto.[43]

But repudiation is not a politically viable response to the overall problem. We might be willing to eliminate a phrase here, a minor symbol there. But not many Americans—including law professors and justices—will cheerfully denounce all the significant parts of Jefferson's Virginia Statute, the Declaration of Independence, Lincoln's Second Inaugural, and on and on. The strategy would amount to a massive repudiation of much in our history that we have thought to be the most inspiring and praiseworthy.

So, what other responses are available? One tempting possibility is denial or repression, in the psychological sense. We might just try to avoid thinking about the discrepancy—to put the offending past out of mind. The Supreme Court's majority opinion in the *Newdow* case could be taken as a technical instance of this response. The dilemma facing the Court was apparent: on any honest view, the words "under God" in the Pledge *do* send a message endorsing religion, but it would also have been extremely inexpedient as a political matter for the Court to order that the words be stricken. So the Court understandably might have wished that the problem would just go away, and it used standing doctrine to achieve that happy evasion—at least for a year or so.[44]

---

42. Newdow v. United States Congress, 328 F. 3d 597 (9th Cir. 2002), rev. sub. nom. Elk Grove Unified School Dist. v. Newdow, 542 U.S. 1 (2004).

43. See, e.g., Douglas Laycock, "Comment: Theology Scholarships, the Pledge of Allegiance, and Religious Liberty; Avoiding the Extremes but Missing the Liberty," *Harvard Law Review* 118 (2004): 155, 223–31; Steven H. Shiffrin, "The Pluralistic Foundations of the Religion Clauses," *Cornell Law Review* 90 (2004): 9, 65–73; Steven G. Gey, "'Under God,' the Pledge of Allegiance, and Other Constitutional Trivia," *North Carolina Law Review* 81 (2003): 1865. See generally Steven B. Epstein, "Rethinking the Constitutionality of Ceremonial Deism," *Columbia Law Review* 96 (1996): 2083.

44. Actually, the Court conceded that Michael Newdow satisfied constitutional standing requirements. But there is a separate "prudential" standing component, the majority hastened to explain, that can be invoked to avoid deciding cases that there is good reason not to decide, and the majority grasped at this doctrine to avoid addressing the question on the merits.

PART 3: PROVIDENTIALISM AND THE TRAVAILS OF LIBERALISM

But again, the strategy of ignoring or forgetting is not promising as an overall response to the problem. The Pledge of Allegiance case will come up again; indeed, it is already pending. More generally, it is very hard just to forget our history, and hard to remember it while studiously neglecting to notice the discrepancies between what revered figures like Jefferson and Lincoln did and said and what current doctrine says public officials must *not* do. So perhaps we might try to rewrite our history so that the basic facts are acknowledged but the incongruities are removed. I have already suggested that Jefferson is often subjected to this sort of secularizing revisionism. Some commentators take the Rehnquist concurring opinion in *Newdow* as an example of this strategy: they read Rehnquist as saying that the addition of "under God" to the Pledge was a *patriotic* expression and therefore *not* a religious one. I happen to think that this is a misreading of Rehnquist's opinion,[45] but for present purposes it doesn't really matter: if Rehnquist didn't make this argument, other people and justices clearly have made arguments of this kind.[46]

Critics usually find this sort of revisionism unsatisfying, with good reason. The revisionism involves a deliberate distortion of the historical

---

45. Rehnquist did assert that the Pledge is "a patriotic exercise," but this assertion can be taken as a denial that the Pledge affirms a religious idea only if "patriotic" exercises and religious affirmations are somehow mutually exclusive or incompatible. Nothing in Rehnquist's opinion suggests that he perceives any such incompatibility. Rehnquist also asserted that recitation of the Pledge is not a "religious exercise" in the sense that prayer is, and is not an "establishment" of religion. But his assumptions seem to be that it is possible to affirm a religious idea without actually engaging in a religious or devotional exercise and without "establishing" religion. And this assumption seems eminently plausible. Suppose a public official is asked, "Do you believe in God?" and she replies, with apparent sincerity, "Yes, I do." She has thereby made a religious affirmation, but it would be odd to say that she has either engaged in a "religious exercise" or that she has "established" religion.

46. For example, Justice O'Connor has explained that the reason why expressions like the national motto, In God We Trust, or the announcement "God save the United States and this Honorable Court" are not unconstitutional is that those expressions serve to solemnize public occasions, or to express confidence in the future, or to encourage recognition of what is worthy in society. See, e.g., *Lynch*, 465 U.S. at 693 (O'Connor, J., concurring). The claim seems to be that because these expressions serve those secular purposes, they are therefore not endorsements of religion, which would be unconstitutional.

record. In addition, the particular version of the argument ascribed by critics to Rehnquist—and plainly discernible, I would say, in some of Justice O'Connor's explanations—insults our intelligence, because it tries to get us to accept a blatant non sequitur. Patriotic expressions and religious expressions are not mutually exclusive—far from it—so the argument "patriotic, therefore *not* religious" seems an error that even a child could spot. It brings to mind the *Dilbert* cartoon in which Dogbert says: "I was wondering, Dilbert, whether you were stupid or just incredibly ignorant. But then I thought to myself, 'Whoa, Dogbert, you're being narrow-minded. He could easily be both.'"[47]

Despite these embarrassments, the revisionist strategy is a way to avoid repudiating a vast portion of our political heritage. Or perhaps not—because if we formally preserve our past only by fundamentally transforming its meaning—its substance—haven't we thereby repudiated our heritage *as it actually was* and as we have heretofore accepted it?

There might be a way to avoid these problems: perhaps we could acknowledge that the expressions of Jefferson and Washington and Lincoln, and the 1954 Congress, were in fact religious *at the time they were made*, so that they would be constitutionally objectionable if made in the same sense and spirit today: but in fact we do not have to disavow them because, *by now*, for us—for us *as a people*, that is—they have lost their religious character (though they may still have that character for some citizens *as individuals*). This is essentially the tactic adopted by Justice O'Connor in her *Newdow* concurrence.[48]

The appeal of this approach is apparent, I think: it lets us keep the Pledge intact without either trying to avoid the problem (as the majority did) or falsifying history and offending logic (as some said Rehnquist did). But there are still problems, and they are not small ones. The first is probably the most obvious: what Justice O'Connor says about even the current meaning of the Pledge is manifestly implausible. It simply is not true that today the words

---

47. Dilbert's response is: "It only looks easy."
48. See 542 U.S. at 33–45 (O'Connor, J., concurring) ("Whatever the sectarian ends its authors may have had in mind, our continued repetition of the reference to 'one Nation under God' in an exclusively patriotic context has shaped the cultural significance of that phrase to conform to that context. Any religious freight the words may have been meant to carry originally has long since been lost").

PART 3: PROVIDENTIALISM AND THE TRAVAILS OF LIBERALISM

"under God" in the Pledge have lost their religious significance for anyone who pays any attention to them. Thus, Douglas Laycock observes that "this rationale is unconvincing both to serious nonbelievers and to serious believers."[49] Steven Shiffrin concurs. "I am sure," Shiffrin reports, "that a pledge identifying the United States as subject to divine authority is asserting the existence and authority of the divine." And he adds that "pretending [that this and similar expressions] are not religious is simply insulting."[50]

I tried an unscientific test of these observations by giving a multiple choice test regarding the *Newdow* case to my law and religion seminar. I asked the students to choose among four options:

1. The words "under God" in the Pledge are constitutional because they do not actually endorse religion.
2. The words are *unconstitutional* because they *do* endorse religion.
3. The words are constitutional because, although they endorse religion, the endorsement is *de minimis*.
4. The whole approach to this issue needs to be rethought.

Options 2, 3, and 4 each received some support from the class. Not a single student voted for option 1, which is in fact Justice O'Connor's rationale.

It is worth pausing to appreciate this situation. Justice O'Connor has all along been the major sponsor of the "no endorsement" doctrine, and her account of why the Pledge of Allegiance does not violate that doctrine probably comes as close as any interpretation can to being the official explication of the doctrine. By that interpretation, we can and will save portions of our national heritage by clenching our teeth and making representations about that heritage that, even as we make them, we have to know are simply not believable. Not true.

And it is not just Justice O'Connor who finds herself in this position. Other justices will do the same. Public officials who want to defend traditional, revered practices and expressions are forced to resort to the same sorts of transparent misdescriptions. There is no time here to discuss the details, but we will see—we have already seen—a similar phenomenon in

49. Laycock, "Comment: Theology Scholarships," 235.
50. Shiffrin, "The Pluralistic Foundations," 70–71.

recent controversies about the Ten Commandments.[51] We see it in establishment clause controversies of various types, around the nation. It is a troubling jurisprudence, I think, that places citizens and officials in the position of routinely having to make affirmations that they cannot seriously believe to be true. Or, to put the point more crudely, of *lying*.

But suppose I am wrong about this—along with Laycock and Shiffrin and all the students in my seminar. Suppose Justice O'Connor is right in saying that the words "under God" in the Pledge originally had religious significance but that for us as a people (as distilled into an "objective observer") they no longer have that significance and hence are constitutionally permissible. The implication is that if Congress were to reenact the 1954 provision today, or were to enact it for the first time today, the exact same words would in that case be unconstitutional. That seems curious. And it provokes questions.

For example, does O'Connor's view entail that the words "under God" in the Pledge actually were unconstitutional at the time they were added, so that in theory if they had been challenged in a lawsuit at that time they should have been declared unconstitutional by a prescient court? So was it only thanks to a fortuity—that no one sued, that the courts did not yet adequately understand the First Amendment—that the words survived

---

51. See Dahlia Lithwick, "The High Court Should Stop Its Disingenuous Sidestep of the Church-State Debate," *American Lawyer* 26 (December 2004): 122:

> This same duality will be apparent in the arguments advanced by each side of the Decalogue Debate. Next winter, we will witness oral advocates arguing before the high court—with a straight face, mind you—that the commands possess absolutely no spiritual significance for anyone; they are purely "historical artifacts." And precisely as they intone this constitutional equivalent of the philanderer's mantra ("She means nothing to me, honest!"), angry citizens on the marble plaza before the Court will be waving signs saying, "Put God back into Government" and "Yahweh or the Highway."
>
> By the same token, atheists and civil libertarians on the other side—folks who have survived decades of Sunday School and reruns of CBS's Touched by an Angel—will insist, in Court and out on the plaza, that even a passing glance at "Honor Thy Father and Mother" will either turn their children into mad evangelicals, or open the door to a lifetime of religious persecution and ostracizing.

long enough to achieve constitutional status? The words were unconstitutional *then*, in 1954, and they would also be unconstitutional *now*, if freshly enacted, but under some sort of constitutional laches notion words that both *were* and *would be* unconstitutional are not?

Or should we rather say that the constitutional principle itself changed, so that it was all right for government to endorse religion in 1954 but it became unacceptable later on? So the words were constitutional then and now—though only because their meaning has fortuitously changed in beautiful parallel with changes in the governing constitutional principle?

Either way, I can't help thinking that there is something very odd about this position. Suppose we try to apply the same logic to some other classic statement from our history. Can a public school teacher, for example, display the national motto—In God We Trust—in class? Can she recite the Declaration of Independence to students—in particular the part about "Nature and Nature's God" or the affirmation that we are "endowed by our Creator with certain unalienable rights"? The answer is contested, no doubt, and the issues are just beginning to surface in actual disputes. Thus far, the litigation has mostly focused on more conspicuous expressions, such as prayers and reproductions of the Ten Commandments.

But the essence of the precedents and of Justice O'Connor's explanations is this, I think: it is all right for the public schools to read from the Declaration of Independence so long as they are engaged in an objective teaching of the facts of our history. Conversely, if a public school teacher reads from the Declaration as a way of promoting the theistic beliefs expressed in that document, she endorses religion and thereby violates the First Amendment as the Court currently construes it. On television I recently heard a civil rights attorney give exactly this explanation in connection with a recent case in which a Cupertino, California, public school teacher had been disciplined for his use of the Declaration of Independence and similar documents in class. And as an interpretation of existing doctrines and precedents, I think the attorney's explanation was persuasive.

And yet this seems to me a very peculiar instruction to give to teachers or other public officials and employees: "You are permitted to talk about and even read from the document which more than any other has been thought to express this nation's most fundamental commitments—but only so long as you do not actually mean to affirm and promote the rationale for those commitments that is explicitly asserted in that document." How can it be that the government of a country and its officials are permitted to *report* but not actually to *affirm* the beliefs on which the country was founded?

GEORGE ORWELL AND THE DISAVOWAL OF HISTORY

In contemplating this state of affairs, an adjective that naturally comes to mind is "Orwellian," and though it is probably overused, in this case I believe that the adjective comes close to being apt. The term is understood, of course, as an allusion to George Orwell's chilling dystopian novel[52] about a society that is horrible in many respects; but one of them is that the government—Big Brother—is engaged in a massive, ongoing effort (implemented in the Ministry of Truth) to reshape history to fit current political needs and enhance the power of the Party. If the nation, Oceania, is currently at war with Eurasia, then citizens must and do believe that the nation was *always* at war with Eurasia. If tomorrow foreign policy shifts so that Oceania is at peace with Eurasia but at war with Eastasia, then citizens must and will believe that the nation has always been at peace with Eurasia and at war with Eastasia. History is what the nation, or at least the Party, needs it to be.

This manipulation is possible only through the cultivation of a technique known as "doublethink." The master of doublethink must be able "to tell deliberate lies while genuinely believing in them, to forget any fact that has become inconvenient, and then, when it becomes necessary again, to draw it back from oblivion for just so long as it is needed."[53]

The protagonist in the story, Winston Smith, quietly resists the government in various respects, but perhaps above all he resists its efforts to manipulate history. In a struggle to remember the past as it was, he clings to memories (even painful ones) of his own childhood; he questions people who lived before the present tyranny; he finds and treasures objects from an earlier time. At great risk to himself he saves, in his memory, a document that he once held in his hand and that, while inconsequential in itself,

---

52. George Orwell, *1984* (New York: Signet Classics, 1961; original 1949).
53. Orwell, *1984*, 177.

PART 3: PROVIDENTIALISM AND THE TRAVAILS OF LIBERALISM

proves that at least one event in the past did not happen in the way Big Brother currently represents it. When he undertakes the almost suicidally dangerous task of meeting and speaking openly with O'Brien, whom at that point Winston believes to be part of the resistance, his last toast upon parting emphasizes the importance of truthfully remembering the past.

> "What shall it be this time?" [O'Brien] said, still with the same faint suggestion of irony. "To the confusion of the Thought Police? To the death of Big Brother? To humanity? To the future?"
> "To the past," said Winston.
> "The past is more important," agreed O'Brien gravely.[54]

In the end, Winston's efforts come to naught: the Party's power to rewrite—and thus, in effect, destroy—history overwhelms him.

Today we have nothing quite like the Ministry of Truth; cynics might propose analogies, but the differences, fortunately, are large. (Even in the novel, one difficulty is that it is hard to imagine how such a massive effort in manipulation could succeed.) But although this is not *1984*, it is arguable that similar processes (and a large measure of doublethink) are at work in the Court-directed effort to avoid the embarrassment that so much in our history—so much that we have previously revered and celebrated and regarded as foundational for our political community—is at odds with what currently articulated constitutional doctrine prescribes. So it was a fitting fortuity, perhaps, that it was in 1984 that the "no endorsement" doctrine entered constitutional jurisprudence.

As I have suggested, that doctrine has in some unmeasurable proportion reflected or brought about a sort of constitutional revolution. As a result, in 1952 constitutional decisions could be based on the truism (as it then seemed) that "we are a religious people whose institutions presuppose a Supreme Being," whereas a half century later not only is that truism no longer deemed true, its utterance as an official matter by public officials is at least in principle forbidden by prevailing constitutional doctrine. What *was* true then *now* cannot even be said—not officially, at any rate, not if current doctrine is faithfully followed.

54. Orwell, *1984*, 145–46.

Canceling the American Past?

As I have tried to argue, this transformation entails a disowning of our history in one way or another. To summarize, current constitutional doctrine would seem to require that we repudiate the official vestiges of the religious aspects of our past. Or, if we find that prescription unacceptable, we may try to ignore or forget about the past. Insofar as we are unable or unwilling to adopt one of these measures—insofar, that is, as we are determined to remember and maintain our history—it seems we must choose between rewriting that history to eliminate its religious character, or else acknowledging the religious character of our past but insisting that this religious quality has dissipated with the passage of time. Either of these alternatives is likely to require an effort in falsification or doublethink: the first alternative involves falsifying the past (as in the secularist interpretation of Jefferson), while the second will usually involve falsifying the present (as in Justice O'Connor's *Newdow* opinion). And either alternative deprives us of the privilege and possibility of actually affirming our past—celebrating it for *what and how it actually was* and ascribing to it a continuing validity and authority.[55]

So, what is so regrettable about this disowning of actual history and this fabrication of a newer, more acceptable history? From some points of view—from a darkly cynical perspective, for instance, or conversely, from a highly sanguine and secular progressive perspective—the answer is probably "nothing."[56] Holmes said it: "Continuity with the past is only a necessity and not a duty."[57] So to the extent that we can escape from a questionable past, we should do so. It is lamentable that our governments,

---

55. It is perhaps a symptom of the contempt for historical truth that the current doctrinal regime promotes that the one opinion in *Newdow* that tried honestly to face up to the historical fact that modern establishment doctrine and decisions are based on demonstrable misreadings of the past causes its author—Justice Clarence Thomas—to be promptly denounced as being on the "lunatic fringe." See Brian Leiter, "The U.S. Supreme Court Dodges a Bullet," *Leiter Reports*, June 15, 2004, https://tinyurl.com/bdebttzw.

56. In Orwell's novel, not everyone who acknowledges the falsification cares: Winston's lover Julia sees nothing especially troubling in the fact that the government routinely tells lies, including lies about history. Orwell, *1984*, 127–29.

57. Oliver Wendell Holmes, *Collected Legal Papers* (New York: Harcourt, Brace & Howe, 1920), 211.

PART 3: PROVIDENTIALISM AND THE TRAVAILS OF LIBERALISM

by endorsing religion in a variety of ways, have often caused some citizens to feel like outsiders; but that is no excuse for causing such offense in the future.

In response, I would very quickly offer three observations. First, it seems to me that we are sometimes unjustifiably complacent in taking national continuity for granted. What is it that holds a diverse group of people with different languages, backgrounds, and interests together as a political community? The matter is surely complex and even, I think, mysterious. Nations, we are plausibly told, are "imagined communities"[58]—it is perceived or imagined bonds that cause us to think of ourselves as a continuing nation called "The United States of America"—and a common revered history is surely one of the most important bases of such imaginings. Insofar as we treat our history as something to be forgotten or disowned or overcome, these bonds are broken and cast off, and the question "Why are we a nation?" becomes more urgent, and more troubling. We might have learned from the twentieth century that even nations that appeared formidable and secure can unexpectedly come apart, sometimes with devastating consequences. In this situation, I would suggest that complacency toward the historical foundations of our community is reckless and irresponsible.

Second, the progressive rejection of history depends on the assumption that things are getting better, not worse. And most of us probably believe that in many important respects, our current constitutional self-understanding *is* an improvement over past versions—slavery is again the most salient case in point. But at least for myself, I would not place the affirmations in the Declaration of Independence—neither the conclusions nor the premises—in the same category as slavery. More generally, if we have to choose between the providential understanding of America articulated in different ways by people like Jefferson and Lincoln, and the secularized understanding advanced by the likes of Professor Rawls, Professor Ackerman, and Justice O'Connor, while others may differ, I do not think this is a close question.

Orwell's novel suggests a third reason why we might regret the disavowal or falsification of the past. Why, after all, does Winston place so

---

58. Benedict Anderson, *Imagined Communities: Reflections on the Origin and Spread of Nationalism* (London: Verso, 2006).

much importance on remembering the past? In part, because the memory gives him hope that things have been, and hence could be, better than they are now. And he regrets the loss of a past that included "Chaucer, Shakespeare, Milton, Byron."[59] (An American version of this list might include the Declaration of Independence and Lincoln's Second Inaugural.) Winston knows that the Party's ability to manipulate the past is also a central source of its power over people, so that remembering the past may be a way of resisting that power.

But it seems to me that something more is at work. Winston is fighting to maintain the possibility of being actually human. He is not sanguine about the possibility: his last words before being arrested are "We are the dead"—an assertion immediately echoed by his lover Julia and then by the agent of the Thought Police.[60] But Winston senses that part of being human is an ability to believe things because they seem to be true, and this commitment to truth seems to have special force for him with respect to the past. Why?

Perhaps the answer is something like this: We human beings are finite creatures situated in place and time, in history, and we maintain our identity and continuity—our mortal reality, really—by maintaining our connection to a history. Conversely, if we are cut off from our history, or if we degrade our history into a mutable fabrication fashioned not according to truth but rather by present perceived needs, then we lose our identity and become merely transitory phantoms of shifting consciousness and conversation, without continuity or substance. One of Winston's colleagues, Syme, is at one point a character in the story, but then his name and identity are blotted out and he becomes an "unperson." In this way, a person can be "lifted clean out of the stream of history," as Orwell puts it, as if he never existed. Our reality is inextricably tied, we might say, to our historicity.

I am not sure whether this is a valid account of personal identity. But the account seems worth entertaining, and it seems even more cogent for a *people*, or a community or nation, than for individuals. For a nation, history is not merely what holds it together: it is only as a historical entity

---

59. Orwell, *1984*, 47.
60. Orwell, *1984*, 182.

that a nation enjoys reality in the first place. After all, does anyone believe that a political community has anything like an immaterial soul that might give it identity independent of its temporal history?

And in this view, it seems that whether this nation can "long endure," as Lincoln put it, depends among other things on having leaders who are bold enough, or at least reckless enough, to proclaim the large, enduring truths that constitute it. Truths like "we are a religious people whose institutions presuppose a Supreme Being."

Postscript: The Orwellian Rewriting of History

One possible approach to a history that under the modern orthodoxy is constitutionally dubious, as the lecture suggests, is to rewrite that history in Orwellian fashion; but the lecture adds that nothing in modern jurisprudence or scholarship is as overt and deliberate in this respect as what happens in Orwell's novel. "Today," the lecture observed, "we have nothing quite like the Ministry of Truth; cynics might propose analogies, but the differences, fortunately, are large."

Or perhaps not so large.

One recent and prominent example occurs in the book *The Religion Clauses: The Case for Separating Church and State*, written by Howard Gillman and Erwin Chemerinsky and published by Oxford University Press.[61] Both authors are major academic figures. Gillman has been chancellor of the University of California at Irvine. Chemerinsky, a well-known and respected legal academic and the author of outstanding treatises in constitutional law and federal courts, has been dean of the law school at the University of California at Berkeley and past president of the Association of American Law Schools.

Gillman and Chemerinsky's central contention is that "the Constitution meant to and should be interpreted as creating a secular republic, meaning that the government has no role in advancing religion and that religious belief and practice should be a private matter."[62] That view is common enough today, as we have seen: it has basically been the constitutional orthodoxy since

---

61. Howard Gillman and Erwin Chemerinsky, *The Religion Clauses: The Case for Separating Church and State* (New York: Oxford University Press, 2020).

62. Gillman and Chemerinsky, *The Religion Clauses*, 19.

the 1960s. And we have seen how, on the "repository of principles" conception of the Constitution, it is at least possible to argue that the Constitution or the First Amendment prescribes a secular republic, even if the founders mostly did not draw that conclusion for their own times and indeed repeatedly and unapologetically mixed religion and governance in various ways.

Gillman and Chemerinsky want to make a stronger argument, however; they want to contend that the founders themselves consciously intended to create a secular republic, even for their own times. They are like the Big Brother who is not content to have people believe that we are at war with Eurasia *now*; people must believe that we have *always* been at war with Eurasia. So then, how do these distinguished authors deal with the mountain of evidence that seems to contradict their thesis?

Basically, by careful selection, recharacterization, and if necessary misrepresentation of the evidence.

Thus, pressing their argument, Gillman and Chemerinsky claim that "by the time the American Republic was founded there would be no references in the founding documents to a Supreme Being."[63] That statement is sufficiently important, and audacious, that it bears repeating. *"By the time the American Republic was founded there would be no references in the founding documents to a Supreme Being."*

This seems a heroic claim given that, as Laura Underkuffler-Freund has written, at the time of the founding,

> governmental papers were replete with mention of "God," "Nature's God," "Providence," and other religious references. Religious references on the Great Seal of the United States were apparently deemed desirable by conservatives and reformers alike. When proposed designs were solicited, Franklin suggested an image of Moses lifting up his wand and dividing the Red Sea, with the motto "Rebellion to tyrants is obedience to God," and Jefferson proposed the children of Israel in the wilderness "led by cloud by day and a pillar of fire by night." Reformers tolerated such references, apparently, because they were not believed to implicate core concerns.[64]

---

63. Gillman and Chemerinsky, *The Religion Clauses*, 32.
64. Laura Underkuffler-Freund, "The Separation of the Religious and the Secular," *William & Mary Law Review* 36 (1995): 954–55 (footnotes omitted).

PART 3: PROVIDENTIALISM AND THE TRAVAILS OF LIBERALISM

But perhaps the "Great Seal of the United States" and all of the founding-era "governmental papers" referred to by Underkuffler-Freund do not count as "founding documents"? If Gillman and Chemerinsky meant to limit their claim to the Constitution itself, then their assertion would be plausible enough, as we have seen. And yet it would seem odd to say that the Constitution was the *only* founding document, and indeed the authors' use of the plural—"founding documents"—suggests that they intend no such limit. So then, what else might count as a founding document?

Perhaps the Declaration of Independence? For many (like Lincoln and, as we have seen, John Courtney Murray), the Declaration is *the* quintessential founding document. After all, the "four score and seven years ago" of Lincoln's Gettysburg Address dated the nation (the "nation, under God") back to the Declaration, not to the Constitution. Now, it is true that the Declaration does not use the exact words "Supreme Being." But the document does appeal, not peripherally but in its essential argument, to "the Creator" and to "Nature and Nature's God." And the Declaration concludes with a statement of trust in "Divine Providence."

Or what about Jefferson's seminal Virginia Statute for Religious Liberty? Though formally applicable only within the state of Virginia, that statute has often been invoked as the nation's pathbreaking legal commitment to religious freedom, and the Supreme Court has more than once cited it as such.[65] The eminent historian Bernard Bailyn described the Statute as "the most important document in American history bar none."[66] Gillman and Chemerinsky do not appear to disagree; they discuss Jefferson's Statute at some length, and with obvious approval. And yet the Statute would seem to be an embarrassment to their central thesis. It begins, after all, with an eloquent and thoroughly theism-laced preamble:

> Whereas *Almighty God* hath created the mind free; that all attempts to influence it by temporal punishments, or burdens, or by civil in-

---

65. See, e.g., Flast v. Cohen, 392 U.S. 83, 104 (1968); McGowan v. Maryland, 366 U.S. 420, 437 (1961); Everson v. Board of Education, 330 U.S. 1, 12–13 (1947).

66. Quoted in Vincent Phillip Munoz, *Religious Liberty and the American Founding: Natural Rights and the Original Meaning of the First Amendment Religion Clauses* (Chicago: University of Chicago Press, 2022), 69.

capacitations, tend only to beget habits of hypocrisy and meanness, and are a departure from the plan of *the Holy Author of our religion*, who being *lord both of body and mind*, yet chose not to propagate it by coercions on either, as was in *his Almighty power* to do; that the impious presumption of legislators and rulers, civil as well as ecclesiastical, who, being themselves but fallible and uninspired men, have assumed dominion over the faith of others.[67]

The preamble continues at considerable length, but the first clauses are obviously replete with references to God (which I have italicized).

So then, how do Gillman and Chemerinsky explain away this language, or square it with their contention that there were "no references in the founding documents to a Supreme Being"?

Simple: they edit the theistic language out of their quotation. Gillman and Chemerinsky do give an extended quotation from the preamble. But they simply omit to quote the first clauses, and instead begin with "the impious presumption of legislators and rulers . . ."[68]

Consider a second example. It is well known—and thus hardly to be overlooked—that both the House and the Senate in the first Congress appointed chaplains to begin legislative sessions with prayer. The first Congress and its actions have often been regarded as entitled to special deference in constitutional interpretations, in part because many of the drafters and enactors of the Constitution were serving in that Congress. So the legislators' approval of chaplains stands as an obstacle to the claim that the founders intended to establish a secular republic in which religion and governance would not be mixed. Advocates of the secular republic position have often noticed this difficulty and have tried to deflect it in various ways—by, for example, contending that Congress was acting from "unreflective bigotry" and in violation of constitutional principles. We considered these arguments in chapter 2.

So then, how do Gillman and Chemerinsky address the difficulty? Here is their treatment: "The first Congress hired Christian chaplains (of dif-

---

67. "Bill for Establishing Religious Freedom, 1786," reprinted in *The Founding Fathers and the Debate over Religion in Revolutionary America*, ed. Matthew L. Harris and Thomas S. Kidd (New York: Oxford University Press, 2012), 79 (emphasis added).
68. Gillman and Chemerinsky, *The Religion Clauses*, 33.

PART 3: PROVIDENTIALISM AND THE TRAVAILS OF LIBERALISM

ferent denominations) to offer prayers but did so over the objections of James Madison, who argued that such a practice violated the Establishment Clause and also discriminated against religious groups such as Quakers and Catholics 'who could scarcely be elected to office.'"[69] If this report were accurate, it would still leave the authors' strong "secular republic" thesis in a perilous state, because it would seem that the large majority of founders saw no problem with legislative chaplains. Still, Gillman and Chemerinsky at least might claim the weighty support of James Madison, often described as the "Father of the Constitution" and a leading sponsor of the Bill of Rights.

But in fact the report is profoundly misleading.[70] What Gillman and Chemerinsky fail to tell readers is that at the time of Congress's chaplain decision, Madison apparently did *not* raise any objection. On the contrary, he sat on the committee that recommended the appointment of chaplains, and he seems to have supported the recommendation. Later—decades later—Madison did indeed come to hold the objection referred to by Gillman and Chemerinsky;[71] but even then he did not assert that objection publicly. Rather, he expressed his view in a private memorandum that was not even made public during Madison's lifetime.[72] Readers, of course, would be unable to discern any of this from Gillman and Chemerinsky's description, which clearly implies that Madison made his constitutional objection openly in Congress at the time of the chaplain decision.

There is in America today no official Ministry of Truth. But there are nonetheless those who are willing and able to perform a similar function.

---

69. Gillman and Chemerinsky, *The Religion Clauses*, 40.

70. The inaccuracy of the report is actually apparent on the face of the description. Madison could hardly have argued that the appointment of chaplains "violated the Establishment Clause" because at the time of the appointment the establishment clause had not yet been enacted.

71. James Madison, "Detached Memoranda," *The Founders' Constitution*, ed. Philip B. Kurland and Ralph Lerner, vol. 5 (Chicago: University of Chicago Press, 1987), document 64.

72. See Mark David Hall, *Did America Have a Christian Founding?* (Nashville: Nelson, 2019), 82.

EPILOGUE

"Only a God Can Save Us"

Through much of the country's history, Americans understood themselves as constituting a nation "under God." And this understanding was not merely peripheral; it was constitutive, or essential to what made America the nation it was.

The providentialist understanding provided Americans with a sense of purpose: their republic was not just an association formed for the benefit of its members, but rather a crucial chapter in a larger providential narrative. This understanding informed public discourse, and sometimes managed to elevate that discourse at its best into, as John Coleman observed, "a rhetoric contain[ing] rich, polyvalent symbolic power to command commitments and of emotional depth, when compared to 'secular' language."[1] Indeed, nations being "imagined communities,"[2] the providential perspective was central to Americans' ability to imagine themselves as a community, or as a nation. And Americans understood their Constitution, in itself religiously agnostic, not as mandating a providentialist public philosophy, but as permitting such a philosophy. This providentialist self-understanding lasted at least through the mid-twentieth century. It was conspicuous in public rhetoric in the 1950s—the era of "piety on the Potomac"—as the nation acted to distinguish itself from "godless Communism."

By now, conversely, as the twenty-first century unfolds, public providentialism has been largely lost. Who knows? Perhaps providentialism

---

1. John Coleman, *An American Strategic Theology* (Eugene, OR: Wipf & Stock, 2005), 193–94.
2. See Benedict Anderson, *Imagined Communities: Reflections on the Origin and Spread of Nationalism* (London: Verso, 2006).

would have faded anyway, as Americans increasingly follow the rest of the Western world into a secularist individualism in which the prevailing object of obeisance is not God but rather something like personal fulfillment or authenticity.[3] But what *might* have happened is a matter of counterfactual speculation. What actually *did* happen was that the Supreme Court officially banished the providential perspective and thereby—we borrow from the assessment of John Courtney Murray—effectively established atheism, not, to be sure, as any comprehensive philosophy (as it had been in Marxist regimes), but as a component of or constraint on the *public* philosophy. Perhaps unwittingly, the Court instigated this transformation when it reconstrued or reconstructed the Constitution to require government to be "neutral" toward religion and to confine governance to the domain of the secular.

In an odd reversal, it is now the formerly Communist and atheistic countries (along with the Islamic nations, of course) that, however opportunistically, publicly embrace God and religion in order to distinguish themselves from the (officially) godless, secular West.[4]

And what has replaced providentialism as the foundation for national purpose and public discourse, and for a sense of national identity as a community? Perhaps nothing. Perhaps the nation's destiny, as thinkers like John Rawls and Richard Rorty have contended, is to manufacture its own destiny—to do without foundations. But is nationhood without foundations a viable project?

It is a hard question, but the indications as of now are not encouraging. The highest purpose currently imaginable that might inform some public philosophy is to facilitate each individual in satisfying personal preferences and achieving personal fulfillment or authenticity in whatever form he, she, they, or it may prefer. This highly individualistic and self-centered ideal[5] is

---

3. See Steven D. Smith, *The Disintegrating Conscience and the Decline of Modernity* (Notre Dame: University of Notre Dame Press, 2023), chapter 3.

4. For an essay criticizing Russia's proreligious stance as purely cynical and opportunistic, see Cyril Hovorun, "'Traditional Values' Are Russia's Geopolitical Weapons," *Public Discourse*, July 26, 2023, https://tinyurl.com/3xswkmnn. For a somewhat more sympathetic treatment, see Matthew Del Santo, "Theopolitics of Ukraine," *First Things*, August 2023, https://tinyurl.com/mwwemrhp.

5. For insightful studies of this modern condition, see Carl Trueman, *The Rise and

pervasively reflected in our public discourse—when it manages to remain civil and positive, that is; increasingly those qualities seem to elude us, and our discourse deteriorates into clashing accusations of irrationality, selfishness, and bigotry. And instead of conceiving of America as a community engaged in some common project, "often it feels," as longtime foreign correspondent Nick Bryant observes, "as if the only thing that unites the nation is mutual loathing. America seems to be engaged in a forever war with itself."[6]

So then, what is to be done? *Can* anything be done? The foregoing discussion might seem to generate an obvious prescription: the nation needs to return to its providentialist foundations. This is after all the course often taken in the biblical history that served as a sort of paradigm for America and Americans (the "new Israel") at an earlier period, as we saw in chapter 3. The people of Israel are depicted in the Hebrew scripture that Christians call the Old Testament as following a cyclical path in which they fall away from worship of the One God; they accordingly forfeit the support and protection of that God; they are conquered by a foreign power (the Philistines, the Assyrians, the Babylonians); they are humbled by this adversity into an awareness of their transgressions and thus into a condition of humility and repentance; and they are eventually restored to self-rule and prosperity. Might America today follow a similar path?

It's conceivable—but hardly probable. At least as a formal constitutional matter, actually, such a return seems more permissible today than it once did: to the consternation of the devotees of the "secular neutrality" regime,[7] the Supreme Court has of late been discarding some of that regime's precedents

---

Triumph of the Modern Self (Wheaton, IL: Crossway, 2020); O. Carter Snead, *What It Means to Be Human* (Cambridge, MA: Harvard University Press, 2020); Charles Taylor, *Sources of the Self: The Making of the Modern Identity* (Cambridge, MA: Harvard University Press, 1989).

6. Nick Bryant, "Joe Biden One Year On: Has the United States Become Ungovernable?" BBC, January 19, 2022, https://tinyurl.com/2vsz9h4f.

7. See, e.g., Kate Shaw, "The Supreme Court's Disorienting Elevation of Religion," *New York Times*, July 8, 2023, https://tinyurl.com/bdejrsc7; Ira C. Lupu and Robert W. Tuttle, "The Remains of the Establishment Clause," *Hastings Law Journal* 74 (2023): 1763; Justin Driver, "Three Hail Marys: Carson, Kennedy, and the Fractured Detente over Religion and Education," *Harvard Law Review* 136 (2022): 208, 219.

and commitments[8] (though not the ideal of neutrality itself). Even so, it is hard to be hopeful. If anything, current trajectories are moving in the opposite direction, as more and more Americans abandon churches and reject any sort of traditional faith. Ours is the age of the "nonverts," as Stephen Bullivant has said,[9] or of the "nones."[10] And the dominant modern conceptions of history are not cyclical but rather progressive: we do not return to earlier conditions but rather continually move forward, or at least onward, into . . . something else. "You can't turn back the clock," as the saying goes.

At this point, though, we might notice an obvious objection to this tentative conclusion, and indeed to all of the discussion in this book. ("*Finally*!" a devout reader might be thinking.) Or at least the objection would have seemed obvious to anyone immersed in the providentialist mind-set of earlier periods. In considering the effects of providentialism for America, an objector might say, the book's discussion has persistently focused on the consequences or implications of *believing* in God, or of believing that God directs the courses of nations. Nothing has turned, it may seem, on whether there actually *is* a God who directs the course of nations; the benefits of national identity and purpose and of occasionally searching public debate and discourse flowed from the fact that Americans believed in a providential God.

Now, believing in God—the psychological and sociological fact of believing—surely does have consequences or implications, however difficult it might be to track these with any exactitude. And yet, a genuine providentialist might protest, this focus entirely misses the primary point—which is that there actually *is* a God who directs the course of history. And this believer might issue an impatient indictment: even in writing a book about providentialism, he might say, and even in worrying about the results of the modern turn against providentialism, you as an author—as a professor in a secular academy—have utterly succumbed to the postprovidentialist and indeed atheistic culture. You have offered an analysis that declines to assert or assume at any point that God is actually real, and is a real force in

---

8. See, e.g., Kennedy v. Bremerton School District, 597 U.S. 507 (2022).

9. See, e.g., Stephen Bullivant, *Nonverts: The Making of Ex-Christian America* (New York: Oxford University Press, 2022).

10. See, e.g., Mark Movsesian, "The Nones and the Religion Clauses," *Reason*, March 30, 2022, https://tinyurl.com/4rma8xc7.

"Only a God Can Save Us"

the shaping of our lives and our history. You may or may not *be* an atheist, but you write *as if* you were an atheist.

The believer who offered this critique would of course be correct. Such are the conditions and constraints of the contemporary secular academy. But maybe, just maybe, there is in this criticism also a glimmer of hope.

How so? Well, if from a purely human perspective we merely look at current trajectories and project them forward, any sort of return to a providentialist foundation seems unlikely; and it is hard to see either what new foundation might be found to replace the former one or how a deeply polarized nation can long endure without any common foundation. The "House Divided" teachings of Jesus—and of Abraham Lincoln—almost seem devised for times like ours.[11] But if there actually *is* a God ... well, who knows?

In a famous interview in which he attempted (unpersuasively) to explain away his earlier association with Nazism, the philosopher Martin Heidegger was asked whether he believed that any philosophy could rescue life and politics from the ills that afflict modernity. Heidegger replied that no philosophy could perform these restorative functions. The most that philosophy could do would be to render us open and potentially receptive to the possibility of extrahuman assistance. "Only a god can save us."

> SPIEGEL: Now the question naturally arises: Can the individual man in any way still influence this web of fateful circumstance? Or, indeed, can philosophy influence it? Or can both together influence it, insofar as philosophy guides the individual, or several individuals, to a determined action?
>
> HEIDEGGER: If I may answer briefly, and perhaps clumsily, but after long reflection: philosophy will be unable to effect any immediate change in the current state of the world. This is true not only of philosophy but of all purely human reflection and endeavor. Only a god can save us. The only possibility available to us is that by thinking and poetizing we prepare a readiness for the appearance of a god.[12]

---

11. Matt. 12:25. On Lincoln's "House Divided" speech, see David Herbert Donald, *Lincoln* (New York: Simon & Schuster, 1995), 206–9.

12. "'Only a God Can Save Us': The Spiegel Interview (1966)," https://tinyurl.com/3uadk7ys.

EPILOGUE

Only a god can save us. But *will* God save us, as a nation? Why on earth, why for heaven's sake, should he?

Here we might turn again to the reflections of a humbler but wiser and more admirable figure. "Fondly [may] we hope, fervently [may] we pray," for some sort of divine, restorative intervention. Ultimately, though, as Abraham Lincoln acknowledged, "the Almighty has his own purposes." We cannot know what they are. And whatever may come, "still it must be said 'the judgments of the Lord are true and righteous altogether.'"

Acknowledgments

With a book like this one, which is the product of exchanges and conferences and conversations over a period of decades, it is impossible to thank everyone who has contributed to and shaped the book. In a feeble effort at acknowledgment, though, I want to thank some people who have read and commented on some or all of these chapters: Larry Alexander, Nathan Chapman, Marc DeGirolami, David DeWolf, Don Drakeman, Rick Garnett, Rosemary Getty, Mark David Hall, Sandy Levinson, Michael Moreland, Bob Nagle, Jeff Pojanowski, Merina Smith, George Wright, and John Wright.

Index

Abington Township v. Schempp, 118
Ackerman, Bruce, 180, 202
Adams, John, 11, 39, 61, 65, 74, 120, 183, 191
Adams, Sam, 82
Adler, Gary, Jr., 105
age of the earth, 70
agnosticism: hybrid, 24–25; of the Constitution, 14, 27; meaning of, 14–15; possibility of, 15–21
alienation, 93–97
Alternative für Deutschland, 108–9
American Revolution, 55, 60, 79, 83
antifoundationalism, 151–53
atheism: establishment of, vii, 113–14, 123–26; methodological, 126; and neutrality, 127–28; types of, 114n5
Augustine, 178
authoritarianism, 103, 104, 105, 148

Bailyn, Bernard, 206
Balkin, Jack, 115n6
Banner, Stuart, 81–82, 185
Barlow, Joel, 95

beliefs: detached, 22–24; layered nature of, 21–24; operative, 22–24
Bellah, Robert, 89–104
Bentham, Jeremy, 160
Berman, Mitchell, 47n39
Beveridge, Senator Albert, 101
Bible, 53, 65–68, 75, 85–88, 121, 138, 182
biblical literacy, 138
Big Brother, 200, 205
Black, Hugo, 200, 205
Blackstone, William, 144, 185
Book of Mormon, 182
Boorstin, Daniel, 69–72, 154, 158, 187
Bostock v. Clayton County, 40–43
Bradfield v. Roberts, 44
Bradley, Gerard, 118n18, 126
Brennan, William, 36, 45–46, 131, 134, 135
Breyer, Stephen, 47
Brown v. Board of Education, 38, 115, 121
Bullivant, Stephen, 212

INDEX

Bush, George W., 92, 107

Campbell, David, 113
Carter, Stephen, 131
Case, Mary Ann, 122n38
chaplains, legislative, 35–36, 39, 59, 121, 207–8
Chapman, Nathan, 11n5, 131n51
Chappel, David, 88
Chavez, Cesar, 102
Chemerinsky, Erwin, 204–8
Cherry, Conrad, 59n15, 78n93, 91n10, 100n45
"Chester," 60
"Christian nation," 44, 51, 82, 83, 86, 190
Christian nationalism, 89–90, 92, 103–10
"City on a Hill" speech, 59, 172
civil religion, 89–103
Civil War, 56, 74–80, 83, 84–85, 98
Clifford, William, 18–19
Clinton, Bill, 92, 107
Coke, Edward, 185
Coleman, John, 82, 209
Communism, and communist countries, x, 209
communities, imagined, 82, 202, 209
Constitutional Convention, 1, 12, 38, 58, 81, 183
constitutions: American, vii, 1–15, 27–32, 33–50, 112–23, 189–99; foreign, 3–4; interpretation of, 34–49; "living," 45; proposed amendments to, 6; and providential language, 1–5, 9–10; as quasi-sacred text, 90; as repository of "principles," 45–48, 205; of states, 3–4
Continental Congress, 60–62, 79, 99
Cooper, Kody, 57n7, 69n59, 81n105
Cremer, Tobias, 108–10
Crevecoeur, Hector St. John de, 52
Cumings, Henry, 61, 63

Darwinism, 151–52, 175
Declaration of Independence, ix–xi, 3, 38, 71, 81, 90, 121, 142, 149, 154, 158, 184, 186, 191, 193, 198, 202, 203, 206
deism, 186, 187
Descartes, René, 18, 53
Dewey, John, 116
Dickinson, John, 62
Dierenfield, Bruce, 121
Dignitatis Humanae, viii
"doublethink," 199–201
Douglas, William O., 113, 121, 178
Douglass, Frederick, 67, 76, 82
Douthat, Ross, 148n24
Drakeman, Donald, 42
Driver, Justin, 121
Duche, Jacob, 99–100
Dworkin, Ronald, 48, 164
Dyer, Justin, 57n7, 69n59, 81n105

Eberstadt, Mary, 148
Eisenhower, Dwight D., x, 85, 87, 94
"Elihu," 95
Emerson, Ralph Waldo, 98
endorsement of religion, 93, 119, 143, 181, 190–96, 200

Index

Engel v. Vitale, 118, 121–22, 174
Enlightenment, ix, 186–87
Enlightenment in America, The (May), 187
Epperson v. Arkansas, 127
equality, 38–39, 71, 102, 115, 130, 142, 145, 151, 167–76, 186
Ervin, Sam, 113
establishment clause, 7, 31, 33–50, 114–40, 189–90, 197, 208
evangelicals, 109–10
Everson v. Board of Education, 117–18
"evolutionary explanation," 45–49

fascism, viii, 99, 103, 148
fasts, public, 24, 61, 63, 68, 79
Fea, John, 83
Federalist Papers, 12
First Amendment, meaning of, 33–50, 114–40
Fletcher, George, 71, 184
"forced options," 19–21, 26
Foucault, Michel, 175
Franklin, Benjamin, 11, 65, 183, 205
Freedom from Religion Foundation, 122
"freestanding" commitments, 152, 154, 160, 177
French, David, 147
French Revolution, viii–ix
Froese, Paul, 106
Fukuyama, Francis, 146

Galston, William, 147
Garnett, Richard, 47n40
Gauland, Alexander, 109
Gedicks, Frederick, 96n32

Gettysburg Address, 80, 86, 182, 206
Gillman, Howard, 204–8
Glendon, Mary Ann, 162n28
Godless Constitution, The (Kramnick and Moore), 4, 9
godlessness: of the Constitution, xii, 4–15, 28; meaning of, 13; in politics, xii, 5–7, 28, 31–36, 49
Gorski, Philip, 92, 106–7
Gorsuch, Neil, 41
Great Chain of Being, The (Lovejoy), 53
Great Seal of the United States, 187, 205
Green, Steven, 64
Greene, Jamal, 161–65
grievance culture, 168–76
Griswold v. Connecticut, 179
Gutman, Amy, 180
Guyatt, Nicholas, 56–62, 84, 101, 107, 141

Hall, Mark David, 11n7, 36n6, 51n2, 208n72
Hamilton, Alexander, 12, 159
Hamilton, Marci, 11n4
Harris, Katherine, vii
Heidegger, Martin, 213
Helmholz, R. M., 81n106, 159
Herberg, Will, 86, 89
history, value of, 203–4
Holmes, Oliver Wendel, Jr., 185, 201
Horwitz, Paul, 15n16
"House Divided" speech, 213
"hubris of the elect," 97–100
Hunter, James Davison, 149, 169

INDEX

Huxley, Thomas, 14
"hypocrisy story," 36–39

Imagined Communities (Anderson), 82, 202, 209
Ingersoll, Robert, 96
Islamic nations, 4, 210

James, William, 18–26, 123
Jay, John, 12
Jefferson, Thomas, ix–x, 2, 35, 38, 62–64, 68–72, 81, 90, 94, 112, 113, 120, 142, 154–58, 167, 180, 184, 191–95, 202, 205, 206
Jesus, 20–21, 26, 124, 154, 172, 213
"Jim Crow," 145

Kant, Immanuel, 178
Karamazov, Fyodor, 24
karma, 54
Kennedy, John F., 87, 96
Kennedy v. Bremerton School District, 93
Kenny, Anthony, 16, 24–25
Keteltas, Abraham, 60
Khrushchev, Nikita, xi
King, Martin Luther, Jr., 82, 87, 90, 102, 115, 172, 173
Kingdom of God in America, The (Niebuhr), 98
Koppelman, Andrew, 129n49
Kramnick, Isaac, 4–7, 9, 12–13, 28, 31, 34

Laycock, Douglas, 37, 190, 196
League of the Militant Godless, 13
Ledewitz, Bruce, 13n14, 116n9
legitimation of oppression, 100–102
Lemon test, 119, 189

Lemon v. Kurtzman, 119
"Letter from a Birmingham Jail," 87
Li, Ruiqian, 106
liberalism: embattled, 145–50; and foundations, 151–54; meaning of, 141–42; and secularism, 144–45
Liberalism Against Itself (Moyn), 148
Liberal League, 6
Lincoln, Abraham, 39, 65, 68, 73–76, 78, 80, 82, 86, 90, 94, 98, 108, 112, 120, 124, 145, 164, 180, 182, 183, 191, 193, 194, 195, 202, 203, 204, 206, 213, 214
Lithwick, Dahlia, 197n51
Livermore, Samuel, 42
Lloyd, Genevieve, 53, 54
Lost World of Thomas Jefferson, The (Boorstin), 187
Lovejoy, Arthur, 53
Lu, Rachel, 168
Lupu, Ira, 47n43

Macedo, Stephen, 136, 180
Maclure, Jocelyn, 144
Madison, James, 12, 35, 36, 64, 79, 120, 208
MAGA populism, 108
Magnalia Christi Americana (Mather), 59
mammoths, 69–70
"Manifest Destiny," 101
Marbury v. Madison, 27
Marcus Aurelius, 53
marriage, 139, 179
Marshall, John, 37
Martin, Luther, 38

Index

Marx, 174, 175
Mason, George, 39, 81
Mather, Cotton, 59
May, Henry, 71, 187
McConnell, Michael, 131n51, 137n67
Melville, Herman, 82
Middlekauf, Robert, 55, 56, 86
Milke, Mark, 168n36
Mill, John Stuart, 5
Miller, Paul, 106–7
Miller, Perry, 65
Ministry of Truth, 199, 200, 208
Moore, R. Laurence, 4–7, 9, 12–13, 28, 31, 34
Morris, Gouverneur, 38, 81
Moyn, Samuel, 148
Munoz, Philip, 41n22, 155n11
Murray, John Courtney, SJ, viii–xiii, 28, 113, 123, 127, 149–50, 206, 210

national anthem, 86
national motto, x, 30, 31, 86, 121, 136, 190, 193, 198
National Reform Association, 6
natural law, x, 81, 159
negative partisanship, 147
neutrality: and "baselines," 129n49; constitutional requirement of, 113, 118–19; impossibility of, 123–24, 127–28; necessity of, 129–31
Newdow, Michael, 122
Newdow case, 193–95, 201
Niebuhr, H. Richard, 82, 87, 99–100
Niebuhr, Reinhold, 98
Nietzsche, Friedrich, 116, 175–76

nihilism, 174–76
"no endorsement" test, 93, 190, 192, 196, 200
Noll, Mark, 65–67, 79, 85, 90, 97–98
"nones," 212
Nonverts: The Making of Ex-Christian America (Bullivant), 212
Novak, David, 15, 24, 26
Nussbaum, Martha, 45

Obama, Barack, 92, 107, 173
Obergefell v. Hodges, 162
O'Connor, Sandra Day, 47, 119, 132, 190
Old Testament, 1, 65–68, 88, 182, 211
"originalism," 45, 48
Orwell, George, 199–208
Owen, J. Judd, 135

Pascal's wager, 25
Peace of Westphalia, 130
Peguy, Charles, 21–22
Pentateuch, 66
Perry, Michael, 184
Perry, Samuel, 89n3
Philadelphia convention, 1, 12, 38, 58, 81, 183
Philippines, 101
"Piety on the Potomac," x, 85, 112, 209
Plato, 27, 53
Pledge of Allegiance, x, 30, 31, 86, 121, 136, 137, 180, 181, 190, 193, 194, 196
Pojanowski, Jeff, 116n10
Pojman, Louis, 184

INDEX

prayer: days of, 61, 63, 126; as expression of providential perspective, 58–59; official, xiii, 35, 44, 58, 137, 183, 207, 208; school, 118, 133, 138
presidential inaugurations, xiii, 35, 91, 137, 191
Protestant-Catholic-Jew (Herberg), 86
Providence and the Invention of the United States (Guyatt), 56
providentialism: and Christian nationalism, 89–90, 104, 110–11; and civic religion, 89–92; as constitutive of community, 82–84, 93–97, 149, 170, 176, 202, 209; and equality, 167–76; functions of, 76–84, 209–10; and injustice, 100–102, 167–76; judicial, 56–57; national, 56–57; and national purpose, 77–80, 112, 149, 210; optimistic, 68–72; as protean concept, 64–65, 85, 94, 112; and public discourse, 57, 65, 80–82, 93, 102, 112, 149, 209–12; and religion, 52–54; and rights, 69, 71, 154–67; tragic, 73–76
Puritans, 78
Putnam, Robert, 113

Ratzinger, Joseph, 17, 116
Rauschenbusch, Walter, 82
Rawls, John, viii, 130, 143, 145, 152, 153, 177, 180, 202, 210
Reagan, Ronald, 92, 107, 122
Rehnquist, William, 36, 194–95
Religion Clauses, The: The Case for Separating Church and State (Gillman and Chemerinsky), 204
religious freedom, viii–xi, 142, 191, 206
religious tests, 6, 49
Reuben Quick Bear v. Leupp, 44
rights: "bubbling of," 163–66; and "interests," 156–59, 164–66; and law, 156–66; natural, 160; and needs, 157; positive, 160; as presumptively categorical, 163–64; "proportionality" approach to, 165; and providential plan, 69, 71, 154–67; as rhetorical exclamation mark, 163; and wants, 157
"rightsism," 161–64
"rights revolution," 115, 161–64
Roosevelt, Franklin D., 192
Rorty, Richard, 153, 210
Rousseau, Jean-Jacques, 89
Ryrie, Alec, 21

Scalia, Antonin, 36, 45, 180
Schragger, Richard, 145, 147
Schwartzman, Micah, 145, 147
Searle, John, 151n2
Second Inaugural Address (Lincoln), 75, 82, 183, 193, 203
secularism, constitutional requirement of, 113, 118–20, 122–23, 125–26, 189
Sehat, David, 7n18, 94n20
self-righteousness, 97–100
separation of church and state, vii–xiii, 8, 28, 35, 63, 64, 105, 113, 117

Index

sexual revolution, 139
Shiffrin, Steven, 196
slavery, 38–39, 68, 74–76, 80–81, 83, 84, 85, 100, 102, 145, 149, 159, 172, 192, 202
Smith, Christian, 87
Smith, Jesse, 104n60, 104n63, 105, 106
Smith, Winston, 199–203
Snead, O. Carter, 211n5
social contract, 78, 155, 186
Souter, David, 36
Spanish-American War, 101
Spinoza, Baruch, 53
Stiles, Ezra, 62–63
Stone, Geoffrey, 6n15, 139, 161n25
Stout, Harry, 84
Sunstein, Cass, 146

Taylor, Charles, 144
Thomas, Clarence, 180, 201n55
Thought Police, 200, 203
Tillich, Paul, 96
Tocqueville, Alexis de, 52, 84, 89, 135, 143
Tri-Faith America (Schultz), 85
Trollope, Francis, 52
Trueman, Carl, 210n5
Trump, Donald, 92, 103, 109–10

Turner, James, 95
Turner, Nat, 68
Tuttle, Robert, 47n43

Underkuffler-Freund, Laura, 205
"undetected meaning" account, 36, 39–43
utilitarianism, 5

Vermeule, Adrian, 146n13
Virginia Statute for Religious Liberty, ix, 193, 206–7

Waldron, Jeremy, 184
War of 1812, 79
wars of religion, 130
Washington, George, 2, 11, 29, 35, 39, 57–58, 61, 63, 65, 74, 79, 90, 97, 120, 124, 183, 191, 192, 195
"Western Civ," 116
Whitehead, Andrew, 89n3
Why Liberalism Failed (Deneen), 146
Winthrop, John, 59, 82, 172
Witherspoon, John, 65, 79
Witte, John, Jr., 47n39
Woodward, Kenneth, 105

Zeitz, Joshua, 67
Zorach v. Clauson, 179

TITLES PUBLISHED IN
EMORY UNIVERSITY STUDIES IN LAW AND RELIGION

Thomas C. Berg, *Religious Liberty in a Polarized Age* (2023)

Harold J. Berman, *Faith and Order: The Reconciliation of Law and Religion* (1993)

Stephen J. Grabill,
Rediscovering the Natural Law in Reformed Theological Ethics (2006)

Johannes Heckel,
Lex Charitatis: A Juristic Disquisition on Law in the Theology of Martin Luther (2010)

Timothy P. Jackson, ed., *The Best Love of the Child:
Being Loved and Being Taught to Love as the First Human Right* (2011)

Timothy P. Jackson, *Political* Agape: *Christian Love and Liberal Democracy* (2015)

Paul Grimley Kuntz, *The Ten Commandments in History:
Mosaic Paradigms for a Well-Ordered Society* (2004)

Douglas Laycock, *Religious Liberty*, Volume 1: *Overviews and History* (2010)

Douglas Laycock, *Religious Liberty*, Volume 2: *The Free Exercise Clause* (2011)

Douglas Laycock, *Religious Liberty*, Volume 3: *Religious Freedom Restoration Acts, Same-Sex Marriage Legislation, and the Culture Wars* (2018)

Douglas Laycock, *Religious Liberty*, Volume 4: *Federal Legislation after the Religious Freedom Restoration Act, with More on the Culture Wars* (2018)

Douglas Laycock, *Religious Liberty*, Volume 5: *The Free Speech and Establishment Clauses* (2018)

W. Bradford Littlejohn, *The Peril and Promise of Christian Liberty:
Richard Hooker, the Puritans, and Protestant Political Theology* (2017)

Ira C. Lupu and Robert W. Tuttle, *Secular Government, Religious People* (2014)

Martin E. Marty, *Building Cultures of Trust* (2010)

R. Jonathan Moore, *Suing for America's Soul:
John Whitehead, The Rutherford Institute, and Conservative Christians in Court* (2007)

Joan Lockwood O'Donovan,
Theology of Law and Authority in the English Reformation (1991)

Jean Porter, *Ministers of the Law: A Natural Law Theory of Legal Authority* (2011)

Charles J. Reid Jr., *Power over the Body, Equality in the Family:
Rights and Domestic Relations in Medieval Canon Law* (2004)

Liam de los Reyes, *The Earth Is the Lord's: A Natural Law Theory of Property* (2025)

Noel B. Reynolds and W. Cole Durham Jr., eds.,
Religious Liberty in Western Thought (1996)

A. G. Roeber, *Hopes for Better Spouses: Protestant Marriage and Church Renewal in
Early Modern Europe, India, and North America* (2013)

James W. Skillen and Rockne M. McCarthy, eds.,
Political Order and the Plural Structure of Society (1991)

Steven D. Smith, *The Godless Constitution and the Providential Republic* (2025)

Steven D. Smith, *Pagans and Christians in the City:
Culture Wars from the Tiber to the Potomac* (2018)

Brian Tierney, *The Idea of Natural Rights:
Studies on Natural Rights, Natural Law, and Church Law, 1150–1625* (1997)

Glenn Tinder, *The Fabric of Hope: An Essay* (1999)

Glenn Tinder, *Liberty: Rethinking an Imperiled Ideal* (2007)

David VanDrunen, *Divine Covenants and Moral Order:
A Biblical Theology of Natural Law* (2014)

David VanDrunen, *Natural Law and the Two Kingdoms:
A Study in the Development of Reformed Social Thought* (2009)

Johan D. van der Vyver and John Witte Jr., eds.,
Religious Human Rights in Global Perspective: Legal Perspectives (1996)

David A. Weir, *Early New England: A Covenanted Society* (2005)

John Witte Jr., *God's Joust, God's Justice:
Law and Religion in the Western Tradition* (2006)

John Witte Jr. and Johan D. van der Vyver, eds.,
Religious Human Rights in Global Perspective: Religious Perspectives (1996)

Nicholas Wolterstorff, *Justice in Love* (2011)